Elisha Benjamin Andrews

The History of the Last Quarter-Century in the United States 1870-1895

Volume I

Elisha Benjamin Andrews

The History of the Last Quarter-Century in the United States 1870-1895
Volume I

ISBN/EAN: 9783743399730

Manufactured in Europe, USA, Canada, Australia, Japa

Cover: Foto ©ninafisch / pixelio.de

Manufactured and distributed by brebook publishing software (www.brebook.com)

Elisha Benjamin Andrews

The History of the Last Quarter-Century in the United States 1870-1895

Drawn by R. West Clinedinst

THE CROWD IN FRONT OF THE NEW YORK TIMES OFFICE ON THE NIGHT OF THE
TILDEN-HAYES ELECTION, 1876

THE HISTORY OF THE LAST QUARTER-CENTURY IN THE UNITED STATES
1870-1895

BY

E. BENJAMIN ANDREWS
PRESIDENT OF BROWN UNIVERSITY

WITH MORE THAN
THREE HUNDRED AND FIFTY
ILLUSTRATIONS

VOLUME I

NEW YORK
CHARLES SCRIBNER'S SONS
MDCCCXCVI

Press of J. J. Little & Co.
New York, U. S. A.

PREFACE

FEW quarter-centuries in the world's life bristle with salient events as does that following the year 1870. Recognizing this the writer recently undertook, in a series of papers published in Scribner's Magazine, to portray the chief of these events so far as they relate to the United States. In the opinion of the publishers the series met with gratifying success, which suggested the preparation of the present work. While based on the Magazine articles it is essentially new. The original matter has been carefully revised, much of it, in fact, re-written, while extensive and valuable additions have been made, securing to the narrative a consecutiveness which the separate papers forbade. A detailed national history since 1870 the reader must not expect. He is going upon a rapid excursion through vast tracts, with frequent use of the camera, and not upon a topographical survey. Happenings of mere local moment are ignored altogether; legal and constitutional developments we can only

PREFACE

sketch; while many other interesting and even vital matters are barely brought to notice. The task is certainly arduous and hazardous. None of the sources for our most recent history have as yet been sifted. On each specially critical occurrence studied by them congressional committees report contradictorily. State and private papers needed fully to explain the acts of public men and the policies of administrations falling within the period covered by this History are still under seal. A writer treating of affairs so uncertainly vouched must keep in tense exercise a form of discretion which in better trodden fields predecessors have made unnecessary. At best he will err, and he will often be thought to err when he does not. In discussions of yesterday's transactions statements the most true are sure to be challenged from some quarter. If you are right in essentials, your ideas of proportion and of the relative importance of things may to many seem strange. And, however sincere and unremitting the effort to treat all sections, parties, and persons with perfect fairness, perhaps no man can judge his contemporaries without a degree of prejudice. To write freshly made history would thus be difficult enough had one ample space for all necessary modifications and explanations; being obliged to condense the narrative as these chapters require doubly aggravates the undertaking. A labor so forbidding in these many ways

PREFACE

might well be declined but for the following considerations: It is hoped that precisely on account of their occurrence in recent time the doings set forth will have a peculiarly living interest; that the work may here and there rescue from oblivion some significant deed which would surely meet that fate were the recording deferred; and that prospectors traversing this forest hereafter may get on better for our toil in blazing the path.

CONTENTS

I The United States at the Close of Reconstruction 1

Land and people in 1870.—Territories.—Railroads in the West.—Fenian Movements.—Boston's Peace Jubilees.—The Great Cities.—The Chicago Fire.—The Boston Fire.—The Tweed Ring.—Tweed's Escape and Capture.—Financial Condition of the Nation.—Ships.—Army and Navy.—Reconstruction, the Problem.—The Presidential and the Congressional Plan.—Iron Law of March 2, 1867.—The Process of Reconstruction.—Situation in 1870.—Debate on the Coercion of States.—Outcome.—The Test.—All States at Last Again Represented in Both Houses of Congress.

II General Grant as a Civil Chief . . . 23

The Republican Party in 1870.—Its Defects.—President Grant's Shortcomings.—His First Cabinet.—The Party's Attitude Toward the Tariff.—Toward the Democracy.—Toward Re-enfranchisement at the South.—The Liberal Movement.—The Democrats.—The "New Departure" Among Them.—Vallandigham.—John Quincy Adams.—Reconstruction.—Errors Committed Therein.—The Fifteenth Amendment.—The Ku-Klux Klan.—The Force Bill—Re-enfranchisement at the South.—Grant and the Nation's Finances.—Gould and Fisk.—Black Friday.—The Treaty of Washington.—Relations with Cuba.—Proposed " Annexion " of Santo Domingo.—Sumner and the Administration.

III The Greeley Campaign 57

The Rise of Horace Greeley.—The *Tribune*.—Greeley and Grant.—The Liberal-Republican Movement.—The Spoils System.—Shepherd at Washington.—Scandals Connected With the Collection of the Revenues.—Reversal of Hepburn *vs.* Griswold.—Grant and Greeley Nominated.—Mixed Politics.—Both Candidates Severely Criticised.—A Choice of Evils.—A Bitter Campaign —Difficulties Confronting Greeley.—Grant Elected.—Greeley's Death.—His Character.—Continuation of Republican Policy at the South.—Force and Anarchy in Louisiana.

CONTENTS

IV The Geneva Award and the Credit Mobilier 87
Outcome of the Washington Treaty.—The "*Alabama* Claims."—Vain Efforts at Settlement.—The Geneva Tribunal.—Rules for its Guidance.—Questions Answered by It.—Its Decision.—The Northwestern Boundary Settlement.—The Credit Mobilier Story.—Enthusiasm for the West.—Vastness of that Section.—The Rush Thither.—The Pioneers.—Land Grabbing.—Grants for Transcontinental Railways.—Inception of the Union Pacific Company.—The Credit Mobilier Company.—Oakes Ames and His Contract.—Stock Sold to Congressmen.—The "Sun's" Publication.—The Facts.—Ames's Defense.—Censure of Him by the House of Representatives.—His Death.—Reasons for the Sentiment Against Him.

V "Carpet-Bagger" and "Scalawag" in Dixie 111
Grant's Re-election and the South.—Court Decisions Confirming State Sovereignty.—The Louisiana "Slaughter House Cases."—Osborn *vs.* Nicholson.—White *vs.* Hart.—Desolation at the South After the War.—Discouragement, Intemperance, Ignorance.—Slow Revival of Industry.—Social and Political Conflict.—The "Scalawag."—The "Carpet-Bagger." Good Carpet-Baggers.—Their Failings.—Resistance.—Northern Sympathy With This.—The Freedmen.—Their Vices.—Their Ignorance.—Foolish and Corrupt Legislation.—Extravagant Expenditures in Various States—In Mississippi.—In Georgia.—In South Carolina.—Overthrow of Many Carpet-Bag Governments.—Violence Still, But Often Exaggerated.

VI Decline of the Transitional Governments in South Carolina, Mississippi, Arkansas and Louisiana 131
Gen. Sherman on the Southern Problem.—Reckless Legislation in South Carolina.—Appeal of the Taxpayers' Union.—Gov. Chamberlain's Reforms.—The Conflict in Arkansas.—Factions.—The Stake Fought For.—A New Constitution.—Gov. Garland Elected.—Report of the Poland Committee.—The Vicksburg "War."—Mayor *vs.* Governor.—President Grant Will Not Interfere.—Senator Revels on the Situation.—The Mississippi Reconstructionists.—The Kellogg-McEnery Imbroglio in Louisiana.—Metropolitans and White Leaguers Fight.—The Kellogg Government Overthrown but Re-established by Federal Arms.—Protests. —The Election of November 2, 1874.—Methods of the Returning Board. —Gen. Sheridan in Command.—Legislature Organized Amid Bayonets.—Members Removed by Federal Soldiers.—Sheridan's Views.—Allegations Contra.—Public Opinion at the North.—The "Wheeler Adjustment."

VII Indian Wars and the Custer Death . . 169
Civilized Indians in 1874.—Grant's Policy for the Wild Tribes.—Difficulties of the Indian Commissioners.—Indians' Wrongs and Discontent.—Troubles in Arizona.—Gov. Safford's Declaration.—Massacre of Apaches in 1871.—Report of Federal Grand Jury.—The Apaches Subdued.—Grievences of the Sioux.—The Modoc War and Gen. Canby's Death.—Troubles in 1874.—The Mill River Disaster in Massachusetts.—The Sioux Rebellion.—The Army's Plan of Campaign.—Custer's Party.—His Death.—How the Battle Went.—"Revenge" of Rain-in-the-Face. —Custer Criticised.—And Defended.

CONTENTS

VIII "The Year of a Hundred Years"—The Centennial Exposition and the Hayes-Tilden Imbroglio 195

Origin of the Centennial Exposition.—Philadelphia Landmarks.—The Exposition Buildings.—The Opening.—The Various Exhibits.—Attendance. —A Political Crisis.—Grant and Jewell.—The Belknap Disgrace.—Another Reform Movement.—Fear of a Third Term for Grant.—Issues Between the Parties.—Hayes and Tilden Nominated.—Their Letters of Acceptance.—The Campaign.—Prophecy of Trouble Over the Presidential Count.—The Twenty-second Joint Rule.—Result of the Election in Doubt.—Cipher Dispatches.—Queer Ways of Returning Boards.—Fears and Hopes.—The Electoral Commission.—The Case of Florida, of Louisiana, of Oregon, of South Carolina.—Hayes Declared Elected.—An Electoral Count Law.

IX Hayes and the Civil Service . . . 223

Hayes's Character.—His Cabinet.—End of Bayonet Rule at the South.— This the Result of a "Deal."—"Visiting Statesmen" at the Louisiana Count.—Hayes Favors Honesty.—His Record.—Hayes and Garfield Compared.—The Spoils System.—Early Protests.—A Civil Service Commission.—Its Rules.—Retrogression Under Grant.—Jewell's Exit from the Cabinet.—Hoar's.—Butler's "Pull" on Grant.—Collector Simmons.— The Sanborn Contracts.—Bristow a Reformer.—The Whiskey Ring.— Myron Colony's Work.—Plot and Counter-Plot.—"Let no Guilty Man Escape."—Reformers Ousted.—Good Work by the Press.—The "Press-gag."—First Democratic House Since the War.—Hayes Renews Reform. —Opposed by Conkling.—Fight Over the New York Collectorship.—The President Firm and Victorious.

X "The United States Will Pay" . . 249

Back to Hard Money.—Act to Strengthen the Public Credit.—Difficulty of Contraction.—Ignorance of Finance.—Debtors Pinched.—The Panic of 1873.—Causes.—Failure of Jay Cooke & Co., and of Fiske & Hatch. —Black Friday No. 2.—On Change and on the Street.—Bulls, Bears and Banks.—Criticism of Secretary Richardson.—First Use of Clearing-House Certificates.—Effects and Duration of the Panic.—An Important Good Result.—Resumption and Politics.—The Resumption Act.—Sherman's Qualifications for Executing It.—His Firmness.—Resumption Actually Begun.—Magnitude and Meaning of This Policy.—Our Bonded Debt Rapidly Reduced.—Legal Tender Questions and Decisions.—Juilliard *vs.* Greenman.—The "Fiat-Greenback" Heresy.—"Dollar of the Fathers" Demonetized.—Not By Fraud But Without Due Reflection.— The Bland Bill and the "Allison Tip."—The Amended Bill Vetoed, But Passed.—Subsequent Silver Legislation.

XI Agrarian and Labor Movements in the Seventies 281

The "Grangers."—Their Aims.—Origin of the Inter-State Commerce Act.—Demand for Cheap Transportation.—Illinois's "Three-Cent War." —Court Decisions.—Land-Grant Colleges.—Their Significance.—Various Labor Congresses and Platforms.—Rise of Labor Bureaus.—The National Department of Labor.—Its Work, Methods, and Influence.—Value of the State Bureaus.—Contract-Labor Law.—The Greenback Party.—Peter

CONTENTS

Cooper and Gen. Butler.—Violence in the Labor Conflict.—Causes.—Combinations of Capital.—Of Laborers.—Black List and Boycott.—Labor War in Pennsylvania.—Methods of Intimidation.—The "Mollie Maguires."—Murder of Alexander Rea.—Power and Immunity of the Mollies.—Plan for Exposing Them.—Gowen and McParlan.—Assassination of Thomas Sanger.—Gowen's Triumph and the Collapse of the Conspiracy.—Great Railway Strike in 1877.—Riot at Pittsburg.—Death and Destruction.—Scenes at Reading and Other Places.—Strikes Common From This Time On.

XII "Anything to Beat Grant" . . . 307

Presidential Possibilities in 1880.—Grant the Lion.—Republican Convention.—A Political Battle of the Wilderness.—Garfield the Dark Horse.—Grant's Old Guard Defeated But Defiant.—Democrats Nominate Hancock.—"The Ins and the Outs."—Party Declarations.—The Morey Forgery.—Blaine Can't Save Maine.—Conkling's Strike Off.—Garfield Elected.—"Soap" *vs.* Intimidation and Fraud.—From Mule Boy to President.—Hancock's Brilliant Career.—The First Presidential Appointments.—Conkling's Frenzy and His Fall.—The Cabinet.—Garfield Assassinated.—Guiteau Tried and Hanged.—Star Route Frauds.—Pendleton Civil Service Act.

XIII Domestic Events During Mr. Arthur's Administration 343

Mr. Arthur's Dilemma.—His Accession.—Responsibility Evokes His Best.—The Presidential Succession Question.—Succession Act Passed.—Electoral Count Act Passed.—Arthur's Cabinet.—Condition of the Country in 1881.—Decadence of Our Ocean Carrying.—Tariff Commission of 1882 and the Tariff of 1883.—Mahone and the Virginia "Readjusters."—Mahone's Record.—His Entry Into the Senate.—President Arthur and the Chinese.—Origin of the Chinese Question.—Anson Burlingame.—The 1878 Embassy.—Chinese Throng Hither.—Early California.—The Strike of 1877 Affects California.—Rise and Character of Denis Kearney.—His Program.—The "Sand-Lot" Campaign.—Kearney's Moderation.—He Is Courted.—And Opposed.—His Constitutional Convention.—Its Work.—Kearneyism to the Rear.—The James Desperadoes.—Their Capture.—The Yorktown Celebration.—Mementoes of Old Yorktown.—The Pageant.—"Surrender" Day.—The Other Days.—Close of the Fête.—Flood and Riot in Cincinnati.

LIST OF ILLUSTRATIONS

SCENES AND VIEWS

TITLE	PAGE
Crowd in Front of the New York Times Office on the Night of the Tilden-Hayes Election, 1876 . . . . Frontispiece *Drawn by B. West Clinedinst*	
Driving the Last Spike of the Union Pacific. Scene at Promontory Point, May 10, 1869 . *Drawn by B. West Clinedinst from photographs loaned by General G. M. Dodge*	3
The Court House at Chicago before the Fire *From a photograph*	6
The Chicago Court House after the Fire . *From a photograph*	6
The Chicago Court House in 1895 . . . . . *From a photograph*	7
The Reconstruction Committee . . *Drawn by W. R. Leigh from photographs*	25
The High Commissioners in Session at Washington *Drawn by E. B. Child from photographs*	33
Fisk and Gould's Opera House in a State of Siege *Drawn by B. West Clinedinst*	41
Scene in the New York Gold Room on Black Friday . . . *Drawn by C. S. Reinhart from photographs and descriptions by eye witnesses*	49
Horace Greeley Signing the Bail Bond of Jefferson Davis . . . . . *Painted by W. R. Leigh from photographs, and sketches made at the time by W. L. Sheppard*	63
Mr. Greeley Receiving the Democratic Committee which Notified him of his Nomination . *Painted by W. R. Leigh from photographs and descriptions*	65
Dispersal of the McEnery Legislature at Odd Fellow's Hall, New Orleans *Drawn by C. K. Linson from photographs and descriptions*	81
Three Famous Confederate Cruisers : The *Florida*, the *Shenandoah* and the *Alabama* . . *Drawn by M. J. Burns from photographs*	89
Count Sclopis Announcing the Decision of the Geneva Tribunal . . . . . *Painted by W. R. Leigh from photographs and diagrams loaned by J. C. Bancroft Davis, Esq.*	93
The South Carolina Legislature of 1873 Passing an Appropriation Bill . . *Painted by W. R. Leigh from photographs, plans, and a description by an eye-witness*	123
Beginning of the Conflict in Front of the Anthony House, Little Rock, Arkansas *Painted by W. R. Leigh from photographs and descriptions*	133
The Brooks Forces Evacuating the State House at Little Rock *Painted by Howard Pyle from photographs and descriptions*	137

LIST OF ILLUSTRATIONS

The Scene of the Conflict at the Pemberton Monument, near Vicksburg, December 7, 1874 143
From a photograph made for this work

The Mississippi Legislature Passing a Resolution Asking for Federal Aid after the Attack on Vicksburg 146
Drawn by B. West Clinedinst from photographs and descriptions

General Badger in Front of the Gem Saloon, New Orleans . . . 149
Drawn by C. K. Linson from photographs

The Mass Meeting of September 14, 1874, at the Clay Statue, New Orleans . . 154
Drawn by C. K. Linson from photographs

L. A. Wiltz Taking Possession of the Speaker's Chair in the Louisiana State House, January 4, 1875 163
Drawn by W. R. Leigh from photographs and plans

The Lava Beds 178
From a photograph by Taber

Scene of the Canby Massacre . . 179
From a photograph by Taber

Indian Trader's Store at Standing Rock, North Dakota . 185
Drawn by W. A. C. Pape from a photograph by Barry

The Custer Monument 190
Drawn by Harry Fenn from a photograph by Barry

Old Swedes' Church, Philadelphia, Built in 1700 . 195
Drawn by Harry Fenn from a photograph by Rau

State House Row, Philadelphia . . . 197
Drawn by Harry Fenn from a photograph by Rau

Centennial Opening Ceremonies on May 10, 1876 . 199
Drawn by Harry Fenn from a photograph

View From Photographic Hall Looking Toward Machinery Hall . . 203
Drawn by C. K. Linson from a photograph

Fountain Hall . . . 206

Exterior of Horticultural Hall . . 206

Interior of Horticultural Hall . . 207

The Main Building at Philadelphia . . 209
After a photograph

The Trial of Thomas Munley, the "Mollie Maguire," at Pottsville, Pa. . . 297

The Attempt to Fire the P. R.R. Roundhouse in Pittsburg, at daybreak of Sunday, July 22, 1877 301
Painted by W. R. Leigh from photographs by Robinson

Burnt Freight Cars at Pittsburg . 303
From a photograph by Robinson

Union Station and Interior of Roundhouse after the Riot of 1877 . . 304
From photographs by Robinson

The Interview at the Riggs House Between Conkling and Garfield . 322
Drawn by B. West Clinedinst from photographs and descriptions

Conkling's Speech Before the "Committee of Conciliation" 325
Drawn by C. K. Linson from photographs, and a diagram and description furnished by Mr. H. L. Dawes

The Anti-Chinese Riot of 1880, in Denver, Col. 328
Drawn by C. K. Linson from a photograph and a sketch made by an eye-witness

LIST OF ILLUSTRATIONS

President Garfield's Remains Lying in State at the Capitol 335
Drawn by W. R. Leigh from photographs

Scene at a Station on the P. R. R. as the Garfield Ambulance Train Passed on its Way to Elberon 337
Drawn by C. K. Linson

The Garfield Funeral Car About to Start from the Public Square, Cleveland, Ohio, for the Cemetery 339
Drawn by T. de Thulstrup from a photograph by Ryder

President Arthur Taking the Inaugural Oath at his Lexington Avenue Residence . . 345
Drawn by W. R. Leigh

President Hayes and his Cabinet Receiving Chen Lan Pin and the First Resident Chinese Embassy to the United States, September 28, 1878 358
Drawn by W. R. Leigh from photographs

The Chinese Consulate in San Francisco 360
Drawn by A. F. Jaccaci from a photograph by Taber

A "Mixed Family" in the Highbinders' Quarter, "Chinatown" 361
From a photograph by Taber

God in Joss Temple, "Chinatown," San Francisco 362
Drawn by Harry Fenn from a photograph by Taber

Chinese Accountants 363
Drawn by E. B. Child from a photograph by Taber

Alley in "Chinatown" 365
Drawn by F. H. Lungren from photographs by Taber

Dining Room of a Chinese Restaurant in Washington Street, San Francisco . . 366
Drawn by Harry Fenn from photographs by Taber

A "Sand Lot" Meeting in San Francisco 368
Composition of B. West Clinedinst with the assistance of photographs by Taber

Denis Kearney Addressing the Workingmen on the Night of October 29, on Nob Hill, San Francisco 372
Drawn by G. W. Peters from photographs, and diagrams and descriptions by eye-witnesses

Denis Kearney Being Drawn Through the Streets of San Francisco After his Release from the House of Correction 375
Painted by Howard Pyle from photographs by Taber and a description by Kearney himself

The Old *Chronicle* Building in San Francisco 377
Drawn by Otto H. Bacher from a photograph by Taber

Procession Wong Fong in San Francisco 379
Drawn by T. de Thulstrup from a photograph by Taber

The Nelson House in 1881 383

The West House at Yorktown 384

The Yorktown Memorial Monument 385

Lawrenceburg, Indiana, During the Floods of 1884 387
From a copyrighted photograph by Rombach & Groene

Second Street, Cincinnati, Looking East 388

Gas Tanks in Second Street, Cincinnati 388

Cincinnati Riots of 1884—Barricade in South Sycamore Street 389
From a photograph by Rombach & Groene

PORTRAITS

William M. Tweed . . . . . *Drawn by Alfred Brennan from a photograph*	12
Hiram R. Revels, of Mississippi	20
Joseph F. Rainey, of South Carolina	20
George E. Harris, of Mississippi . . . . . *Drawn by Alfred Brennan from a photograph*	21
John F. Lewis, of Virginia . . . *Drawn by Alfred Brennan from a photograph*	21
James Fisk, Jr. . . . . *Drawn by Alfred Brennan from a photograph by Rockwood*	28
Jay Gould .	28
President Grant . . . . *From a photograph by Hoyt in 1869*	29
Fred. Douglass	30
Buenaventura Baez, President of Santo Domingo . *From a photograph in the collection of James E. Taylor*	30
President Grant's First Cabinet—Borie, Creswell, Hoar, Washburne, Cox, Schofield and Boutwell . . . . *Drawn by Alfred Brennan from photographs*	35
Alexander T. Stewart . . . . *After the portrait by Thomas Le Clear*	36
Stanley Matthews . ..	37
Oliver P. Morton	45
Clement L. Vallandigham . . . . . *From a photograph in the collection of James E. Taylor*	53
Horace Greeley . . . . . *From a photograph by Sarony*	59
William Henry Fry . . . . *After a daguerreotype in the possession of Horace B. Fry*	60
Count Adam Gurowski . . . . . . *After a daguerreotype in the possession of Charles A. Dana*	60
George Ripley . . . . *After a daguerreotype in the possession of Charles A. Dana*	60
Margaret Fuller . . . . . . *After a daguerreotype in the possession of H. W. Fay*	60
Bayard Taylor . . . *From a photograph by Sarony*	60

LIST OF ILLUSTRATIONS

Thomas Hicks
Charles A. Dana 61
George William Curtis
From a daguerreotype by Brady, 1852, in the possession of Charles A. Dana

Zebulon B. Vance 69
Drawn by Alfred Brennan from a photograph

Lyman Trumbull 70
Drawn by Alfred Brennan from a photograph

Henry Wilson 72
Drawn by Alfred Brennan from a photograph

B. Gratz Brown 72
Drawn by Alfred Brennan from a photograph

Charles O'Conor 76
Drawn by Alfred Brennan from a photograph

John Quincy Adams, in 1870 . . . 77
Drawn by Alfred Brennan from a photograph

Henry Clay Warmoth 79
Drawn by Alfred Brennan from a photograph

P. B. S. Pinchback 79
Drawn by Alfred Brennan from a photograph

Charles Sumner 90

The English Representatives at Geneva—Tenterden, Bernard, Cockburn and Palmer . . 96
Drawn by Orson Lowell from photographs

The American Representatives at Geneva—Cushing, Evarts, Adams, Davis and Waite 97
Drawn by Orson Lowell from photographs

U. S. Grant 99
From a very rare photograph by Walker, June 2, 1875

George Bancroft 101
Drawn by Alfred Brennan from a photograph in the historical collection of H. W. Fay

Emperor William I. of Germany 105

Oakes Ames 107
Drawn by Alfred Brennan from a photograph

Daniel H. Chamberlain 113

W. Beverley Nash 121

Charles Hayes, of Alabama . . . 128

Elisha Baxter 135
Drawn by J. Brittain from a photograph

Joseph Brooks 135
Drawn by J. Brittain from a photograph

Chief Justice John McClure . . . 135
Drawn by J. Brittain from a photograph

Augustus H. Garland . . . 139

Adelbert Ames 142

Richard O'Leary, Mayor of Vicksburg in 1874 . . 144

William Pitt Kellogg 156
Drawn by Alfred Brennan from a photograph

PLANS, MAPS, FACSIMILES, ETC.

TITLE	PAGE
Railroads of the United States in 1870	4
Railroads of the United States in 1894	5
Chicago in 1869, Showing the Burned District	8
Chicago in 1894	9
Autograph Telegram from General Sheridan to the Secretary of War, Announcing the Great Fire at Chicago *In the collection of C. F. Gunther*	10
Nast Caricature: "The Brains that Achieved the Tammany Victory at the Rochester Convention"	13
Nast Caricature: "Who Stole the People's Money?"	15
Fragment from the Original Engrossed Text of the Fourteenth Amendment at the State Department, Washington	24
A Ku-Klux Warning in Mississippi, put in Evidence Before the Congressional Committee	27
A Newspaper Cutting put in Evidence Before the Congressional Committee	27
Signatures to the Treaty of Washington *From the original at the State Department, Washington*	32
Grant and Wilson Campaign Medal	74
Greeley Campaign Medals and Badge	75
Map of the Northwest Water Boundary	102
Summary of the Amounts Paid to One Firm for Furniture by the South Carolina Legislature of 1872-74 *From the Report of the Investigating Committee*	115
"Gratuity" Voted to Governor Moses by the South Carolina Legislature of 1871 *From the original at the State House, Columbia*	116
A Bill for Furnishing the State House at Columbia, South Carolina, in 1872 *From the original at the State House, Columbia*	119
Map of the Region Occupied by the Modocs, Showing the "Lava Beds"	174
Ku-Klux Notice Posted up in Mississippi During the Election of 1876	214
One of the Cipher Dispatches Sent During the Election Deadlock with Translation *From the original put in evidence before the Congressional Committee*	217
Two Chamberlain-Hampton Letters After the State Election of 1876 in South Carolina *From the originals at the State House, Columbia*	229
A "Mollie Maguire" Notice	293
A Notice put in Evidence During the "Mollie Maguire" Prosecutions	294
A "Mollie Maguire" Notice	295
Front Page of the Issue of *Truth* Containing the Morey Letter	315

THE LAST QUARTER-CENTURY
IN THE UNITED STATES

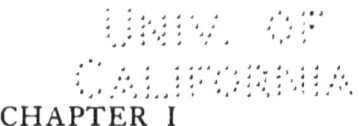

CHAPTER I

THE UNITED STATES AT THE CLOSE OF RECONSTRUCTION

LAND AND PEOPLE IN 1870.—TERRITORIES.—RAILROADS IN THE WEST.—FENIAN MOVEMENTS.—BOSTON'S PEACE JUBILEES.—THE GREAT CITIES.—THE CHICAGO FIRE.—THE BOSTON FIRE.—THE TWEED RING.—TWEED'S ESCAPE AND CAPTURE.—FINANCIAL CONDITION OF THE NATION.—SHIPS.—ARMY AND NAVY.—RECONSTRUCTION, THE PROBLEM.—THE PRESIDENTIAL AND THE CONGRESSIONAL PLAN.—IRON LAW OF MARCH 2, 1867.—THE PROCESS OF RECONSTRUCTION.—SITUATION IN 1870 —DEBATE ON THE COERCION OF STATES.—OUTCOME.—THE TEST OATH.—ALL STATES AT LAST AGAIN REPRESENTED IN BOTH HOUSES OF CONGRESS.

IN 1870 the United States covered the same tract of the globe's surface as now, amounting to four million square miles. Hardly more than a fifth of this represented the United States of 1789. About a third of the vast domain was settled, the western frontier running irregularly parallel with the Mississippi, but nearer to that stream than to the Rocky Mountains. The centre of population was forty-eight miles east by north of Cincinnati, having moved westward forty-two miles since 1860. Except certain well-peopled sections on the Pacific slope, and small civilized strips in Utah, Colorado, and New Mexico, the Great West had but a tenuous white population. Over immense regions it was still an Indian fastness, rejoicing in a reputation, which few could verify, for rare scenery, fertile valleys, rich mines, and a delightful climate.

The American people numbered 38,558,371 souls. Not quite one in seven had colored blood, while a little more than that proportion were of foreign birth, most of these Irish and German. In the settled parts of our country the population had a density of 30.3 persons to the square mile, southern New England being the most closely peopled. Much of western Pennsylvania was in the condition of the newest States, railroads building as never before, population increasing at a remarkable rate, and industries developing on every hand. Petroleum, which before the Civil War had been skimmed off the streams of the oil region and sold for medicine, in 1870 developed a yield of over five and a half million gallons in Pennsylvania alone, more than eleven times as much as a decade previous. The West was rapidly recruiting itself from the East, the city from the country. Between 1790 and 1860 our urban population had increased from one in thirty to one in six; in 1870 more than one in five dwelt in cities.

There were now thirty-seven States, nine organized territories, and two unorganized ones, these being Alaska and the Indian Territory. Noteworthy among the territories was Washington, whose population had doubled in the preceding decade and was now 24,000. Colorado had about 40,000. Utah boasted 86,000, one-third of whom were foreigners. New Mexico numbered in 1870, 91,874, in 1871, 114,000, less than one to each square mile. Arizona was still much harried by Indians, and contained hardly 10,000 civilized men. This year female suffrage, hitherto unknown in America, if not in the world, gained a foothold in Wyoming and in Utah.

During the ten years preceding 1870 the railroad mileage of the country nearly doubled. The Union and Central Pacific Roads, forming the only transcontinental line then in existence, had been completed on May 10, 1869. Into Denver already came, besides the Union Pacific, three other railroads, all short, while Washington Territory contained the germ of the Northern Pacific, whose eastern extremity had just been begun at Duluth. Dakota had sixty-five miles of railway, Wyoming four hundred and fifty-nine. With the above exceptions the territories were wholly without railroads.

DRIVING THE LAST SPIKE OF THE UNION PACIFIC. SCENE AT PROMONTORY POINT, UTAH, MAY 10, 1869

Drawn by B. West Clinedinst from photographs in the possession of General G. M. Dodge

THE LAST QUARTER-CENTURY

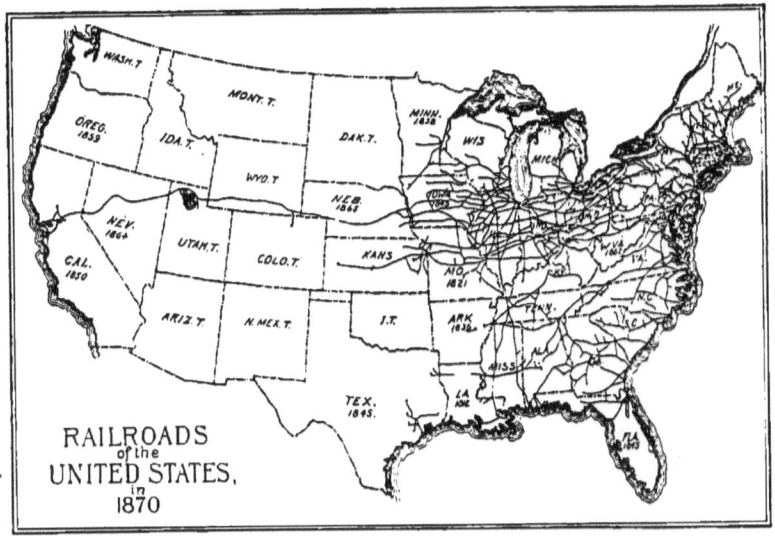

RAILROADS of the UNITED STATES, in 1870

The close of the long Civil War had gladdened all true American hearts. Only the Fenians sought further bloodshed, and even they pursued their aim rather feebly. Their attempt, in April, 1866, to capture the British island of Campobello, near Eastport, Me., collapsed on the approach of Gen. Meade with United States troops. On June 1 a detachment of Fenians succeeded in capturing Fort Erie, across from Buffalo, and on the 7th another company occupied St. Armand, just over the Vermont border; but both parties were speedily dislodged and routed. The heart of the nation delighted in peace. In 1869, carrying out a conception of Mr. P. S. Gilmore, Boston held a great Peace Jubilee to celebrate the end of the late fraternal strife. An immense coliseum was erected for the performances, which began on June 15 and lasted till June 20. A choir of 10,000 singers, an orchestra of over 1,000 pieces, a battery of artillery, and an anvil chorus of 100 men beating anvils made up the unique musical *ensemble*. So great was the success, financially and other-

THE GREAT CITIES

RAILROADS of the UNITED STATES. in 1894.

wise, of this scheme, that in 1872 Mr. Gilmore undertook an international Peace Jubilee. This, too, was held in Boston, opening June 17 and lasting till July 4. Twenty thousand voices and an orchestra 2,000 strong joined in it, parts being taken also by choice military bands from France, Germany and England, and from the United States Marine Corps. Vast crowds were attracted, but the receipts this time fell far short of the expenditures.

In 1870, New York, with 942,292 inhabitants, Philadelphia, with 674,022, Brooklyn, with 396,099, St. Louis, with 310,864, and Chicago, with 298,977, were, as in 1890, our five largest cities, and they had the same relative size as in 1890, save that Chicago meantime passed from the fifth to the second place. This in the face of adversity. In October, 1871, the city was devastated by one of the most terrible conflagrations of modern times. It began on Sunday evening, the 8th, in a wooden barn on DeKoven Street, in the West Division. Lumber yards were numerous there, and through

THE LAST QUARTER-CENTURY

The Court House at Chicago before the Fire

these the flames raged, leaping across the stream before a strong westerly wind into the Southern Division, which was closely built up with stores and warehouses. The fire continued all Monday. It crossed the main channel of the Chicago River into the Northern Division, sweeping all before it.

"Niagara sank into insignificance compared with that towering wall of whirling, seething, roaring flame. It swept on and on, devouring the massive stone blocks as though they had been the cardboard playthings of a child. Looking under the flame one could see, in the very centre of the furnace, stately buildings on either side of Randolph Street whose beauty and magnificence and whose wealth of contents were admired by thousands the day before. A moment and the flickering flame crept out of a window; another and another hissing tongue followed; a sheet of fire joined the whirling mass above, and the giant structure was gone. One pile after another thus dissolved like snow on the mountain. Loud

The Chicago Court House after the Fire

THE CHICAGO FIRE

The Chicago Court House in 1895

detonations to the right and left, where buildings were being blown up, the falling of walls and the roaring of flames, the moaning of the wind and of the crowd, and the shrill whistling of tugs endeavoring to remove the shipping out of the reach of danger, made up a frightful discord of sounds that will live in every hearer's memory while his life shall last."

The glare could be seen for hundreds of miles over the prairie and the lake. The river seemed to boil and mingle its steam with the smoke. Early Monday morning the Tribune building, the only structure left in the business quarter, remained intact. Two patrols were constantly at work; one sweeping away live coals and brands, the other watching the roofs. Till four o'clock the reporters passed in regular reports of the fire. At five the forms were sent down. In ten minutes the cylinder presses would have been at work. At that moment the front basement is discovered on fire. The water-plug at the corner is opened, but the water-works have been destroyed. The pressmen have to fly for their lives. By ten o'clock the block is in ashes.

THE LAST QUARTER-CENTURY

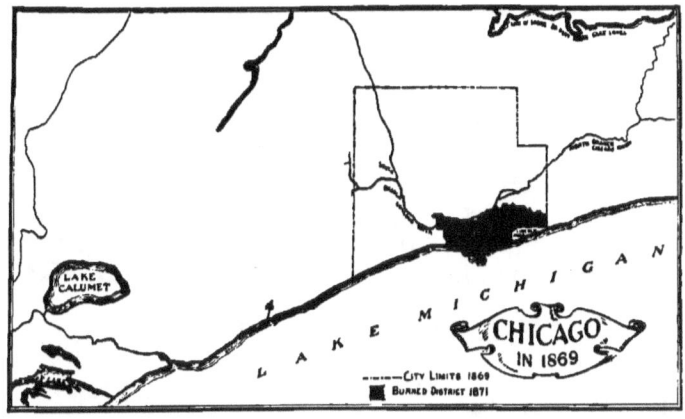

Streets, bridges, parks are gorged with panic-stricken throngs. Not a few are crazed by terror. One old woman stumbles along under a great bundle, crooning Mother Goose melodies. Anarchy reigns. The horrors of the night are multiplied by drunkenness, arson, burglary, murder, rape. Vigilance committees are formed. It was estimated that fifty ruffians first and last were shot in their tracks, among them five notorious criminals. Convicts locked in the court-house basement would have been burnt alive but for the Mayor's timely order, which his son, with the utmost difficulty and danger, delivered after the building had began to burn.

The morning after the fire the indomitable Chicago pluck began to show itself. William D. Kerfoot knocked together a shanty, facetiously called "Kerfoot's block," an unrivalled structure, for it was the only one in the neighborhood. To it he nailed a sign which well typified the spirit of the city. "Wm. D. Kerfoot, all gone but wife, children, and ENERGY." The next Sunday the Rev. Dr. Collyer preached where his church had formerly stood, in the midst of the city, yet in the heart of a wilderness, more than a mile from human habitation.

Not till Tuesday morning was the headway of the fire checked, and parts of the charred *débris* smouldered on for

THE BOSTON FIRE

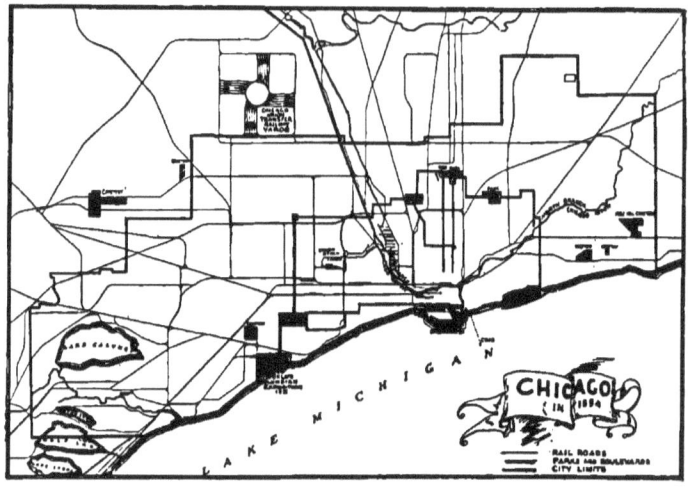

months. Nearly three and a third square miles were burned over; 17,450 buildings were destroyed; 98,500 persons rendered homeless; and over 250 killed. The total direct loss of property amounted to $190,000,000, which indirect losses, as estimated, swelled to $290,000,000. Fifty-six insurance companies were rendered insolvent by the fire. A Relief and Aid Society was at once formed, which within a month had subscriptions from all over the country amounting to three and a half million dollars, was aiding 60,000 people, and had assisted in building 4,000 temporary shelters. Later the Illinois legislature voted aid.

Next after that of Chicago the most destructive conflagration ever known in the United States visited Boston in 1872. It originated during Saturday evening, November 9, on the corner of Kingston and Summer Streets, spread with terrible rapidity east and north, and raged with little abatement till nearly noon next day. During Sunday afternoon the flames seemed well under control, but an explosion of gas about midnight set them raging afresh, and much of Monday had passed before they were subdued. Ordinary appliances for fighting

THE LAST QUARTER-CENTURY

Facsimile of the Autograph Telegram from General Sheridan to the Secretary of War, announcing the Great Fire at Chicago; in the collection of C. F. Gunther

fire were of no avail, the demon being at many points brought to bay only by the free use of dynamite to blow up buildings in his path. Sixty-five acres were laid waste. Washington Street from Bedford to Milk formed the western limit of the tract, which, at Milk, receded to Devonshire, lying east of this from Milk to State, which formed its northern term. Nothing but the waters of the harbor stayed the eastern march of the fire. The district burned had been the home of Boston's wholesale trade, containing the finest business blocks which the city could boast. Fourteen or fifteen lives were lost, and not far from eight hundred buildings consumed. The property loss was placed at $80,000,000.

THE TWEED RING

Meantime New York City was suffering from an evil worse than fire, the frauds of the "Tweed Ring," notorious forevermore. In the summer of 1870 proof was published of vast frauds by leading city officials, prominent among them "Boss" William M. Tweed, who, in the language of Judge Noah Davis, "saw fit to pervert the powers with which he was clothed, in a manner more infamous, more outrageous, than any instance of a like character which the history of the civilized world afforded."

William Marcy Tweed was born in 1823, at 24 Cherry Street, New York City. A youth devoted to business made him a fair penman and an adept reckoner, but not a business man. He, indeed, once attempted business, but, as he gave his chief attention to speculation, gambling and ward politics, completely failed, so that he seems forever to have renounced legitimate money-making. As a volunteer fireman, known as "Big Six," a gross, licentious Falstaff of real life, albeit loyal and helpful to his friends, Tweed led the "Roughs," being opposed by his more decent fellows, the "Quills." The tide of "respectability," receding uptown, left Tweed's ward in the hands of poor immigrants or the sons of such, who became partly his willing accomplices, partly his unwitting tools, in his onslaughts upon taxpayers. He began these forays at twenty-seven, as Alderman, suspended them for a time in Congress, resumed them in 1857 as Public School Commissioner, continued and enlarged them as member and four times President of the Board of Supervisors, and brought them to a climax as a functionary of the Street Department. He thus became, in time, the central sun in the system of brilliant luminaries known as the "Tweed Ring."

The multitudinous officials of the city were the Ring's slaves. At one time eight hundred policemen stood guard to prevent a hostile majority, in Tammany Hall itself, from meeting. The thugs of the city, nick-named "Tweed's lambs," rendered invaluable services at caucus and convention. Two

THE LAST QUARTER-CENTURY

days before election these venal cohorts would assemble in the 340 election districts, each man of them being listed and registered under several assumed names and addresses. From Tweed's house in 1868 six registered, from Justice Shandley's nine, from the Coroner's thirteen. A State Senator's house was put down as the home of thirty voters. One Alderman's residence nominally housed twenty, another's twenty-five, an Assemblyman's fifteen. And so it went. Bales of fictitious naturalization papers were secured. One year 105,000 blank applications and 69,000 certificates were ordered printed. In one case thirteen men, in another fifteen, were naturalized in five minutes. The new citizens "put in" election day following their leaders from polling place to polling place as needed.

When thieves could be kept in power by such means plunder was easy and brazen. Contractors on public works were systematically forced to pay handsome bonuses to the Ring. One of them testified: "When I commenced building I asked Tweed how to make out the bills, and he said: 'Have fifteen per cent. over.' I asked what that was for, and he said, 'Give that to me and I will take care of your bills.' I handed him the percentage after that." Innumerable methods of fraud were successfully tried. During the year 1863 the expenditures of the Street Department were $650,000. Within four years Tweed quadrupled them. A species of asphalt paving, dubbed "Fisk's poultice," so bad that a grand jury actually declared it a public nuisance, was laid in great quantities at vast cost to the city. Official advertising was doled to twenty-six daily and fifty-four weekly sheets, of which twenty-seven vanished on its withdrawal. But all the other robber enterprises paled before the city Court House job. This structure, com-

TWEED

THE TWEED RING

menced in 1868, under stipulation that it should not cost more than $250,000, was in 1871 still unfinished after an outlay of $8,000,000, four times as much as was spent on Parliament House in London. Its ostensible cost, at last, was not less than $12,000,000. As by witchcraft the city's debt was in two years more than doubled. The Ring's operations cheated the city's tax-payers, first and last, out of no less than

[Reproduced from Harper's Weekly (October 21, 1871) by permission of Messrs. Harper & Brothers. Copyright, 1871, by Harper & Brothers]

THE BRAINS
that achieved the Tammany Victory at the Rochester Democratic Convention

$160,000,000, "or four times the fine levied on Paris by the German army." Though wallowing in lucre, and prodigal withal, Tweed was yet insatiably greedy. " His hands were everywhere, and everywhere they were they were feeling for money." In 1871 he boasted of being worth $20,000,000, and vowed soon to be as rich as Vanderbilt.

With his coarse nature the Boss revelled in jibes made at the expense of his honor. He used gleefully to show his friends the safe where he kept money for bribing legislators, finding those of the " Tammany Republican " stripe easiest game. Of the contractor who was decorating his country place at Greenwich he inquired, pointing to a statue, " Who the hell is that ? " " That is Mercury, the god of merchants and thieves," was the reply. " That's bully ! " said Tweed. " Put him over the front door." His donation of $100 for an altar cloth in the Greenwich Methodist Church the trustees sent back, declaring that they wanted none of his stolen money. Other charitable gifts of his were better received.

The city papers, even those least corruptible, were for long either neutral or else favorable to the Ring, but its doings were by no means unknown. They were matters of general surmise and criticism, criticism that seemed hopeless, so hard was it to obtain exact evidence.

But pride goeth before a fall. Amid its greatest triumph the Ring sowed the wind whence rose the whirlwind which wrought its ruin. At a secret meeting held in the house of John Morrissey, pugilist member of Congress, certain of the unsatisfied, soon known as the " Young Democracy," planned a revolt. Endeavoring to prevent the grant by the New York legislature of a new charter which the Ring sought, the insurgents met apparent defeat, which, however, ultimately proved victory, Tweed building for himself far worse than he knew. The new charter, abstractly good, in concentrating power concentrated responsibility also, showing the outraged people, when awakened, where to strike for liberty. In spite of whitewashing by prominent citizens, of blandishments and bulldozing, of attempts to buy the stock of the *Times* and to boycott *Harper's Weekly*, where Nast's cartoons—his first work of the kind—gave the Ring international notoriety, the reform spirit proved irresistible. The bar had been servile or quiet, but the New York Bar Association was now formed, which at once became what it has ever since been, a most influential censor of the bench. The Young Democracy grew powerful. Public-spirited citizens organized a Council of Political Reform.

The occasion of conclusive exposure was trivial enough. Sheriff O'Brien was refused part of what he thought his share of the sheriff fees. An expert accountant in the Comptroller's office supplied him with damning evidence against the Ring. On July 18, 1871, Mr. O'Brien walked into the *Times* office and, handing the editor a bundle of documents, said : " There are all the figures : you can do with them just what you please." The figures were published on the 20th in an exhibit printed in English and German, causing excitement compared with which that arising from the Orange Riot of July 12th seemed

THE TWEED RING

[Reproduced from Harper's Weekly (August 19, 1871) by permission of Messrs. Harper & Brothers. Copyright, 1871, by Harper & Brothers]

trifling. The sensation did not end with talk. On September 4th a mass-meeting of citizens was held at Cooper Institute and a committee of seventy prominent men chosen to probe the frauds and to punish the perpetrators. For the work of prosecution the Attorney-General appointed Charles O'Conor, who associated with himself the ablest counsel. Samuel J. Tilden was conspicuously active in the prosecution, thus laying the foundation for that popularity which made him the Governor of New York, 1875-'77, and in 1876 the Democratic candidate for the presidency of the United States.

On October 28, 1871, Tweed was arrested and gave a million dollars bail. In November, the same year, he was elected to the State Senate, but did not take his seat. On December 16th he was again arrested, and released on $5,000 bail. The jury disagreed on the first suit, but on the second he was convicted and sentenced to pay a fine of $12,550 and to suffer twelve years imprisonment. This sentence was set aside by the Court of Appeals and Tweed's discharge ordered. In the meantime other suits had been brought, among them one to recover $6,000,000. Failing to find bail for $3,000,000, he was sent to the Ludlow Street Jail. Being allowed to ride in the Park and occasionally to visit his residence, one day in December he escaped from his keepers. After hiding for several months he succeeded in reaching Cuba. A fisherman found him, sunburnt and weary but not homesick, and led him to Santiago. Instead of taking him to a hotel, Tweed's guide handed him over to the police as probably some American filibuster come to free Cuba. The American consul procured his release (his passports had been given him under an assumed name), but later found him out. The discovery was too late, for he had again escaped and embarked for Spain, thinking there to be at rest, as we then had no extradition treaty with that country. Landing at Vigo, he found the governor of the place with police waiting for him, and was soon homeward bound on an American war-vessel. Caleb Cushing, our Minister at Madrid, had learned of his departure for that realm, and had put the authorities on their guard. To help them identify their man he furnished them a caricature by Nast, representing Tweed as a Tammany policeman gripping two boys by the hair. Thus it came about that "*Twid antelme*" was apprehended by our peninsular friends as a *child-stealer*. Though everything possible was done to render him comfortable in jail, Tweed sighed for liberty. He promised, if released, to turn State's evidence and to give up all his property and effects. Some papers suggested that the public pitied the man and would be glad to have him set free. No compromise with him was made, however, and he continued in jail till his death in 1878.

In 1870 the national debt amounted to a little less than $2,500,000,000, nearly three times the sum of all the country's

SHIPS

State, county and municipal indebtedness combined. Yet the revenues sufficed to meet the interest and gradually to pay off the principal. Reduction in the rate of taxation was recommended in the President's Message, as also a refunding of the debt, but this latter was postponed for the time by the outbreak of the Franco-Prussian war. Our imports for the year ending June, 1870, were worth $462,377,587, which exceeded the figure for any previous fiscal year. The duties on these imports footed up nearly $195,000,000. The imports for the year fell short of the exports by over $36,000,000.

Painful to notice was the small proportion of our commerce which was carried on in American vessels. Between 1850 and 1855 we had outstripped England both in shipbuilding and in tonnage. Seventy-five per cent. of our ocean traffic was then borne in American vessels; in 1869 the proportion had fallen to thirty per cent. The decay of our merchant marine was originally due to the fatal enterprise of Confederate privateers during the war, and to the change now going on from wood to iron as the material for ships. This transferred to British builders the special advantage which Americans had so long as wood was used. Why the advantage continued with the British was a much-disputed question, not yet separating the two political parties. Protectionists found it in British labor and British subsidies to steamship lines, and wished to offset it by bounties and by still higher subsidies to American shipping enterprise. Anti-protectionists traced all the difficulty to protection, particularly denouncing the duties on materials imported for ship-building. They urged free United States registry for foreign-built ships, or at least the privilege of importing free of duty all stock to be used in the construction of ships.

The United States navy was neglected after the war and soon became antiquated, being occupied mainly with the most peaceful enterprises, such as hydrographic and coast surveys. Indeed, it was fitted only for such. The destruction of the pirate Forward on the coast of Mexico and the bombardment of certain Corean forts were its only warlike deeds during 1870. The army, this year, numbered 34,000 enlisted men, soon to be reduced to the legal number of 30,000. It was busied in making surveys, in protecting settlers against Indians, and one-sixth of it in assisting Government officials to keep order in the South. Some of the army officers and men were also busy in taking and publishing over the country scientific observations of the weather, an extremely useful form of public service then in its infancy. The United States Weather Bureau dates from 1870, its origin and organization mainly due to the then Chief Signal Officer of the Army, General Albert J. Myer.

When the resuscitation of the South began, it raised a most interesting constitutional question, viz., what effect secession had upon the States guilty of it; whether or not it was an act of State suicide. That it amounted to suicide, leaving, of the State that was, "nothing but men and dirt," was held by many, among them Sumner and Stevens. Both these men conceived the problem of the disordered States as that of an out-and-out "reconstruction;" and they ascribed to Congress the right to work its will in the conquered region, changing old State lines and institutions as it might please, and postponing settlement for any convenient length of time. Against this theory a strong party maintained that of State indestructibility, asserting the total nullity of secession acts.

The universal supposition at first was that the Southern States needed only "restoration," to be conducted by the President. "Restoration" was the policy of Presidents Lincoln and Johnson; as also of the entire Democracy. Following the idea of simple restoration, Lincoln had recognized loyal State governments in Virginia at the beginning of the war, and in Louisiana, Arkansas, and Tennessee later. During 1865 Johnson did the same in all the other States lately in secession.

THE IRON LAW OF MARCH 2, 1867

Strong considerations had led Congress, at this point, to assume charge of the restitution of the States, and, braving President Johnson's uttermost opposition and spite, to rip up the entire presidential work. "The same authority which recognized the existence of the war" seemed "the only authority having the constitutional right to determine when, for all purposes, the war had ceased. The Act of March 2, 1867, was a legislative declaration that the war which sprang from the Rebellion was not, to all intents and purposes, ended; and that it should be held to continue until State governments, republican in form, and subordinate to the Constitution and laws, should be established."*

On March 2, 1866, it was enacted that neither House should admit a member from any seceder-State till a congressional vote had declared the State entitled to representation. The ratification of the Fourteenth Amendment, making negroes citizens of the United States and forbidding legislation to abridge their privileges, was made prerequisite to such vote. Tennessee accepted the terms in July, but, as action was optional, all the other States declined, thus defeating for the time this amendment. Congress now determined not to wait for the lagging States, but to enforce their reconstruction. The iron law of March 2, 1867, replaced "secessia" under military rule, permitted the loyal citizens of any State, blacks included, to raise a convention and frame a constitution enfranchising negroes, and decreed that when such constitution had been ratified by the electors to the convention and approved by Congress, and when the legislature under it had ratified the Fourteenth Amendment and this had become part of the Constitution, then the State might be represented in Congress. The supplementary law of March 19th hastened the process by giving district commanders the oversight of registration and the initiative in calling conventions.

* Opinion of Attorney-General E. R. Hoar, May 31, 1869.

THE LAST QUARTER-CENTURY

HIRAM R. REVELS
of Mississippi
The first colored member of the U. S. Senate. Admitted February 25th, 1870

JOSEPH F. RAINEY
of South Carolina
The first colored member of the U. S. House of Representatives. Admitted December 12, 1871

THE FIRST COLORED MEMBERS OF CONGRESS

After this the work went rapidly on. Registration boards were appointed, the test-oath* applied, delegates elected, and constitutions framed and adopted. These instruments in all cases abolished slavery, repudiated the Confederate debt and the pretended right of a State to secede, declared the secession acts of 1861 null and void, ordained manhood suffrage, and prohibited the passage of laws to abridge this.

Congress then acted. Alabama, Arkansas, North and South Carolina, Florida, Georgia and Louisiana, were admitted to representation in June, 1868, agreeing never to revoke universal suffrage. As Georgia was suspected of evading some of the requirements, the senators from the State were refused seats at Washington, and did not obtain them till the last of January, 1871. Georgia's representatives were given seats, but

---

TEST OATH.—Act of July 2, 1862. Be it enacted, etc. That hereafter every person elected or appointed to any office of honor or profit under the Government of the United States, either in the civil, military, or naval departments of the public service, excepting the President of the United States, shall, before entering upon the duties of such office, and before being entitled to any of the salary, or other emoluments thereof, take and subscribe the following oath or affirmation : " I, A. B., do solemnly swear (or affirm) that I have never voluntarily borne arms against the United States since I have been a citizen thereof; that I have voluntarily given no aid, countenance, counsel or encouragement to persons engaged in armed hostility thereto ; that I have neither sought nor accepted nor attempted to exercise the functions of any office whatever, under any authority or pretended authority in hostility to the United States, that I have not yielded a voluntary support to any pretended government, authority, power or constitution within the United States hostile or inimical thereto. And I do further swear (or affirm) that, to the best of my knowledge and ability, I will support and defend the Constitution of the United States against all enemies, foreign and domestic ; that I will bear true faith and allegiance to the same ; that I take this obligation freely, without any mental reservation, or purpose of evasion, and that I will well and faithfully discharge the duties of the office on which I am about to enter, so help me God."

ALL STATES AGAIN REPRESENTED

subsequently, in 1869, these were vacated, and they remained empty till 1871. To regain representation in Congress this State, too, was obliged to ratify the Fifteenth Amendment.

Thus stood matters in 1870: all but four of the late Confederate States nominally back in the Union, these still contumacious, but confronted by an inflexible Congress, which barred them from every national function of statehood till they had conformed to all the conditions above described.

Representative George E. Harris, of Mississippi. Admitted February 23, 1870

Senator John F. Lewis, of Virginia. Admitted January 27, 1870

"*RECONSTRUCTED CONGRESSMEN*"

Virginia, Mississippi, and Texas held out the longest. The Act of April 10, 1869, was passed to hasten their action, authorizing the President to call elections for ratifying or rejecting the new constitutions in those States. To punish the States' delay, their new legislatures were required to ratify the proposed Fifteenth Amendment, guaranteeing the negro's right to vote, as well as the Fourteenth. When it passed the House the bill lacked such a provision, which was moved by Senator Morton, of Indiana, an ultra Republican. Morton urged the adoption of the amendments as of vast importance to the country. If the three recalcitrant States were commanded to ratify and did so, the negroes' ballot would be once for all assured, placing the South forever in loyal hands. The unreconstructed States, he said, ought not to oppose this requirement, and their opposition was sad evidence of their treacherous purpose later to amend their constitutions so as to strike down colored suffrage. Senator Thurman replied that the question concerned every State in the Union. By forcing these three States to ratify this amendment, he declared, "you do not coerce them alone. You coerce Ohio, you coerce Illinois, you coerce every State whose people are unwilling to adopt the amendment." Senator Bayard thought it a most dangerous Federal encroachment to take from the States and deposit with the Federal Government the regulation of the elective franchise, " the power of all powers, that which underlies and creates all other powers." The opposition was, however, overborne, and by February, 1870, the new constitutions, together with the Fourteenth and Fifteenth Amendments to the United States Constitution, had been ratified, and the three belated States again stood knocking at the doors of Congress.

The House of Representatives began by declaring Virginia entitled to representation in the national legislature. The Senate, more radical, influenced by the still lurking suspicion of bad faith, amended this simple declaration with a provision requiring the " test-oath " of loyalty from members of the Legislature and public officers before they should resume their duties, at the same time making it a condition that the constitution of the State should never be so amended as to restrict the suffrage, the right to hold office, or the privilege of attending public schools. Similar provisos were attached to the resolution admitting senators and representatives from the other two States. Out of sheer weariness the House concurred. By January 30, 1871, all the States were again represented in both Houses, as in 1860.

CHAPTER II

GENERAL GRANT AS A CIVIL CHIEF

THE REPUBLICAN PARTY IN 1870.—ITS DEFECTS.—PRESIDENT GRANT'S SHORTCOMINGS.—HIS FIRST CABINET.—THE PARTY'S ATTITUDE TOWARD THE TARIFF.—TOWARD THE DEMOCRACY.—TOWARD RE-ENFRANCHISEMENT AT THE SOUTH.—THE LIBERAL MOVEMENT.—THE DEMOCRATS.—THE "NEW DEPARTURE" AMONG THEM.—VALLANDIGHAM.—JOHN QUINCY ADAMS.—RECONSTRUCTION.—ERRORS COMMITTED THEREIN.—THE FIFTEENTH AMENDMENT.—THE KU-KLUX KLAN.—THE FORCE BILL.—RE-ENFRANCHISEMENT AT THE SOUTH.—GRANT AND THE NATION'S FINANCES.—GOULD AND FISK.—BLACK FRIDAY.—THE TREATY OF WASHINGTON.—RELATIONS WITH CUBA.—PROPOSED "ANNEXION" OF SANTO DOMINGO.—SUMNER AND THE ADMINISTRATION.

THE year 1870 found the Republican party in full power. In the Senate of the Forty-first Congress sat but nine Democrats, and out of its two hundred and thirty Representatives only seventy-five were Democrats. Spite of differences in their own ranks, spite of the frantic struggles of the opposition, the Republican policy of reconstruction had been put through and consummated by the Fifteenth Amendment, "making all men equal." Sweepingly victorious upon every issue recently tried, freed, moreover, from the incubus with which President Johnson had weighted them, having elected to the executive chair of the nation a hero whom practically the entire party and country trusted, the Republicans could not but be in a happy mood. No wonder that the Republican platforms of the different States in 1870 and 1871 breathed utmost satisfaction and hope.

This self-gratulatory spirit among the Republicans was an unhealthy sign. Honest as were its rank and file and a majority of its leaders, much corruption defiled the party's

Article XIV.

Section 1. All persons born or naturalized in the United States, and subject to the jurisdiction thereof, are citizens of the United States and of the State wherein they reside. No State shall make or enforce any law which shall abridge the privileges or immunities of citizens of the United States; nor shall any State deprive any person of life, liberty, or property, without due process of law; nor deny to any person within its jurisdiction the equal protection of the laws.

A Fragment in Facsimile from the Original Engrossed Text of the Fourteenth Amendment, at the State Department, Washington. Adopted July 28, 1866

high places. "The early movements of Grant as President were very discouraging. His attempt to form a cabinet without consultation with any one, and with very little knowledge, except social intercourse, of the persons appointed, created a doubt that he would be as successful as a President as he had been as a general, a doubt that increased and became a conviction in the minds of many of his best friends. . . The impression prevailed that the President regarded the heads of departments, invested by law with specific and independent duties, as mere subordinates, whose functions he might assume. . . It can hardly be said that we had a strictly Republican administration during Grant's two terms. While Republicans were selected to fill the leading offices, the policy adopted and the controlling influence around him were purely personal. He consulted but few of the Senators or members, and they were known as his personal friends. Mr. Conkling, by his imperious will, soon gained a strong influence over the President, and from this came feuds, jealousies and enmities, that greatly weakened the Republican party and threatened its ascendancy."* In the questions of taxation, debt and finance, so important to the welfare of all, Grant showed little interest. " His veto of the bill to increase the amount of United States notes, on the 22d of April, 1874, was

---

* John Sherman's Recollections of Forty Years in the House, Senate and Cabinet.

THE RECONSTRUCTION COMMITTEE

Drawn by W. R. Leigh

The Joint Committee of Fifteen, appointed to "inquire into the condition of affairs in the so-called Confederate States," who finally adopted, April 28, 1866, a series of resolutions embodying a recommendation which afterward took form at the Fourteenth Amendment. Senators W. P. Fessenden, Maine, Chairman; J. W. Grimes, Iowa; Ira Harris, New York; J. M. Howard, Michigan; George H. Williams, Oregon. Representatives: Thaddeus Stevens, Pennsylvania; E. B. Washburn, Illinois; Justin S. Morrill, Vermont; J. A. Bingham, Ohio; G. S. Boutwell, Massachusetts; Roscoe Conkling, New York; H. T. Blow, Missouri; H. M. Grider, Kentucky; A. J. Rodgers, New Jersey; Senator Reverdy Johnson, Maryland. The last three voted against the resolutions.

PRESIDENT GRANT'S SHORTCOMINGS

"Dam Your Soul. The Horrible Sepulchre and Bloody Moon has at last arrived. Some live to-day to-morrow "*Die.*" We the undersigned understand through our Grand "*Cyclops*" that you have recommended a big Black Nigger for Male agent on our no rods; wel, sir, Jest you understand in time if he gets on the rode you can make up your mind to pull rope. If you have any thing to say in regard to the Matter, meet the Grand Cyclops and Conclave at Den No. 4 at 12 o'clock midnight, Oct. 1st, 1871.
  When you are in Calera we warn you to hold your tounge and not speak so much with your month or otherwise you will be taken on supprise and led out by the Klan and learnt to stretch hemp. Beware. Beware. Beware. Beware.
  (Signed) "PHILLIP ISENBAUM,
               "*Grand Cyclops.*
           "JOHN BANKSTOWN
           "ESAU DAVES.
           "MARCUS THOMAS.
"You know who. And all others of the Klan." "BLOODY BONES.

Facsimile of a Ku-Klux "Warning" in Mississippi—put in evidence before the Congressional Committee

an exception, but on this he changed his mind, as he had expressed his approval of the bill when pending."*

"General Grant became afterward so thoroughly a party man that it is necessary to recall by a positive effort that his position was looked upon as very uncertain when his administration began. His report to President Johnson on the condition of the Southern States had indicated that he was not in sympathy with the congressional plan of reconstruction, which was the burning question of the time. Party leaders were nervous lest he should prove unwilling to conduct his administration in harmony with them, and in case of a break they feared a total loss of party control in the country. Members of the administration were therefore urged strenuously to make no issue on what might be regarded as a personal wish of the President,

[From the Independent Monitor, Tuscaloosa, Alabama, September 1, 1868.]
A PROSPECTIVE SCENE IN THE CITY OF OAKS, 4TH OF MARCH, 1869.

"Hang, curs, hang! * * * * *Their* complexion is perfect gallows. Stand fast, good fate, to *their* hanging! * * * * If they be not born to be hanged, our case is miserable."
  The above cut represents the fate in store for those great pests of Southern society—the carpet-bagger and scalawag—if found in Dixie's land after the break of day on the 4th of March next.

A Newspaper Cutting put in Evidence before the Congressional Committee

*John Sherman's Recollections of Forty Years in the House, Senate and Cabinet

JAMES FISK, Jr.
(After a photograph by Rockwood)

and they shared the opinions of their party friends enough to make them feel the importance of avoiding collision."*

General Grant's deficiencies in the presidential office were, however, nearly all due to faults of his character which were based in virtues. To the man's moral and physical courage, and his calm, but all but stubborn bearing, he added a magnanimity and an unsuspecting integrity, which were at once his strength and his weakness. Herein lay the secret of the love men bore him and of their trust in him. But these characteristics combined with his inexperience of civil life to disarm him against the dishonorable subtleties of pretended friends, thus continually compromising him. "A certain class of public men adopted the practice of getting an audience and making speeches before him, urging their plans with skillful advocacy and impassioned manner. They would then leave him without asking for any reply, and trust to the effect they had produced. Perhaps their associates would follow the matter up in a similar way. It would thus sometimes happen that, for lack of the assistance which a disinterested adviser could give, his habitual reticence would make him the victim of sophistries which were not exposed, and which his tenacity of purpose would make him cling to when once he had accepted them."† General Sherman thought that his old friend, Grant, would be "made miserable to the end of his life by his eight

JAY GOULD

*J. D. Cox, *Atlantic Monthly*, August, 1895, p. 167.
†J. D. Cox, ibid., p. 173.

GRANT'S FIRST CABINET

years' experience" in the presidency. As we shall see, there was considerable reason for this foreboding. He evidently had Grant's case chiefly in mind in regretting "the reputations wrecked in politics since 1865," and "the many otherwise good characters" whom political life had "poisoned."

Grant's first cabinet was on the whole not strong, though comprising several thoroughly competent men. Hon. E. B. Washburne, of Illinois, was at first Secretary of State, but resigned to accept the position of Minister to France. He was succeeded by Hon. Hamilton Fish, of New York, a gentleman of great ability, who had been honorably prominent in the politics of his State, and had served a term in Congress. The Interior Department was placed in charge of J. D. Cox. A. E. Borie was made Secretary of the Navy. This appointment was much criticised, and Borie soon resigned, when the place was given to George M. Robeson. President Johnson's Secretary of War, General Schofield, Grant retained for a time. General Rawlins, an excellent and useful officer, succeeded him, but died soon. His successor was William W. Belknap. J. A. J. Creswell was Postmaster-General, E. Rockwood Hoar, Attorney-General. A. T. Stewart, the New York millionaire merchant, was named for the Treasury portfolio, and the Senate confirmed him with the rest, but the appointment was found to be contrary to a statute of 1789, pro-

PRESIDENT GRANT
(*From a photograph by Hoyt, in 1869*)

viding that no person engaged in trade or commerce should hold that office. Efforts were made to remove the legal barrier, which failed, and George S. Boutwell was appointed.

No strictly positive policy at this time inspired the Republican body. Republicans certainly opposed any repudiation of the war debt, whether by taxing bonds or by paying the principal or the interest of them in dollars less valuable than gold dollars. But this was only a phase of the party's war zeal, which always carried men's thought backward rather than to the future. Upon the tariff question it was impossible to tell where the party stood, though, clearly, the old Whig high-tariff portion of its constituency did not yet dominate. Nothing bolder than "incidental protection" was urged by anyone, except where a State or section, like Maine, tentatively commended some interest to the "care, protection, and relief" of the Government. In their public utterances touching the tariff the two great parties differed little. In each, opinion ran the gamut from "incidental protection," where Democrat met Republican in amity, to "approximate free trade," which extreme there were not lacking Republicans ready to embrace had the tariff been then a party issue.

FRED. DOUGLASS
(From a photograph by Handy)

BUENAVENTURA BAEZ
President of Santo Domingo
(From a photograph in the collection of James E. Taylor)

Instead of looking forward and studying new national interests, the party grounded its claims too exclusively upon the "glorious record" which truly belonged to it, and upon the alleged total depravity of the Democrats with the eternal incorrigibleness of the South. Said Senator Morton, of Indiana: "The Republican

THE LIBERAL MOVEMENT

Party . . . could not afford to make a distinct issue on the tariff, civil service reform, or any other individual measure; it must make its stand on these assertions: The Democrats, if they return to power, will either take away the pensions of the loyal soldiers, or else will pension Confederate soldiers also; will, when they have a majority in Congress, quietly allow the Southern States to secede in peace; will tax national bonds and unsettle everything generally." In January, 1871, Senator Henry Wilson wrote: "To keep out of power the Democratic party and its semi-rebellious adherents both North and South, has became a matter of supreme importance to the nation and to the cause of humanity itself."

There were, however, Republicans who by no means shared these views, and the lifting of their hands already foreshadowed the bolt of 1872. Not a few Republican participants in the war wished the earliest possible re-enfranchisement of the Southern whites. It was this sentiment that carried West Virginia for the Democrats in 1870. Re-enfranchisement was a burning question also in Missouri. At the Republican convention in that State the same year, after a hot discussion, General McNeill mounted a chair and shouted "to the friends of the enfranchisement of the white man, that they would withdraw from this convention to the senate chamber." About a third of the delegates, led by Carl Schurz, retired, and nominated a Liberal-Republican State ticket, headed by B. Gratz Brown. Supported by most of the Democrats who could vote, this ticket was triumphant.

Early in the year 1871, at a political meeting in St. Louis, was manifested the first overt hostility on the part of the Liberals, or "Brownites," to President Grant. This sign of the times was followed on March 10th by a meeting of a dozen prominent Republicans in Cincinnati, Ex-Governor Cox and Stanley Matthews being of the number. They drafted a report, which was signed by a hundred well-known Republicans, advancing four principles: (1) general amnesty to the late Confederates, (2) civil service reform, (3) specie payments, and (4) a revenue tariff. During the year the "bolt" took on national importance. Sympathy with it appeared throughout the country and in Congress, and existed where it did not appear. Influenced by Mr. Sumner, even the Massachusetts Republican Convention, without going further, condemned, impliedly, Grant's foreign policy. Finally a call was issued from Missouri for a National Convention, to be held at Cincinnati on May 1, 1872, in opposition to Grant and his administration.

FACSIMILE OF SIGNATURES TO THE TREATY OF WASHINGTON
(From the original at the State Department, Washington)

In impotent wrath and bitterness proportioned to the apparent prosperity of the Republicans, stood the Democracy. The more strenuous its opposition to a "godly thorough reformation" of unrepentant rebels, the more determinedly had the people rebuked it at the polls. Hardly more inclined were the people to follow it upon the great question of the public debt, where the party demanded that the five-twenties should be redeemed in greenbacks—"the same money for the plough-holder and the bond-holder"—and that all national

THE "NEW DEPARTURE"

A. E. Borie, Navy.   J. A. J. Creswell, Postm'r-General.   E. R. Hoar, Att'y-General.

E. B. Washburne, State.   J. D. Cox, Interior.   *J. M. Schofield, War.   G. S. Boutwell, Treasury.

PRESIDENT GRANT'S FIRST CABINET

bonds or the interest thereon should be taxed. Even in the South the leaders began to see that the true policy of "The Reform Party"—the Democracy's *nom de guerre*, was that voiced by the South Carolina Convention of 1870, which proposed to "accept the results of the war as settled facts" and make the best of them, striking out for new issues. This was the key-note of the "New Departure" led by Clement L. Vallandigham, of Ohio. Vallandigham had been the most extreme "copperhead" in all the North. By his outspokenness in defence of the Confederacy during the war he had got himself imprisoned and banished to the South. It was significant, therefore, when, in his last public utterance—he accidentally shot himself a month later—his voice once more joined that of South Carolina, this time in accepting "the results of the war, including the three several amendments *de facto*, as a settlement in fact of all the issues of the war."

*Schofield held the office for several months after President Grant's inauguration. The latter then appointed John A. Rawlins.

35

Chief Justice Chase wrote Vallandigham, praising his action as a "great service to the country and the party," and "as the restoration of the Democratic Party to its ancient platform of progress and reform." John Quincy Adams, Democratic candidate for Governor of Massachusetts, like Vallandigham, proposed a hearty acquiescence in what was past, and "deplored the halting and hesitating step with which the Democracy was sneaking up to its inevitable position." "The South," he continued, "is galled to-day not by the presence of the Fifteenth Amendment, but by the utter absence of the Constitution itself. Is it not silly then to squabble about an amendment which would cease to be obnoxious if it was not detached from its context?"

The method of reconstruction resorted to by Congress occasioned dreadful evils. It ignored the natural prejudices of the whites, many of whom were as loyal as any citizens in the land. To most people in that section, as well as to very many at the North, this dictation by Congress to acknowledged States in time of peace seemed high-handed usurpation. If Congress can do this, it was said, any State can be forced to change its constitution on account of any act which Congress dislikes. This did not necessarily follow, as reconstruction invariably presupposed an abnormal condition, viz., the State's emersion from a rebellion which had involved the State government, whose overthrow, with the rebellion, necessitated congressional interference. Yet the inference was natural and widely drawn.

"Congress was wrong in the exclusion from suffrage of certain classes of citizens, and of all unable to take a prescribed retrospective

ALEXANDER T. STEWART
(*Mr. Stewart always refused to sit for a portrait. The accompanying illustration is from a painting, made after his death, by Thomas Le Clear, and now at St. Paul's School, Garden City, Long Island*)

ERRORS COMMITTED IN RECONSTRUCTION

STANLEY MAT-
THEWS

oath, and wrong also in the establishment of arbitrary military governments for the States, and in authorizing military commissions for the trial of civilians in time of peace. There should have been as little military government as possible; no military commissions, no classes excluded from suffrage, and no oath except one of faithful obedience and support to the Constitution and laws, and sincere attachment to the Constitutional Government of the United States."*

"It is a question of grave doubt whether the Fifteenth Amendment, though right in principle, was wise or expedient. The declared object was to secure impartial suffrage to the negro race. The practical result has been that the wise provisions of the Fourteenth Amendment have been modified by the Fifteenth Amendment. The latter amendment has been practically nullified by the action of most of the States where the great body of this race live and will probably always remain. This is done not by an express denial to them of the right of suffrage, but by ingenious provisions, which exclude them on the alleged ground of ignorance, while permitting all of the white race, however ignorant, to vote at all elections. No way is pointed out by which Congress can enforce this amendment. If the principle of the Fourteenth Amendment had remained in full force, Congress could have reduced the representation of any State, in the proportion which the number of the male inhabitants of such State, denied the right of suffrage, might bear to the whole number of male citizens twenty-one years of age, in such State. This simple remedy, easily enforced by Congress, would have secured the right of all persons, without distinction of race or color, to vote at all elections. The reduction of the representation would have deterred every State from excluding the vote of any

* Salmon P. Chase, Letter to Democratic National Committee in 1873.

portion of the male population above twenty-one years of age. As the result of the Fifteenth Amendment, the political power of the States lately in rebellion has been increased, while the population conferring this increase is practically denied all political power. I see no remedy for this wrong except the growing intelligence of the negro race."*

If the South was to become again genuine part and parcel of this Union, it would not, nor would the North consent that it should, remain permanently under military government. Black legislatures abused their power, becoming instruments of carpet-bag leaders and rings in robbing white propertyholders. Only doctrinaires or the stupid could have expected that the whites would long submit. So soon as federal bayonets were gone, fair means or foul were certain to remove the sceptre from colored hands. Precisely this happened. Without the slightest formal change of constitution or of statute the Southern States one by one passed into the control of their white inhabitants.

Where white men's aims could not be realized by persuasion or other mild means, resort was had to intimidation and force. The chief instrumentality at first used for keeping colored voters from the polls was the Ku-Klux Klan, a secret society organized in Tennessee in 1866. It sprung from the old night patrol of slavery times. Then, every Southern gentleman used to serve on this patrol, whose duty it was to whip severely every negro found absent from home without a pass from his master. Its first *post bellum* work was not illmeant, and its severities came on gradually. Its greatest activity was in Tennessee, Arkansas, and Mississippi, where its awful mysteries and gruesome rites spread utter panic among the superstitious blacks. Men visited negroes' huts and " mummicked " about, at first with sham magic, not with arms at all. One would carry a flesh bag in the shape of a heart and go around " hollering for fried nigger meat." Another would

*John Sherman, Recollections.

put on an India-rubber stomach to startle the negroes by swallowing pailfuls of water. Another represented that he had been killed at Manassas, since which time "some one had built a turnpike over his grave and he had to scratch like h—l to get up through the gravel." The lodges were "dens," the members "ghouls." "Giants,' "goblins," "titans," "furies," "dragons," and "hydras" were names of different classes among the officers.

Usually the mere existence of a "den" anywhere was sufficient to render docile every negro in the vicinity. If more was required, a half-dozen "ghouls," making their nocturnal rounds in their hideous masks and long white gowns, frightened all but the most hardy. Any who showed fight were whipped, maimed, or killed, treatment which was extended on occasion to their "carpet-bag" and "scalawag" friends—these titles denoting respectively Northern and Southern men who took the negroes' side. The very violence of the order, which it at last turned against the old Southrons themselves, brought it into disrepute with its original instigators, who were not sorry when Federal marshals, put up to it by President Grant, hunted den after den of the law-breakers to the death.

In 1870 and 1871, by the so-called Force Bills, Federal judges were given cognizance of suits against anyone for depriving another of rights, privileges, or immunities under the Constitution. Fine and imprisonment were made the penalties for "conspiracy" against the United States or the execution of its laws, as by forcibly or through intimidation preventing men from voting. The army and navy were placed at the service of the President to enforce the act, and Federal judges might exclude suspected persons from sitting on juries. By this drastic measure and its rigorous execution in nine counties of South Carolina the organization was by 1873 driven out of existence. But some of its methods survived. In 1875 several States adopted and successfully worked the

"Mississippi plan," which was, by whatever necessary means, to nullify black votes until white majorities were assured. Less violent than the Ku-Klux way, this new one was equally thorough.

Considering the stupendous upheaval in Southern society marked by the erection of bondmen into full citizens, dark days were few. Schools arose. The ballot itself proved an educator, rough but thorough. The negro vote, become a fixed fact, was courted by the jarring factions of whites, and hence to some extent protected. Meanwhile it was plainly to the negro's advantage that he was fighting, not to acquire status and rights, but for status and rights guaranteed in the organic law of his State.

It yet remained to restore the disfranchised whites and to remove the political disabilities imposed by the Fourteenth Amendment. Except in the case of a few leaders, the disabilities were annulled by the Act of Amnesty passed May 22, 1872. At about the same time general re-enfranchisement was accomplished by State legislation, Liberal-Republicans joining with those Democrats, specially numerous in Missouri and West Virginia, who already enjoyed the right of suffrage.

By March, 1866, the price of gold in paper money had fallen from war figures to $130\frac{1}{4}$. There was much illegitimate speculation in the metal, dealing in "phantom gold"—mere betting, that is, on gold fluctuations. Prominent among the operators was the firm of Smith, Gould, Martin & Co. The mind of the firm was Jay Gould, a dark little man, with cold, glittering eyes. Closely associated with him was James Fisk, a vulgar and unprincipled yet shrewd and bold man of business. During the spring of 1869 Gould bought $7,000,000 or $8,000,000 in gold, immediately loaning it again on demand notes. There being not over $20,000,000 gold available outside the Treasury, the business community, in case of any call for gold, was at his mercy, unless the Treasury should sell. This must be prevented.

Drawn by B. West Clinedinst

FISK AND GOULD'S GRAND OPERA HOUSE IN A STATE OF SIEGE

GRANT AND THE NATION'S FINANCES

In June, 1869, President Grant, on a trip from New York to Boston, accepted a place in a private box of the theatre which Fisk owned, and next day took, at the invitation of Fisk and Gould, one of their magnificent steamers to Fall River. After a handsome supper the hosts skillfully turned the conversation to the financial situation. Grant remarked that he thought there was a certain fictitiousness in the prosperity of the country, and that the bubble might as well be tapped. This suggestion "struck across us," said Mr. Gould, later, "like a wet blanket." Another wire must be pulled.

Facts and figures were now heaped together and published to prove that, should gold rise in this country about harvest time, grain, the price of which, being fixed in Liverpool, was independent of currency fluctuations, would be worth so much the more and would at once be hurried abroad; but that to secure this blessing Government must not sell any gold. Gould laid still other pipes. Fisk visited the presidential sphinx at Newport; others saw him at Washington. At New York Gould buttonholed him so assiduously that he was obliged to open his lips to rebuke his servant for giving Gould such ready access to him.

The President seems to have been persuaded that a rise in gold while the crops were moving would advantage the country. At any rate, orders were given early in September to sell only gold sufficient to buy bonds for the sinking fund. The conspirators redoubled their purchases. The price of gold rose till, two days before Black Friday, it stood at 140½.

Though he kept it to himself Gould was in terror lest the Treasury floodgates should be opened to prevent a panic. Business was palsied, and the bears were importuning the Government to sell. At his wits' end he wrote Secretary Boutwell:

"SIR: There is a panic in Wall Street, engineered by a bear combination. They have withdrawn currency to such an extent that it is impossible to do ordinary business. The Erie

Company requires eight hundred thousand dollars to disburse . . . much of it in Ohio, where an exciting political contest is going on, and where we have about ten thousand men employed, and the trouble is charged on the administration. . . . Cannot you, consistently, increase your line of currency?"

Gould, like Major Bagstock, was "devilish sly, sir." In his desperation he determined to turn "bear" and, if necessary rend in pieces Fisk himself. Saying nothing of his fears, he encouraged Fisk boldly to keep on buying, while he himself secretly began to sell. Fisk fell into the trap, and his partner, taking care in his sales to steer clear of Fisk's brokers, proceeded secretly and swiftly to unload his gold and fulfil all his contracts. From this moment they acted each by and for himself, Gould operating through his firm and Fisk through an old partner of his named Belden.

On Thursday, September 23d, while his broker, Speyers, is buying, Fisk coolly walks into the Gold Room and, amid the wildest excitement, offers to bet any part of $50,000 that gold will rise to 200. Not a man dares take his bet.

On Black Friday the Gold Room is crowded two hours before the time of business. In the centre excited brokers are betting, swearing, and quarreling, many of them pallid with fear of ruin, others hilarious in expectation of big commissions. In a back office across from the Gold Room, Fisk, in shirt sleeves, struts up and down, declaring himself the Napoleon of the street. At this time the Ring was believed to hold in gold and in contracts to deliver the same, over $100,000,000.

Speyers, whom all suppose to represent Gould as well as Fisk, begins by offering 145, then 146, 147, 148, 149, but none will sell. "Put it up to 150," Fisk orders, and gold rises to that figure. At 150 a half million is sold him by Mr. James Brown, who had quietly organized a band of merchants to meet the gamblers on their own ground. From all over the country the "shorts" are telegraphing orders to buy. Speyers is informed that if he continues to put up gold he will be shot; but he goes on offering 151, 152, 153, 154. Still none will sell. Meantime the victims of the corner are summoned to pay in cash the difference between 135, at which the gold was borrowed, and 150, at which the firm is willing to settle. Fearing lest gold go to 200, many settle at 148. At 155, amid the tremendous roar of the bull brokers bidding higher and higher, Brown again sells half a million.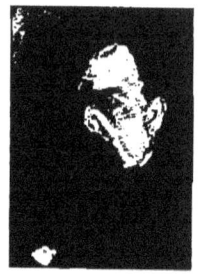

OLIVER P. MORTON

"160 for any part of five millions." Brown sells a million more. "161 for five millions." No bid. "162 for five millions." At first no response. Again, "162 for any part of five millions." A voice is heard, "Sold one million at 162." "163½ for five millions." "Sold five millions at 163½." Crash! The market has been broken, and by Gould's sales. Everybody now begins to sell, when the news comes that the Government has telegraphed to sell four millions. Gold instantly falls to 140, then to 133. "Somebody," cried Fisk, "has run a saw right into us. We are forty miles down the Delaware and don't know where we are. Our phantom gold can't stand the weight of the real stuff."

Gould has no mind permanently to ruin his partner. He coolly suggests that Fisk has only to repudiate his contracts, and Fisk complies. His offers to buy gold he declares "off," making good only a single one of them, as to which he was so placed that he had no option. What was due him, on the other hand, he collected to the uttermost dollar. To prevent being mobbed the pair encircled their opera-house with armed toughs and fled thither. There no civil process or other molestation was likely to reach them. Presently certain of "the thieves' judges," as they were called, came to their relief by issuing injunctions estopping all transactions connected with the conspiracy which would have been disadvantageous for the conspirators.

THE LAST QUARTER-CENTURY

Far the strongest side of Grant's Administration was the State Department, headed by the clever diplomat, Hamilton Fish, one of the most successful Secretaries of State who ever served our country. Here distinguished ability and absolute integrity reigned and few mistakes were made. Were there no other testimony, the Treaty of Washington would sufficiently attest Mr. Fish's mastery of his office. Ever since 1863 we had been seeking satisfaction from Great Britain for the depredations committed during the war by Confederate cruisers sailing from British ports. Negotiations were broken off in 1865 and again in 1868. In 1869 Reverdy Johnson, then our Minister to England, negotiated a treaty, but the Senate rejected it. In January, 1871, the British Government having proposed a joint commission for the settlement of questions connected with the Canadian fisheries, Mr. Fish replied that the adjudication of the "*Alabama* Claims" would have to be first considered, "as an essential to the restoration of cordial and amicable relations between the two governments." England consented to submit this question also to the commission, and on February 27th the High Commissioners met at Washington. The British delegation included, besides several noblemen, Sir E. Thornton the Queen's Minister at Washington, Sir John Macdonald, of Canada, and Mountague Bernard, Professor of International Law at Oxford. The American commissioners were the Secretary of State himself, Justice Nelson of the Supreme Court, Robert C. Schenck our Minister to England, E. Rockwood Hoar late United States Attorney-General, and George H. Williams, Senator from Oregon.

On May 8th the commission completed a treaty, which was speedily ratified by both Governments. It provided for arbitration upon the "*Alabama* Claims," upon other claims by citizens of either country against the other for damages during the Rebellion, upon the fisheries, and upon the northwest boundary of the United States. The principal settlements happily arrived at in this way will be described later.

RELATIONS WITH CUBA

In 1868 the "Junta of Laborers" in Cuba inaugurated a rebellion against the mother country. By 1870 most South American States had recognized them as belligerents, and they were eager that the United States should do the same. The sympathies of our people and Government were with them. In the summer of 1869 Secretary Fish, directed by the President, had prepared and signed a proclamation according to the insurgents the rights of belligerents, but owing to the Secretary's firm unwillingness this document was never issued. In July, 1870, the President changed his mind, heartily thanking Mr. Fish for restraining him from issuing the belligerency message. The good offices of the United States were, however, tendered, with the view of inducing Spain to recognize Cuba's independence, preventing further bloodshed; but the overtures were declined.

Spain's barbarous method of warring excited horror. The Spanish Captain-General in Cuba freely sequestrated property, to whomsoever belonging, ordered shot every male over fifteen years of age found outside his premises without good excuse, burned every uninhabited hut and every hamlet not flying a white flag. Such procedure called forth our remonstrance, which, in conjunction with the known sympathy of Americans for the rebels, greatly irritated Spain. Our legation house at Madrid was threatened, our vessels in one or two instances brought to by Spanish men-of-war, and a number of our citizens in Cuba and on the high seas maltreated or killed. Two American citizens, Speakman and Wyeth, embarked by mistake in a vessel carrying an insurrectionary force destined for Cuba. They gave themselves up, but were brutally murdered after the merest form of a trial. This was exasperating enough; but when, on October 31, 1873, the *Virginius*, belonging to an American citizen, was captured on the high seas off Jamaica by the Spanish man-of-war *Tornado*, the American flag hauled down, and Captain Fry; with fifty-six of his ship's company—nine of them American citizens—

shot, for some weeks hostilities seemed actually imminent. The *Virginius's* errand was in spirit illegal, perhaps literally so. Many revolutionists were on board, also 2,000 Remington rifles, a mitrailleuse, and a large supply of ammunition and provisions for the insurgents. According to the best authorities Spain was quite justified in seizing the vessel, though Attorney-General Hoar denied this, but not in putting to death those on board with no trial but a drumhead court-martial.

When the news of the outrage reached this country innumerable indignation meetings were held. President Grant convoked his Cabinet to deliberate upon the case, and the navy yards were set working night and day. The Spanish Minister of State at first haughtily rejected our protest, saying that Spain would decide the question according to law and her dignity. Madrid mobs violently demonstrated against the American minister, General Sickles. November 4th, Secretary Fish cabled Sickles: " In case of refusal of satisfactory reparation within twelve days from this date, you will, at the expiration of that time, close your legation and will, together with your secretary, leave Madrid." On the 15th, hearing that fifty-seven men had been executed, he sent word: " If Spain cannot redress these outrages the United States will." And on November 25: " If no accommodation is reached by the close of to-morrow, leave." Next day Spain became tractable and Sickles remained. War was happily averted. Spain released the *Virginius* and all the surviving prisoners. Having been on December 16th delivered to officers of our navy, the ship, flying the Stars and Stripes, proudly sailed for New York, but foundered in an ocean storm. The prisoners freed reached New York in safety. Spain solemnly disclaimed all thought of indignity to our flag, and undertook to prosecute any of her subjects guilty, in this affair, of violating our treaty rights.

President Grant's negotiations for the annexation of the turbulent little republic known as Santo Domingo—" Holy Sabbath," a bit of unconscious irony—ended less happily.

THE SCENE IN THE NEW YORK GOLD ROOM ON BLACK FRIDAY, SEPTEMBER 24, 1869

Drawn by C. S. Reinhart from photographs and descriptions by eye-witnesses

PROPOSED "ANNEXION" OF SANTO DOMINGO

The strategic situation of the island is good, and its aspect inviting—luxurious and fertile valleys between grand ranges of volcanic mountains. The heat is tempered day and night by sea-breezes—sometimes rising to hurricanes. The rich mineral and other resources of the island were known in 1870 but little exploited. A tenth of the people were white, living mainly in the sea-board towns. The rest were hybrid descendants of the man-eating Caribs and of the buccaneers and warlike negroes who fought under Toussaint L'Ouverture.

Embarrassed with a rival, President Baez wished to turn his domain over to us, as a predecessor of his had in like case once given it to Spain. He indicated his desire to President Grant, who dispatched Col. Babcock, his assistant private Secretary, to report upon the country, its people, its harbors, etc. No member of the Cabinet favored the mission, yet none officially objected. The State Department had nothing to do with arranging it. New York merchants trading to San Domingo offered Babcock passage thither, showing that his proposed mission was known, and he would have accepted their offered favor but for Secretary Fish's protest. Transportation for him by the navy was then ordered, and it was found that he was to be accompanied by Senator Cole, of California, and an officer from the Inspector-General's department who spoke Spanish. "As the members of the Cabinet were carefully discreet in their reticence, the increase of the party and of the apparent importance of the mission caused a certain uneasiness, especially as rumors began to fly about that business speculations were involved, and that the official character of the affair was much less than its real significance. The members of the Government felt loyally bound to suppress their own doubts, and to attribute to the excitability of the quidnuncs the rumors of important purposes connected with Babcock's voyage."*

---

* This and the next following quotations are from J. D. Cox's interesting article, already cited in this chapter.

Babcock returned bearing a draft of a treaty containing an agreement to cede Santo Domingo to the United States out-and-out for something over a million dollars, or to accept our protectorate over it at the same time giving us a fifty-year lease of the important bay and harbor of Samana. President Grant had become intensely anxious to acquire this realm. It would afford us a coaling and naval station and a commercial entrepot, enrich the United States and extend its power, and open a region which the American negro could colonize and manage. At the first Cabinet meeting after his arrival in Washington Babcock appeared, showing each member as he arrived "specimens of the ores and products of the island and descanting upon its extraordinary value. He met a rather chilling reception, and soon left the room. It had been the President's habit at such meetings to call upon the members of the Cabinet to bring forward the business contained in their portfolios, beginning with the Secretary of State. This would at once have brought the action of Babcock up by Mr. Fish's disclaimer of all part in the matter, and his statement of its utter illegality. On this occasion, however, General Grant departed from his uniform custom, and took the initiative. 'Babcock has returned, as you see,' said he, 'and has brought a treaty of annexation. I suppose it is not formal, as he had no diplomatic powers; but we can easily cure that. We can send back the treaty and have Perry, the consular agent, sign it; and, as he is an officer of the State Department, it would make it all right.'"

"But, Mr. President," said Mr. Secretary Cox, "has it been settled, then, that we *want* to annex San Domingo?"

General Grant "colored, and smoked hard at his cigar. He glanced at Mr. Fish on his right, but the face of the Secretary was impassive, and his eyes were fixed on the portfolio before him. He turned to Mr. Boutwell on his left, but no response met him there. As the silence became painful, the President called for another item of business, and left the

SUMNER AND THE ADMINISTRATION

CLEMENT L. VALLAN-
DIGHAM
(*After a photograph in the col-
lection of James E. Taylor*)

question unanswered. The subject was never again brought up before the assembled Cabinet."

The treaty was put into form, signed on November 29, 1869, and sent to the Senate the following month. Violent opposition to it was at once manifest, of which Mr. Sumner was the soul. Sumner was Chairman of the Senate Committee on Foreign Relations, and in whatever related to this committee's work was inclined to domineer. He had not agreed with Secretary Fish or the President respecting the ground of our war complaint against England. " Sumner insisted that the hasty proclamation by Great Britain of neutrality between the United States and the Southern Confederacy was the gravamen of the *Alabama* claims. The President and Mr. Fish contended that this proclamation was an act of which we could not complain, except as an indication of an unfriendly spirit by Great Britain, and that the true basis of the *Alabama* claims was that Great Britain, after proclaiming neutrality, did not enforce it, but allowed her subjects to build cruisers, and man, arm and use them, under cover of the rebel flag, to the destruction of our commercial navy."

The President, Sumner now said, had violated our Constitution in negotiating the San Domingo treaty as he did ; he was also conniving at an infringement of the Dominican constitution, which forbade alienating any part of that land ; and was traversing international law by a menace to the independence of Hayti. San Domingo, he alleged, with its undesirable population, was in continual turmoil, had cost Spain more blood and treasure than it was worth, and been lost to her after all. Baez he denounced as a " political jockey," and he declared that adventurers were abusing the President's confidence, as it was beginning to be suspected they had done in regard to " Black Friday " the September previous. Writing to Garrison December 29, 1870, and referring to his speech on the "annexion" of San Domingo, Sumner said that the Haytian Minister had previously visited him, " full of emotion at the message of the President as ' trampling his country under foot.' "

President Grant did his utmost to secure ratification for the treaty. Having expired by limitation on May 21st, it was renewed and sent to the Senate again on the 31st. Direct application to Senators in this interest was made on the President's behalf, a course generally felt to be very objectionable. Republican politicians became divided touching annexation, and the utmost bitterness of feeling prevailed. Secretary Fish's position pending this business was extremely embarrassing. An intimate friend of Mr. Sumner, he was accustomed freely to discuss with him all diplomatic affairs. "He had honestly treated the talk of Dominican annexation as mere gossip, without solid foundation, and now he suddenly found his sincerity in question, under circumstances which forbade him to say how gravely the State Department had been compromised." Twice during the episode he offered his resignation, but the President's earnest entreaty, backed by that of leaders anxious to avoid a breach in the party, each time induced him not to insist on its acceptance. " But the progress of the San Domingo business put Mr. Fish in a false position, apparently, and having yielded to the President's urgency that he should remain in the Cabinet he could not, at the moment, explain fully to Mr. Sumner the seeming changes of his attitude. It is in the nature of such differences to grow larger, and in the following winter they led to an open rupture between the old friends."

The President's campaign to secure annexation involved bargaining for the votes of certain "carpet-bag" Senators. " He was told that they desired to please him and to support his plans, but, considering Mr. Sumner's controlling influence

SUMNER AND THE ADMINISTRATION

with their colored constituents, it would be at no small political peril to themselves if they opposed that Senator on the San Domingo question. . . In matters of patronage . . . they found themselves less influential than they had a right to expect. Reciprocity was necessary if the President required their aid. When asked in what departments they found a lack of consideration, the Attorney-General's was named, and it was strongly urged that Judge Hoar should be displaced by a Southern man acceptable to them." Attorney-General Hoar was nominated to the Supreme Court presumably to answer this Southern demand. The Senate refused to confirm his appointment, and Mr. Hoar had to be gotten rid of in some other way. One morning in June, 1870, he received a letter from the President containing the " naked statement that he found himself under the necessity of asking for Hoar's resignation. No explanation of any kind was given or reason assigned." In an interview, subsequently, the President was frank enough to connect this action with " the necessity, to carry out his purposes, of securing support in the Senate from Southern Republicans, who demanded that the Cabinet place should be filled from the South." Amos T. Ackerman, of Georgia, was immediately nominated and soon confirmed. The final vote on the treaty was taken June 30th. A considerable majority of the Senators favored it, but not quite the necessary two-thirds.

The treaty having been refused ratification the matter died out of mind; but an irreparable rift between Grant and Sumner resulted. Shortly after Sumner's speech, above referred to, Grant asked Fred. Douglass, who, friendly to Sumner, yet agreed with Grant: " What do you think of Sumner now?" " I believe that Sumner thought himself doing a service to a down-trodden people, but that he was mistaken," Douglass replied. This answer not seeming to please the President, Douglass asked what he thought of Sumner. After some hesitation Grant replied, with feeling: " I think he is mad." President Grant considered the failure of the treaty a

THE LAST QUARTER-CENTURY

national misfortune, but submitted with patience, not only to the adverse action of the Senate, but to the suspicions of friends and to the attacks of enemies which his San Domingo ambition had aroused.

The annexationists had their revenge when Sumner lost the chairmanship of the Senate Committee on Foreign Relations, which he had held so long and prized so highly. John Lothrop Motley's recall from the British mission was also referred by nearly all to Senator Sumner's course in the Santo Domingo matter. The Saturday Club, of Boston, protested against thus allowing the President's disagreement with Sumner to prejudice Minister Motley by reason of their friendship, considering such treatment certain "to offend all the educated men of New England." Grant's only reply was: "I made up my mind to remove Mr. Motley before there was any quarrel with Mr. Sumner." In his annual message the next December the President proposed a commission to visit San Domingo for additional information about the island and to inquire into the charges of corruption which had been made against the Executive and his agent. With his usual intemperance Sumner opposed this as committing Congress to "a dance of blood;" yet a bill to create the commission passed the Senate unanimously, the House by a majority of 123 to 63. The commissioners were Dr. Samuel G. Howe, President Andrew D. White, and Hon. A. A. Burton. Their report was favorable, making it credible that the President might have secured annexation had he attempted it in a less autocratic way.

CHAPTER III
THE GREELEY CAMPAIGN

THE RISE OF HORACE GREELEY.—THE TRIBUNE.—GREELEY AND GRANT.—THE LIBERAL REPUBLICAN MOVEMENT.—THE SPOILS SYSTEM.—SHEPHERD AT WASHINGTON.—SCANDALS CONNECTED WITH THE COLLECTION OF THE REVENUES.—REVERSAL OF HEPBURN VS. GRISWOLD.—GRANT AND GREELEY NOMINATED.—MIXED POLITICS. —BOTH CANDIDATES SEVERELY CRITICISED.—A CHOICE OF EVILS.— A BITTER CAMPAIGN.—DIFFICULTIES CONFRONTING GREELEY.— GRANT ELECTED.—GREELEY'S DEATH.—HIS CHARACTER.—CONTINUATION OF REPUBLICAN POLICY AT THE SOUTH.—FORCE AND ANARCHY IN LOUISIANA.

ONE hot day in August, 1831, an ungainly journeyman printer from Erie, Pa., was among the "arrivals" in New York City. It was Horace Greeley, born twenty years before, on a farm in Amherst, N. H. From childhood an insatiable reader, at ten he had become the prodigy of his native town. His stump-grubbing on a farm in Vermont, whither poverty drove his father's family, his service as printer's devil there, and later as job and newspaper printer at Erie, paid little. The young man reached the metropolis with only ten dollars in his pocket, while the rest of his earthly goods formed a bundle which he swung in his hand. After long and vain search for work he at last secured a situation so hard that no other printer would take it. In it he wrought twelve or fourteen hours a day at a rate never exceeding six dollars a week.

After various vicissitudes in job-printing and desultory editorial work, where he evinced genius and zeal but no special aptitude for business, Mr. Greeley, in 1841, started the *Tribune*. For this venture he had borrowed $1,000.

THE LAST QUARTER-CENTURY

The first week's losses engulfed nearly half this sum, but at the end of a year the paper was an assured success. It soon became the mouth-piece of all the more sober anti-slavery sentiment of the time, whether within or without the Whig party, and rose to power with the mighty tide of free-soil enthusiasm that swept over the land after 1850. Greeley and his organ were the chief founders of the Republican party, and the most effective moulders of its policy. The influence of the paper before and during the war was incalculable, far exceeding that of any other sheet in America. Hardly a Whig or a Republican voter in all the North that did not take or read it. It gave tone to the minor organs of its party, and no politician on either side acted upon slavery without considering what the *Tribune* would say.

While hating slavery and treason, and hence not averse to the war, Greeley was anxious for peace at the earliest moment when it could be safely had; and forthwith upon the collapse of the Confederacy he dismissed all rancor toward the South. At Jefferson Davis's presentment for treason he stepped forward as bondsman; and in the long friction which followed he persistently opposed all harshness in dealing with the conquered. He disliked Grant as the exponent of severe methods in reconstruction, and, like Sumner, peculiarly abominated his policy of annexing San Domingo.

At length Grant and Greeley became, in effect, foes. They had many party friends in common, who sought by every means to reconcile them, but in vain. Greeley was once induced to call at the White House. Grant invited him to a drive, and he accepted. The horses went, the President smoked, and Greeley kept silence, all with a vengeance. Only monosyllables were uttered as the two stiff men rode side by side, and each was glad when they could alight and separate.

In January, 1872, the Liberal Republicans of Missouri issued a call for a national convention at Cincinnati. Greeley and his *Tribune* took sides with the revolt. Soon they were

THE SPOILS SYSTEM

the life of it. Henceforth the opposition to the Administration increased in strength day by day. The Cincinnati *Commercial* and the Springfield, Mass., *Republican* sided with the *Tribune*, while the New York *Times* and *Harper's Weekly* earnestly advocated Grant's re-election. Sumner had long since broken with Grant. Many other prominent Republicans in Congress and outside had lost confidence in the Administration, and then become hostile thereto. General Banks was one of these, Stanley Matthews another, George W. Julian another. Senator Schurz openly stated that if Grant should be nominated for a second term he would bolt the ticket. Early in the second session of the Forty-second Congress there was question of appointing a committee on Investigation and Retrenchment. Debating this, Senator Trumbull vigorously denounced the prevalent abuses in the civil service.

HORACE GREELEY

The spoils system had been permitted to invade every branch of the Government. The odium heaped upon carpet-bag rule at the South was all along due in large measure to its corruption. By their influence and example many white federal office-holders misled the negro officers, State and national, and the voters as well, to regard office as the legiti-

THE LAST QUARTER-CENTURY

WILLIAM HENRY FRY
After a daguerreotype in the possession of Horace B. Fry

COUNT ADAM GUROW-
SKI
After a daguerreotype in the possession of Charles A. Dana

mate prey of the party triumphant on election day. At the North, no less, appointments in answer to political wire-pulling were the regular order of the time. "Work!" said an office-holder in 1870; "I worked to get here! You don't expect me to work now I am here!"

Federal offices were needlessly multiplied. In March, 1871, a custom-house appraiser was appointed at Evansville, Ind. He informed "his Senator" and the Secretary of the Treasury that his office was a sinecure, writing "his other Senator" soon after that it ought to be abolished. He was removed and a more contented incumbent appointed. "Yet," says the ex-appraiser, "there could be no charge of neglect or incompetency, for no officer was ever more faithful and diligent in drawing his salary than I was during those two years,

GEORGE RIPLEY
After a daguerreotype in the possession of Charles A. Dana

MARGARET FULLER
After a daguerreotype in the historical collection of H. W. Fay

BAYARD TAYLOR
After a photograph by Sarony

SOME NOTED CONTRIBUTORS TO

THOMAS HICKS   CHARLES A. DANA   GEORGE WILLIAM CURTIS
After a daguerreotype by Brady, 1852, in the possession of Charles A. Dana

and absolutely there was nothing else to do." In connection with offices where there were far weightier functions than drawing salaries, extravagance, carelessness, and corruption were exposed with damning iteration.

In 1871 the District of Columbia had been given a territorial government, with a Governor, a Board of Public Works, and a Legislature. The new territory lived too fast to live long, letting out contracts at exorbitant rates, so that they were bought up and sublet, sometimes again and again. It entered upon ambitious schemes of city improvement, which involved the District in a debt far beyond the lawful limit of $10,000,000. These and other evidences of wasteful administration led Congress, in 1874, to abolish the territorial system and again assume direct control of the District. Lapse of time disposed Washingtonians kindly to remember Shepherd, the head of the territorial government during the great transformation, and later not a few wished his statue to appear in the city which had been rendered so beautiful and commodious through his agency.

More notorious than the "Washington Ring" were the scandals connected with the collection of the revenues. Early in April, 1874, a meeting was held in New York to protest against the revenue and "moiety" laws; "moiety," meaning that the law gave to a spy, with certain officials, one-half of the property forfeited to the Government by fraud discovered through such person's agency. Under these laws there were repeated instances of technical forfeitures and condemnation on the ground of constructive fraud, owing to some slight accidental mistake. The laws were often confused and self-contradictory, placing honest officials in danger of committing flagrant wrongs by the effort to execute their terms. A. T. Stewart is said to have been at one time liable to a forfeiture of $3,000,000 for an error of $300.

An informer intimated to a revenue official that an importer had defrauded the Government, paying insufficient duty upon his goods. The official then obtained a secret warrant to seize the importer's books and papers, which was done. The contingent rewards accompanying this business were so enormous that every kind of intrigue, deceit and subornation was practiced. Informers were charged with downright blackmail, for which the power to seize private books and papers gave them exceptional opportunity. They sought to stigmatize the entire mercantile class in the importing cities. The terror in which the house of Phelps, Dodge & Co. was long kept by the lurking agents of the Government would be incredible to most of our citizens now. The system would not have surprised people in Naples, but it was revolting to Americans. "Every clerk might become an informer. The Government stealthily put its hand into every counting-room, as the Church through its agents surreptitiously knew every secret of the household." Vicious as it was, not until after

HORACE GREELEY SIGNING THE BAIL-BOND OF JEFFERSON DAVIS AT THE
RICHMOND, VA., COURT-HOUSE, MAY 13, 1867

REVERSAL OF HEPBURN VS. GRISWOLD

Supreme Court of the United States,' etc., it was enacted 'that no vacancy in the office of Associate Justice should be filled by appointment until the number of Associates should be reduced to six, and thereafter the Supreme Court should consist of a Chief Justice and six Associate Justices.' By an act of 10th April, 1869, to take effect from the first Monday of December, 1869, it was enacted 'that the Court should consist of a Chief Justice and eight Associates, and that, for the purposes of this act, there should be appointed an additional Judge.' Hepburn *vs.* Griswold, it is stated in the opinion of the Court in the case, was decided in conference November 27, 1869 (8 Wallace, 626), there being then eight Judges (the Chief Justice and seven Associates) on the bench, the lowest number to which the Court had been reduced. One of them, Justice Grier, resigned February 1, 1870. The judgment in Hepburn *vs.* Griswold was announced from the bench and entered February 7, 1870. Mr. Justice Strong was appointed February 18, 1870, and Mr. Justice Bradley March 21, 1870, and the order for the present [new] argument was made by, and the argument itself heard before, the Court of nine, as constituted by act of 10th April, 1869."* Both of the new Justices, Strong and Bradley, voted for the reversal. Judgment was rendered in December, 1870, when the Hepburn *vs.* Griswold decision was set aside by a majority of one. The new dictum of the Court was later quite generally accepted as not forced law, as in real accord with the meaning of the Constitution deeply and broadly viewed. We shall recur to the subject again in Chapter X., there arguing that the Court's conclusion was sound; but at the time not a few classed it with the Dred Scott decision, as a partisan and most dangerous attack upon our fundamental law. Said an eminent writer : " When public opinion has reached the point of tolerating such proceedings, paper constitutions may well be consigned to oblivion before they fall into contempt."

*8 Wallace, 528, note.

In spite of all these grounds for criticism, partly solid and partly fanciful, so evidently did the rank and file of the party wish Grant to continue in the White House that his adversaries saw no hope of capturing the Republican convention. Most of them, therefore, allied themselves with the Liberals. The Democrats maintained a policy of "passivity," but long before their convention there were hints that they would accept the bolting Republican candidates as their own, should these not be too radically opposed to democratic ideas. With such aid the separatists expected to carry the country.

The convention of Come-outers assembled at Cincinnati on May 1st, and effected a permanent organization with Carl Schurz as chairman. Touching the South, the platform declared for general amnesty, local self-government, and the abolition of all military authority as superseding civil law. The suspension of *habeas corpus* it especially condemned. It denounced corruption in the civil service, and declared against a second term in the Presidency. It demanded a tariff which should not unnecessarily interfere with industry, advocated a speedy return to specie payments, and ended with a eulogy on the Union soldiers. Mr. Greeley was nominated for the Presidency on the sixth ballot. B. Gratz Brown, Governor of Missouri, received the nomination for Vice-President.

Grant's friends were not frightened. They pretended, rather, to regard the nomination as a huge joke. All conceded that Greeley was an honest man, yet he did not inspire confidence. He had a reputation for doing strange, compromising things. John Sherman thought him "probably the most unfit man for President, except Train, that had ever been mentioned." Many of the Liberals themselves did not fancy him. He was an ultra protectionist, while Schurz and other prominent anti-Administration Republicans leaned toward a revenue tariff. Greeley was understood to intend, in case of his election, to hold his tariff ideas in abeyance in deference to the preferences of his free-trader and low-tariff supporters.

GRANT AND GREELEY NOMINATED

This understanding did not conduce to men's respect for him. Sumner was for radical measures in the South, which most of the Liberals deprecated. It was Sumner who, in the Forty-second and Forty-third Congresses, so earnestly sought to pass the Supplementary Civil Rights Bill, with the aim of securing for the Southern negro social as well as political equality with the white man.

ZEBULON B. VANCE

It imposed heavy penalties on hotel-keepers, theatre and railway managers and others for conducting their businesses so as in any way to discriminate against the blacks. This bill readily passed the Senate whenever moved, but always failed in the House until March 1, 1875, when, a year after Sumner's death, it went upon the statute book—to be, by a Supreme Court decision October 3, 1883, declared unconstitutional and void.* Little as they agreed with one another, however, the majority of the seceders, wishing "anybody to beat Grant," accepted Greeley with no small heartiness.

The Republican Convention met at Philadelphia on June 5th. The platform declared for civil service reform and complete equality in the enjoyment of all civil, political, and public rights throughout the Union, and uttered a somewhat ambiguous statement in regard to the relations of capital and labor. It upheld the President in his Southern policy, though maintaining that State governments should be permitted to function in the fullest degree practicable. The latest amnesty bill of Congress it approved, and it eulogized the President in the highest terms. The Convention exhibited no opposition to Grant, and he was renominated by acclamation. Henry Wilson, of Massachusetts, was given the second place on the ticket, defeating Colfax, who had incurred the enmity of several men influential in the party.

*109 U. S. Supreme Court Reports, 3.

THE LAST QUARTER-CENTURY

LYMAN TRUMBULL

Between the nomination of Grant and the Democratic Convention at Baltimore, over a month later, public attention was centred upon the attitude of the Democratic leaders to the candidacy of Greeley and Brown. That these nominees were not wholly acceptable to the Democracy there could be no doubt. Many of the party chiefs spoke of Greeley with open derision. Yet, as it was evident that if the Liberal candidates did not receive Democratic endorsement all efforts against Grant would prove unavailing, the majority of the party was for Greeley at all hazards. Said ex-Governor Vance, of North Carolina: "If 'Old Grimes' is in the democratic hymn-book, we'll sing him through if it kills us." Accordingly, the Convention, which assembled at Baltimore July 9th, notwithstanding considerable opposition, accepted the Cincinnati candidates and platform, adjourning in some hope of victory. A few dissatisfied Democrats met at Louisville on September 3d and nominated Charles O'Conor for President and John Quincy Adams for Vice-President. Both gentlemen declined, but the nominations were left unchanged.

Greeley accepted the Baltimore nomination in a letter dated July 18th. In this he insisted on the "full enfranchisement" of all the white population at the South, and declared that henceforth Democracy and Republicanism would stand for one and the same idea, "equal rights, regardless of creed or clime or color." The entire effective force of the Democracy, South as well as North, rallied to the Greeley standard, joined, strangely, by Republicans and Abolitionists like Trumbull, of Illinois, Julian, of Indiana, Blair, of Michigan, Sedgwick, of New York, and Bird, of Massachusetts. General W. T. Sherman wrote from Paris to his brother, the Senator: " Of course I have watched the progress of political events from this standpoint, and feel amazed to see the turn things

BOTH CANDIDATES SEVERELY CRITICISED

have taken. Grant, who never was a Republican, is your candidate ; and Greeley, who never was a Democrat, but quite the reverse, is the Democratic candidate." The Senator replied : " As you say, the Republicans are running a Democrat, and the Democrats a Republican. And there is not an essential difference in the platform of principle. The chief interest I feel in the canvass is the preservation of the Republican party, which I think essential to secure the fair enforcement of the results of the war. General Grant has so managed things as to gain the very bitter and active hostility of many of the leading Republicans, and the personal indifference of most of the residue. He will, however, be fairly supported by the great mass of the Republicans, and I still hope and believe will be elected. The defections among Republicans will be made up by Democrats who will not vote for Greeley."

On June 30th George William Curtis wrote : " The best sentiment of the opposition is that both parties must be destroyed and Greeley's election is the way to destroy them. This is Schurz's ground, who likes Greeley as little as any of us. The argument seems to be, first chaos then cosmos. The *Nation* and the *Evening Post* in this dilemma take Grant as the least of evils. He has been foully slandered, and Sumner's speech [of May 31st—see page 75] was unpardonable. He was bitterly indignant at me—said that my course was unspeakable and inconsistent, and that I was bringing unspeakable woe upon my country. I could only reply, ' Sumner, you must learn that other men are as honest as you.' "

Much could be truly said in Greeley's favor. An editor opposed to his election declared " that he was a man of unimpeachable private life, just, charitable, generous ; that like many of our greatest statesmen he had raised himself by his own unaided exertions to a place of great power and distinction ; that though he had been all his life a politician he had never basely sought office and had never held office save once, and then very briefly ; that with all his errors his influence had

THE LAST QUARTER-CENTURY

always been used in favor of every true reform as well as many that merely promised well; and that he was a thorough believer in American ideas and things."

Among Grant's critics the cooler argued about as follows: The war issues, they said, should be treated as settled; in its prosperity the party had become careless; the President was surrounded by unwise counsellors and influenced by unscrupulous men; under him the civil service had been debauched as never before, even in Jackson's time; if he should be re-elected things could not but go from bad to worse. Putting the very best possible construction upon his motives, they declared, it was obvious that Grant was dividing the party, and therefore should no longer continue its official head. Some of the President's antagonists did not hesitate even to impugn his honesty. His advocacy of reform in the civil service they denominated "thin twaddle." He was charged with incorrigible nepotism. The fact that he had been given a house was deemed suspicious. The utmost was made of his incessant smoking and of his love for fast horses.

HENRY WILSON

"It is not a great draft upon the public purse," said one, "nor a creation of a dangerous family influence, when the President appoints a dozen or more of his relatives to office; but it is a bad example, and shows a low view of the presidential office. But far worse than this was the scandal of the President's brother-in-law at the capital following the profession of agent for claims against the Government, carrying his family influence into the subordinate executive departments where such claims are judged, and actually—as he testified before a Congressional Committee—appealing cases

B. GRATZ BROWN

A CHOICE OF EVILS

from the departments to the President and appearing before him to argue them. In effect this was the sale of the President's influence against the ends of justice by his brother-in-law." This criticism was made by an able writer who, after all, preferred Grant to Greeley.

The President's thick and thin supporters pleaded that under his administration the public debt had been decreased, taxes lowered, the utmost honesty and economy introduced in public affairs, industry revived, and confidence restored. They alleged that the cause of the Cincinnati Convention was nothing but selfish discontent. The meeting, they said, had been controlled by scheming politicians and place-hunters, who knew that under Greeley they could have what they wished. If Grant was incompetent, it was asked, what would be the state of affairs should Greeley, who had hardly ever in his life held an office, and never an administrative office, be elected!

A very large class of Republicans admitted as true most that was put forth in criticism of the Administration, yet wished Grant elected. " Of Grant," said one of these Republicans, "we have some reason to think that we know the worst. It appears that he favors civil service reform at least as much as Mr. Greeley does. His relations are now, we believe, all comfortably provided for; gratified citizens have showered upon him as many gifts as he will probably care to receive." " Pitiful as it is to be compelled to choose one of two evidently unfit persons for the highest office in the nation, our preference would be for General Grant. . . Though of proved incapacity in civil government, he is still believed to be honest, cautious and steady, with a reserve of intellectual power and moral purpose which, in any coming crisis of our affairs, might be an invaluable aid to the country." This writer did not doubt that Grant was "stolid, barren of ideas, and below the intellectual level of Jackson, Taylor and Harrison," admitted that vast numbers of Republicans would vote for him merely as a choice of evils, and declared that his re-election could not

THE LAST QUARTER-CENTURY

be taken for an unqualified approval of his administration. "Grant," he said, "conspicuously fails" in obvious desire for the people's good; "his presence inspires no enthusiasm; his pulse does not beat with the popular heart; he has the coldness of Washington without his lofty self-devotion."

As the conflict deepened feeling waxed painfully bitter and the meanest personal allusions were common. Greeley's supporters dubbed their candidate "Honest Old Horace;" the opposition, remembering his bail to Jefferson Davis, whom most abolitionists wished hung, called him "Old Bail-Bonds." "Grant beat Davis," they said, "Greeley bailed him." He was named "Horrors Greeley," and his homely manners were made the subject of innumerable jests. "Greeley"—so ran one relatively sober estimate—"Greeley, with his immense experience and acuteness, and philanthropic philosophy of life, is still unsteady, grotesque, obstinate and ridiculous—epithets never yet justly applicable, all at once, to a President of the United States." Cartoons, which played a great figure in this campaign, vastly exaggerated his corpulency. On the unfortunate B. Gratz Brown the stalwarts heaped the worst disgrace which a political candidate can receive, that of being ignored. His views and his record were never mentioned; only his bare name came before the public. In every cartoon by Nast where Greeley was represented, a tag bearing the legend "and Gratz Brown," hung from his coat-tail. Carl Schurz and Whitelaw Reid, both fighting Greeleyites, were pictured with classical and pedantic features, eye-glasses big as tea-cups, and legs ten feet long.

Such coarseness was not confined to the supporters of the

A BITTER CAMPAIGN

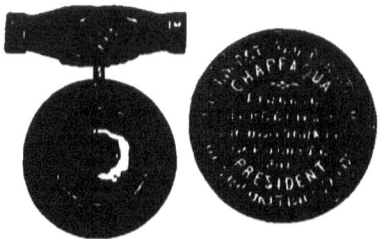

Administration. The Greeley press made Grant call to his intimates to bid him good-by, as he sang:

"My friends are gone to Chappaqua,
Oh, put me in my little bed."

Chappaqua was Greeley's country residence. Greeley was dubbed "Old Whitey" for his coat and hat, his most unique habiliments, and the following doggerel was concocted, equally unique in its good humor:

"Press where ye see my White Hat gleam amid the ranks of war,
And be your oriflamme this day the Coat of Chappaqua."

On May 31st Sumner delivered a speech in which he applied to the President the following extract from a letter of Lord Durham to Henry Brougham: "Among the foremost purposes ought to be the downfall of this odious, insulting, degrading, aide-de-campish, incapable dictatorship. At such a crisis, is this country to be left at the mercy of barrack councils and mess-room politics?"

If the disclosures and falsehoods about the Credit Mobilier, of which we shall give an account in the next Chapter, hurt the party in power, the revelations already made and still coming out concerning the Tweed Ring told against Greeley's cause. Tweed was of Tammany, and Tammany, now in the worst repute it had ever borne, threw to the breeze the Greeley flag. The question of Female Suffrage also plagued Mr. Greeley. The National Women's Suffrage Association met in New York May 9, 1872, and adopted resolutions strongly condemning him for his position in regard to their movement asseverating the right of women to vote under the Fourteenth and Fifteenth Amendments to the Constitution.

THE LAST QUARTER-CENTURY

Nor was this all. As an uncompromising opponent of the Democracy, Greeley had during his editorial career wielded a terribly caustic pen. This fact much aggravated his new position. A cut in *Harper's Weekly* represented him in the act of eating uncomfortably hot soup from a dish bearing the inscription, " My own words and deeds." Greeley had said that the Democratic party would be better off if there were not a school-house in the country, and he had always represented that only people of the lowest sort naturally found their way to its ranks. Now, as " standard-bearer of the great Liberal movement," he had accepted the nomination of that very party. Against Greeley the arch-abolitionist, every fire-eater paper at the South had for twenty-five years been discharging its most venomous spleen. Once, before the war, a Northern sheet characterized the representative plantation lord as sighing:

> "Oh for a nigger and oh for a whip,
> Oh for a cocktail and oh for a nip,
> Oh for a shot at Old Greeley and Beecher,
> Oh for a whack at a Yankee school-teacher ;
> And so he kept ohing for what he had not,
> Not contented with owing for all he had got."

Now the quondam plantation lord was invited to the polls to vote for the " Old Greeley " aforesaid.

Numerous and weighty as were Grant's faults and Greeley's virtues, events or sentiments proved too strong for the bolting movement. Many for a time deluded themselves with the hope of its triumph, but as election day approached it became evident that Grant would receive an overwhelming majority in the electoral college. Most of those Republicans who at first disinclined to vote for Grant, hoping for a better man, determined, as the campaign advanced, to put up with the ills they had rather than fly to the unknown

CHARLES O'CONOR

GREELEY'S DEATH

JOHN QUINCY ADAMS
In 1870

ones which they believed the promotion of Greeley sure to bring. As State after State declared for Republicanism during the late summer and fall, the shadows of defeat lengthened across Greeley's path. Finally he undertook a personal canvass, stumping New Hampshire and Maine in August, Pennsylvania and Ohio in September. From this campaign work he was called to the death-bed of his wife, over whose stricken form he watched with the tenderest love and care until she passed away, a week before the election. His defeat at the polls was overwhelming. He carried but six States, all of them Southern. Grant's popular majority approached three-quarters of a million. Mr. Greeley was quite spent in body and mind by the terrible bitterness of the campaign, by the magnitude of his defeat, and most of all by his deep bereavement. Before his wife's death he had said to an intimate, " I am a broken old man. I have not slept one hour in twenty-four for a month. If she lasts, poor soul, another week, I shall go before her." For six weeks he did not enjoy a night of natural sleep. Malaria had already undermined his system, and on November 29th he succumbed, ere the shouts of the victors had died away. At once all laid aside thoughts of triumph, his bitterest enemies hastening to do honor to the memory of his noble character.

In the death of Horace Greeley the nation lost a citizen of sterling worth and deep patriotism. Opinionated, an idealist rather than a practitioner in his contention for right, he had been led into more than one quixotic error, laying himself open to attacks that left their sting. His judgments were often precipitate and unsound. June 29, 1862, he wrote to J. R. Giddings: " We are going to ruin. McClellan is certainly a fool, probably a traitor, and Halleck is no better. We are doomed." But every one now forgot the man's blunders and remembered only the purity and benevolence of his spirit. No one had ever impeached the honesty of his motives. It was the universal verdict that he had been a man of great soul and lofty devotion, not unworthy the title bestowed upon him by Whittier, of "The Modern Franklin."

As in duty bound, Congress, on February 12, 1873, counted the electoral vote. When the State of Georgia was reached, Mr. Beck, of Kentucky, announced three of the votes of that State for Greeley. The House voting to reject these, since the candidate was dead at the time they were cast, and the Senate voting to receive them, they were thrown out under the Twenty-second Joint Rule, then in force. Upon different objections, but under the same rule, the votes of Arkansas and Louisiana were also rejected. Had Greeley lived he would probably have received sixty electoral votes.

Grant was inaugurated March 4, 1873. In his inaugural address he declared strongly for the establishment of the negroes' civil rights. He maintained that no executive control was exercised in the Southern States which would not be had in others under similar circumstances. He favored the extension of the country's territorial domains, pledging himself to the restoration, so far as possible, of good feeling, and to the establishment of the currency on a solid basis. He urged the construction of cheaper inland routes for travel and trade, and also the re-establishment of our foreign commerce.

The campaign of 1872 naturally sweetened Sumner's temper toward the Southern people. In a letter to the colored voters of the United States, dated July 29, 1872, he said: "Pile up the ashes, extinguish the flame, abolish the hate—such is my desire." In accordance with this sentiment he introduced in the Senate a bill providing that the names of battles against citizens of the United States while in rebellion should not be continued in the army register or placed on the colors of regiments. This failed to pass, but an act did pass which happily reduced to some extent the rancor felt by the

REPUBLICAN POLICY AT THE SOUTH

South against the North. It removed political disabilities from all citizens of the late Confederacy, except Senators and Representatives in the Thirty-sixth and Thirty-seventh Congresses, officers in the judicial, military and naval service, and heads of departments and foreign ministers of the United States. This act was approved May 22, 1872. However, the Republican programme for governing the Southern States was as yet by no means essentially altered.

HENRY CLAY WARMOTH

Congressional discussions over race difficulties were renewed with some bitterness when, in May, 1872, a bill was brought before Congress, extending to all election precincts the act of 1871, whereby Federal Supervisors could be appointed in towns of over 20,000 inhabitants. It passed the Senate without great difficulty. In the House it was strenuously opposed, its enemies dubbing it "election by bayonet." It finally passed the House also, June 8th, as an amendment to an appropriation bill.

During the second session of the Forty-second Congress, there was more or less race trouble in the South, and the anti-Administration forces took occasion to reflect anew on the President's policy under the Force Act. On January 25,

P. B. S. PINCHBACK

1873, the House passed a resolution requesting the President to inform Congress touching the condition of South Carolina, in which State, under the authority of the act of April 20, 1871, he had suspended the writ of *habeas corpus*. The citizens of the State also made a request for a statement of the Government's policy in prosecutions under that act. The reply stated that the Executive was disposed, except in grave cases, to show great

79

THE LAST QUARTER-CENTURY

clemency and to discontinue prosecutions against violators of the law.

The election of November, 1870, gave Louisiana to the Republicans by a substantial majority, but almost immediately the party began to break up into factions. Governor Warmoth was opposed by leading federal officers, who succeeded in gaining control of the Republican State convention. With the assembling of the Legislature in January, 1872, the situation assumed a grave character. On the death of Lieutenant-Governor Dunn, in November of the previous year, P. B. S. Pinchback, a colored adherent of Warmoth, had been elected President of the Senate, but the Administration leaders declared his election illegal. In the House, Speaker Carter, an anti-Warmoth man, was antagonized by Warmoth's friends. After a bitter struggle, during which Warmoth and a number of his supporters were arrested by the Federal authorities, Carter was deposed. A congressional committee investigated the quarrel, but could not quiet it, and the politics of Louisiana continued in an inflamed condition.

Estrangement soon arose between Governor Warmoth and Pinchback, Warmoth heading the Liberal Republican movement in the State. After much manœuvring the Liberals united with the Democratic and "Reform" parties in a fusion ticket headed by John McEnery, with an electoral ticket supporting Greeley and Brown. The Pinchback faction united with the Grant party, nominating W. P. Kellogg for Governor and Pinchback for Congressman-at-large. There can be little doubt that McEnery was elected by a large majority.

The returns of the election were to be submitted to the State Returning Board. At the time of the election the Board consisted of Governor Warmoth, Lieut.-Gov. Pinchback, Secretary of State Herron, John Lynch, and T. C. Anderson. When this board met, Pinchback and Anderson being candidates for office at this election whose result was to be determined, were declared incapable of serving. The Governor

THE DISPERSAL OF THE McENERY LEGISLATURE AT ODD FELLOWS' HALL, NEW ORLEANS

On March 6th, 1873, a body of Metropolitan Police, under orders from General Longstreet, the Commander of the Kellogg militia, marched to Odd Fellows' Hall, where the McEnery Legislature was in session, and arrested the only five members who refused to disperse or to leave the building.

FORCE AND ANARCHY IN LOUISIANA

supplanted Herron with a more trusty friend, and proceeded to fill the other two vacancies. In like manner, Lynch and Herron, professing to be the true board, supplied their own lack in numbers. In December, the Supreme Court of the State declared Herron an intruder into the office of Secretary of State, thus demolishing the Lynch and Herron board, while Federal Circuit Judge E. H. Durell, in answer to Kellogg's prayer, enjoined Warmoth's board from acting. Meantime a legislative act, duly passed and approved, ousted both boards and provided for a new one. This being speedily organized, the returns were canvassed and McEnery was declared elected Governor by a majority of 7,000.

Kellogg's prospects now seemed desperate, but they did not prove to be so. On the night of December 5th, "in his own chambers, without any previous motion in Court," Justice Durell drew up and issued to the United States Marshal, Packard, the following: "It is hereby ordered, that the Marshal of the United States for the District of Louisiana shall forthwith take possession of the building known as the Mechanics' Institute and occupied as the State-house, for the assembling of the Legislature therein, in the city of New Orleans, and hold the same subject to the further order of the Court; and meanwhile to prevent all unlawful assemblage therein under the guise or pretext of authority claimed by virtue of pretended canvass and returns made by said pretended returning officers in contempt and violation of said restraining order; but the Marshal is directed to allow the ingress and egress to and from the public offices in said building, of persons entitled to the same."

This mandate, void in point of law, was efficient, and next morning, obeying the Marshal's order, Captain Jackson, with United States soldiers, began a six weeks' occupation of the State-house. Collector of the Port, Casey, telegraphed the President: "Marshal Packard took possession of State-house this morning, at an early hour, with military posse, in obedience to a mandate of Circuit Court, to prevent illegal assemblage of persons under guise of authority of Warmoth's returning board, in violation of injunction of Circuit Court... The decree was sweeping in its provisions, and if enforced will save the Republican majority and give Louisiana a Republican Legislature and State government."

The same day the Lynch board met and, though without the returns, elected Kellogg Governor by 19,000 majority. They then proceeded by the very easy and summary method set forth in the following bit of testimony, to create a Republican legislature in place of the legal body:

By Mr. Carpenter. Q. "You estimated it, then, upon the basis of what you thought the vote ought to have been?"

By Lynch. A. "Yes, sir. That was just the fact, and I think, on the whole, we were pretty correct."

This Legislature at once impeached Warmoth, thus making Pinchback Governor for the unexpired term. The Court again aided, enjoining all not named on the Lynch list from claiming office, and enjoining Warmoth from interfering with the organization of the Lynch Legislature.

On December 11, 1872, Pinchback telegraphed the Attorney-General at Washington: " May I suggest that the commanding general be authorized to furnish troops upon my requisition upon him, for the protection of the Legislature and the gubernatorial office?" Kellogg, the heir apparent, also telegraphed: "If the President in some way indicates recognition, Governor Pinchback and Legislature would settle everything." Collector Casey co-operated: " The delay in placing troops at disposal of Governor Pinchback, in accordance with joint resolution, is disheartening our friends and cheering our enemies. If requisition of Legislature is complied with, all difficulty will be dissipated, the party saved, . . and the tide will be turned at once in our favor . . . . "

Next day, the 12th, Attorney-General Williams responded: "Acting-Governor Pinchback, New Orleans, Loui-

FORCE AND ANARCHY IN LOUISIANA

siana: Let it be understood that you are recognized by the President as the lawful executive of Louisiana, and that the body assembled at Mechanics' Institute is the lawful Legislature of the State; and it is suggested that you make proclamation to that effect, and also that all necessary assistance will be given to you and the Legislature herein recognized to protect the State from disorder and violence."

In answer to a telegram from McEnery, begging for delay till a committee of citizens could lay the facts before the Executive, came the following: "Hon John McEnery. Your visit with a hundred citizens will be unavailing, so far as the President is concerned. His decision is made and will not be changed, and the sooner it is acquiesced in the sooner good order and peace will be restored. Geo. H. Williams, Attorney-General." Finally this: "Washington, December 14, 1872. General W. H. Emory, U. S. A., Commanding, New Orleans, Louisiana. You may use all necessary force to preserve the peace, and will recognize the authority of Governor Pinchback. By order of the President: E. D. Townsend, Adjutant-General."

On January 7, 1873, the day appointed for the assembling of the Legislature, both the opposing bodies began operations "*inter arma.*" A week later both Kellogg and McEnery took the oath of office. President Grant supported the Pinchback claimants with federal troops. The House of Representatives instructed its Committee on Privileges and Elections to inquire into the dispute. A report was made February 20, 1873, which condemned federal interference. The committee found that McEnery was *de jure* entitled to the governorship, but that Kellogg, supported by the army, was *de facto* Governor. The committee recommended the passage of an act "to secure an honest re-election" in Louisiana. The recommendation was not adopted and anarchy, in effect, followed.

CHAPTER IV

THE GENEVA AWARD AND THE CREDIT MOBILIER

OUTCOME OF THE WASHINGTON TREATY.—THE "ALABAMA CLAIMS."—VAIN EFFORTS AT SETTLEMENT.—THE GENEVA TRIBUNAL.—RULES FOR ITS GUIDANCE.—QUESTIONS ANSWERED BY IT.—ITS DECISION.—THE NORTHWESTERN BOUNDARY SETTLEMENT.—THE CREDIT MOBILIER STORY.—ENTHUSIASM FOR THE WEST.—VASTNESS OF THAT SECTION.—THE RUSH THITHER.—THE PIONEERS.—LAND-GRABBING.—GRANTS FOR TRANSCONTINENTAL RAILWAYS.—INCEPTION OF THE UNION PACIFIC COMPANY.—THE CREDIT MOBILIER COMPANY.—OAKES AMES AND HIS CONTRACT.—STOCK SOLD TO CONGRESSMEN.—THE "SUN'S" PUBLICATION.—THE FACTS.—AMES'S DEFENSE.—CENSURE OF HIM BY THE HOUSE OF REPRESENTATIVES.—HIS DEATH.—REASONS FOR THE SENTIMENT AGAINST HIM.

NOTHING aided President Grant and his party in their 1872 campaign more than the honorable outcome which the Treaty of Washington had in the Geneva Award and the northwestern boundary settlement, both seasonably made known to the world in 1872. The Award related to the famous *Alabama* Claims, and meant that these, or the most important of them, must be paid us by Great Britain. Chief credit for such happy result was due to Hon. Hamilton Fish, Grant's Secretary of State, yet naturally and justly, the Administration as a whole profited by his triumphant diplomacy.

The claims usually denominated "*Alabama*" claims were partly national or, less accurately, "indirect," and partly individual or direct. The national claims were for destruction of United States commerce or its transfer to other flags occasioned by Confederate privateers fitted out wholly or partly in

THE LAST QUARTER-CENTURY

Great Britain, and for enhanced marine insurance and increased cost of the war in life and treasure due to the same cause. The individual or direct claims were for damages through certain specific acts of depredation by Confederate war-vessels, notably the *Alabama*, the *Florida*, and the *Shenandoah*.

In spite of repeated warnings from Hon. Charles Francis Adams, then United States Minister to Great Britain, the Queen's Government had suffered the *Florida*, originally called the *Oreto*, and ostensibly destined for Palermo, Sicily, to be built at Liverpool in 1862, and to receive, at Green Bay, near Nassau, arms and munitions from another vessel. The *Florida* was indeed seized, but soon released. Adams's suspicions were shortly directed against another vessel building at Liverpool, called "the 290," from the number of merchants who contributed to her construction, but later and better known as the *Alabama*. His suspicions were confirmed by evidence which distinguished British counsel declared "almost conclusive," sufficient to impose a "heavy responsibility" upon the collector of customs "if he failed to detain her." Easily dodging the half-hearted reach that was made for her, "the 290" went forth upon her career of devastation, continuing it until she was sunk by the *Kearsage*. The *Shenandoah* cleared from Liverpool as a merchant vessel, the *Sea King*, and when, in November, 1865, she took in supplies and enlisted men at Melbourne, English liability for her acts became definitely fixed. Claims of a less conclusive nature were made on account of the acts of ten other Confederate privateers.

Mr. Adams left England in 1868 without having obtained any satisfaction of these claims. His successor, Hon. Reverdy Johnson, was upon his arrival in London much dined and wined. He made effusive speeches, judging from which one would think that in his view Great Britain could do no wrong. Secretary Seward, too, had a warm regard for England, and was moreover anxious to settle the difficulty before leaving office. But the Johnson-Clarendon Treaty, the off-

THE "ALABAMA CLAIMS"

The Florida   *The Shenandoah*   *The Alabama, or 290*
THREE FAMOUS CONFEDERATE CRUISERS
*The Shenandoah is from a photograph of a drawing owned by John T. Mason, Esq.
The other two are from photographs owned by John M. Kell, Esq.*

spring of this cordial policy, was, in the spring of 1869, unceremoniously drummed out of the Senate to the music of Charles Sumner's famous speech, which, as one paper put it, "set almost all Americans to swinging their hats for eight or nine days, and made every Englishman double up his fists and curse every time he thought of it for several weeks."

That treaty contained not a word of regret for England's unfriendly posture during the war, or the slightest confession of fault. It ignored the national claims of the United States, while its language with regard to British citizens' claims against the United States, whatever was intended by it, was so catholic that when the text of the treaty became known Confederate bonds in England rose from their tomb with ten per cent. of their original vitality about them.

On becoming President, Grant recalled Johnson and sent to succeed him John Lothrop Motley, a firm friend of Sumner's, sharing Sumner's extreme views upon the British question. But the policy of the new Administration was not so radical as Sumner's. It laid little stress upon the recognition of belligerency as a ground for damage, and left Great Britain to take the initiative in coming to an understanding. Like Sumner, Mr. Motley wished to insist upon damages for Eng-

THE LAST QUARTER-CENTURY

CHARLES SUMNER

land's premature recognition of the Confederates as belligerents. He, too, was soon removed.

At the instance of England, a joint High Commission was speedily appointed to sit in Washington. The Treaty of Washington, drawn up by this Commission and proclaimed on July 4, 1871, provided for an adjustment of all outstanding differences between the countries touching the fisheries, the northwestern boundary, and the claims of citizens of either government against the other for acts committed during the Civil War. The Treaty further provided "for the reciprocal free navigation of certain rivers, including the St. Lawrence, for the common use of certain Canadian and American canals, and for reciprocal free transit across the territories of the United States or Canada; these provisions to be enforced by appropriate legislation, to be binding for ten years, and terminable thereafter on two years' notice." In all its articles together the Treaty engaged the co-operation of no fewer than eight sovereign States. The *Alabama* claims it referred to a Tribunal of Arbitration, consisting of one arbitrator from each of the high contracting parties and one each appointed by the executives of Italy, Switzerland, and Brazil. Count Sclopis was the Italian arbitrator, Mr. Jacques Staempfli the Swiss, and Baron Itajuba the Brazilian. The tribunal met at Geneva, December 15, 1871, but, as we have observed, did not render its decision until the succeeding year.

The Treaty of Washington had laid down for the guidance of the tribunal three rules, which form such an important contribution to international law that they deserve quotation in full:

"A neutral government is bound,

RULES FOR GUIDANCE OF GENEVA TRIBUNAL

"First: To use due diligence to prevent the fitting out, arming or equipping, within its jurisdiction, of any vessel which it has reasonable ground to believe is intended to cruise or to carry on war against a power with which it is at peace; and also to use like diligence to prevent the departure from its jurisdiction of any vessel intended to cruise or carry on war as above, such vessel having been specially adapted, in whole or in part, within such jurisdiction, to warlike use.

"Secondly: Not to permit or suffer either belligerent to make use of its ports or waters as the base of naval operations against the other, or for the purpose of the renewal or augmentation of military supplies or arms, or the recruitment of men.

"Thirdly: To exercise due diligence in its own ports and waters, and, as to all persons within its jurisdiction, to prevent any violation of the foregoing obligations and duties."

In the text of the Treaty of Washington Great Britain denied that these rules were a true statement of the principles of international law as that law stood during the American Civil War, but consented that the *Alabama* Claims should be decided in accordance with them notwithstanding. Both countries agreed to abide by these principles in future, and to invite other maritime powers to do the same.

Question being raised as to the interpretation of certain terms and the scope of certain provisions in the three rules, the tribunal made the following preliminary decisions:

1. The meaning of "due diligence." The tribunal took the ground that what constitutes "due diligence" varies with the circumstances of the case. The greater the probable damage to either belligerent, the greater must be the care taken by the neutral government to prevent the escape of cruisers from its ports.

2. Should a neutral detain an escaped cruiser when it re-enters the neutral's jurisdiction, the cruiser having in the meantime been regularly commissioned by its government?

THE LAST QUARTER-CENTURY

The arbitrators decided that the neutral had a right to detain such a cruiser, in spite of its commission, but was under no positive obligation to do so.

3. Does a neutral's responsibility end with the enforcement of its local laws to prevent the escape of cruisers, even if those laws are inadequate? Decision was given that the case must be determined by international law and not by national legislation. If a country's regulations for carrying out its acknowledged international duties are ineffective, they ought to be changed.

Though these decisions touching the law of nations were of world-wide significance, the verdict on the facts in the case had a more immediate interest for the American people. Indirect claims the tribunal dismissed, and it made no award for the expense of pursuing Confederate cruisers, or for any prospective earnings which ships lost through them. But, for Great Britain's negligence in failing to prevent the equipment, arming, and provisioning of the Confederate privateers, the gross sum of $15,500,000 was awarded the United States. Sir Alexander Cockburn, the English "arbitrator," was the only one to take this decree with ill grace. On the announcement of it he seized his hat and left the room without so much as an adieu, getting "leave to print" with the record of the proceedings a choleric document known as his "Opinions."

The dispute as to our northwestern boundary was also decided in our favor during 1872. By a treaty of 1846 the boundary line between the United States and British America was run westward along the 49th parallel "to the middle of the channel which separates the continent from Vancouver's Island, thence southerly through the middle of the said channel and of Fuca's Strait, to the Pacific Ocean." Should "the middle" referred to be interpreted as passing through the Strait of Rosario, on the side next Washington Territory, or through the Canal de Haro, on the Vancouver side of the archipelago there? Should those islands be looped into the

Charles Francis   Jacques   Count   Baron   Sir Alexander
   Adams   Staempfli   Sclopis   Itajubá   Cockburn
              M. Favrot, Secretary

COUNT SCLOPIS ANNOUNCING THE DECISION OF THE GENEVA TRIBUNAL
["Sir Alexander Cockburn . . . left the room without so much as an adieu."]
Painted by W. R. Leigh from photographs and diagrams loaned by J. C. Bancroft Davis, Esq.

ENTHUSIASM FOR THE WEST

territory of Uncle Sam, or given to John Bull? This question the Treaty of Washington referred to Emperor William I., of Germany.

The historian Bancroft, the only surviving statesman save one concerned in negotiating the 1846 treaty, argued our claims in this matter, and on October 21, 1872, had the satisfaction of seeing his plea crowned by a favorable decision. "The award," said President Grant, "leaves us for the first time in the history of the United States as a nation, without a question of disputed boundary between our territory and the possessions of Great Britain." It was a proud result for the President, and assisted not a little in his re-election.

While the consequences of the memorable Treaty of Washington were favorable to the party in power, another revelation of the campaign had much influence in the opposite direction. In August, 1872, when the excitement of the Presidential strife was already high, the New York *Sun* published a story which added fresh fuel to the political fires already raging, and promised to generate much steam to propel the Greeley movement. It related to the Credit Mobilier operations in constructing the Union Pacific Railway. If true, the facts said to exist involved in corruption the Speaker of the House, the Vice-President, the Republican nominee for the vice-presidency, the Secretary of the Treasury, and others high in political life.

Enthusiasm for the Great West kindled again after the war and became a mania. The climate and soil of the region had been persistently misrepresented by the Hudson Bay Company, by Great Britain its successor in title, by influential Southerners jealous of the North, and by numerous exploring parties. The "Great American Desert" was a dragon of which numberless horrors were related. So early as 1850 it had been outflanked by way of the Horn and threatened from the Pacific Coast, but not till after the war, when Southern influence was withdrawn, was it transfixed by any avenue of general travel or trade.

THE LAST QUARTER-CENTURY

The United States west of the Mississippi, leaving out Texas, Minnesota, and California, naturally broke up as follows: (1) The Arkansas District, embracing Arkansas, most of Indian Territory and a portion of Missouri. Here were bottoms of Egyptian fertility and warmth, subject to heavy rainfall, in parts forest-covered. Beyond the Ozarks was a colder and dryer plateau. (2) The Lower Missouri Valley, including nearly the whole State of Missouri, also western Iowa and part of Kansas and Nebraska. This was opened to settlement earlier than (1) and was the sooner populated. The rainfall and temperature here were suited to all northern crops, and the land was nearly level. (3) The Upper Missouri Valley, practically coinciding with North and South Dakota. This tract was higher, dryer and much colder than (2). Fortunately, where it was cold, surface coal was to be had for the digging, and where arid, the earth beneath seemed a vast subterranean sponge, rendering artesian wells a successful means of irrigation. This district was unwooded. (4) The Cordilleran Plateau, extending from 100° W. long.,

Lord Tenterden   *Mountague Bernard*   *Sir Alexander Cockburn*   *Sir Roundell Palmer*
THE ENGLISH REPRESENTATIVES AT GENEVA

westward to the Rocky Mountains, and from near the Canadian border to the Rio Grande. This vast area was too arid for the plow. Formerly a buffalo range, it has become a great cattle pasture, and is apparently destined to continue such.

THE RUSH TO THE WEST

(5) The Mountain Region, in width from 500 miles at the north and south to 1,000 in the middle, composed of basins more or less extensive, enclosed by sharp and high ridges. Irrigation made some farming possible here, but the mineral wealth was immense and mining became the main industry. (6) The Northwestern Country, comprising parts of Wyoming, Idaho, Montana, and the States of Washington and Oregon. Here timber was plentiful and farming profitable. On the Pacific Slope from 50 to 200 cords of wood per acre could be cut, and all ordinary crops and fruits save grapes succeeded.

The settler's way to this Promised Land was in some measure made smooth between 1860 and 1870. Arizona, Colorado, Dakota, Idaho, Montana and Wyoming had been organized as territories; Kansas, Nebraska and Nevada had been admitted to statehood. The status of the West when the rush commenced we set forth in Chapter I. Enormous companies came to the Red River Valley, to Colorado, where raged a mining furor second only to that witnessed by Cali-

Caleb Cushing   William M. Evarts   Charles Francis Adams   J. C. Bancroft Davis   Morrison R. Waite
THE AMERICAN REPRESENTATIVES AT GENEVA

fornia in '49, to Utah, and to the Slope. People pressed along all river courses, especially up and down the valley of the Columbia. Montana received a farming quota. Helena, whose main street was the Last Chance Gulch, was destined, unlike its compeer, Virginia City, to survive and thrive even when the Last Chance Gulch should become a reminiscence. From California and Colorado the Territory caught the gambling spirit. It was said that two Montana mining millionaires were one evening contributing red, white and blue wafers to a goodly pile on the table between them, which in due time was "raked in." As they were about to proceed to a new deal, an Eastern stranger approached, threw down a hundred dollar bill and said: "Gentlemen, I would like to join you. There's the money for some chips." Whereupon one of the players told "Sam," the banker, to "take the gentleman's money and give him a white chip."

Many of the Western pioneers were rough fellows, some of them desperadoes. The orderly population which came later brought the bad element under control, at first by vigilance committees, then by law and order methods, though the pistol long had much to do in keeping as well as in breaking the civil peace. Visitors were early struck with the very considerable culture of the people and by the many articles of comfort and even luxury in those Western towns of a day. Newspapers were common from the first. Asked how a town of a few thousand could support four dailies, a resident replied, "Why, stranger, it takes all those dailies to support the town." "Booming" became a fine art. "No Other Land," said one sheet, "No Other Clime On Top of God's Green Earth, Where Land is Free as Church Bells' Chime, Save the Land of Dakota Dirt. Here For a Year of Honest Toil a Home You May Insure, and From the Black and Loamy Soil a Title in Fee Mature. No Money Needed Until the Day When the Earth Provides; Until You Raise a Crop, no Pay :—What Can You Ask Besides?"

Nevada received an overflow from the West—from California. Here and there, slowly transforming the desert into an empire, were scattered still other pools and lakes of humanity. Not the least important of these was the Black Hills settlement.

U. S. GRANT

From a photograph by Walker, June 2, 1875. General Grant shaved his beard on purpose, the picture being for use in cutting a cameo. Only two copies each of the two views, showing right and left profile, were printed.

LAND GRABBING

GEORGE BANCROFT
After a photograph in the historical collection of H. W. Fay.

The rumor of "Gold in the Black Hills" grew rife in 1874, and the soldiers were in straits to dam the tide of prospectors till a treaty of cession could be obtained to extinguish the Sioux title. "'All same' old story," said a warrior. " White men come, build chu-chu through reservation. White men yawpy-yawpy. Say, 'Good Indian, good Indian; we want land. We give muz-es-kow (money), liliota muz-es-kow (plenty money).' Indian say, 'Yes.' What Indian get? Wah-nee-che (nothing). Some day white man want move Indian. White men yawpy-yawpy. 'Good Indian, good Indian; give good Indian liliota muz-es-kow.' What Indian get? Wah-nee-chee. Some day white man want half big reservation. He come Indian. Yawpy-yawpy: 'Good Indian; we give Indian liliota muz-es-kow.' Indian heap fool. He say, 'Yes.' What Indian get? Wah-nee-chee. All same old story. 'Good Indian, good Indian.' Get nothing!"*

In one way and another speculators seized upon choice slices of the public domain. Often the alternate quarter-sections belonging to a railroad would be bought up, and the other quarter-sections—government land—secured in due time through "dummies" located for the purpose. One Montana land shark gave a series of balls and dinners at a country house, inviting a large number of ladies, and accompanying every invitation with a promise of a $100 present. At each festival, in the midst of the whirl, each guest signed a claim to a homesteader's rights in the adjoining lands. When the "claims" were "proved up" each lady received her $100 and the authors of the scheme got land enough for a dukedom. As many such marches depended upon irrigation for their value, "grabs" for "water-rights" early began.

*"Our Great West," by Julian Ralph.

THE LAST QUARTER-CENTURY

"We who are on the ground," said an enterprising Montanian, "are going to get whatever there is lying around. You don't suppose we are going to let a parcel of strangers pre-empt the water-rights so that we must pay taxes to them? No; we prefer to let them pay the taxes to us." A very reasonable preference.

Queer land laws and railroad bonuses made possible bonanza farming on an enormous scale. In the course of years farming of this sort raised up bands of nomadic farm-hands, who, beginning at the South, worked northward with the advancing season till the ripened year found them beyond the Canada border. There were also companies of sheep-shearing specialists, who usually made two rounds a year, passing their winters riotously in the towns and cities. The great cattle-ranges were traversed by still other nomads, the "cow-boys," in bands known as "trails," traveling about a day apart, each "trail" with its camp equipage and relay of broncos. Texas cattle would be driven northward to fatten upon the Montanian "Bad Lands" as a preparation for their final journey to Chicago.

——— Boundary claimed by England
——— Boundary claimed by the United States

THE NORTHWEST WATER BOUNDARY

Some traits in the foregoing sketch anticipate a little, yet enough of it was true so early as the end of the war to assure a few that the West was to have an enormous development. Two transcontinental railways were planned, one to cross the

GRANTS FOR TRANSCONTINENTAL RAILWAYS

"Great Desert," the other to round its northern end, both to be equipped as soon as possible with branch and connecting lines. The more southerly, the Union and Central Pacific, had the advantage of earlier completion and a more developed western terminus; but the Northern Pacific could cross the Cordilleras at a lower level and need traverse no desert. Both enterprises were unstintedly favored by grants of public land.* This policy was widely condemned, but also vigorously defended.

In 1871 a competent writer discussing the grant to the Northern Pacific declared it self-evident that as a result of the opening of this region the Government would get ample returns for its liberality. It was more than a royal subsidy by which it had secured the construction of that great highway. It had given therefor 50,000,000 acres of land, an area larger than many kingdoms, worth, if sold at the average price of the Minnesota school lands, $350,000,000; if sold like the lands of the Illinois Central Railroad, $550,000,000. Mr. Wilson, for many years Commissioner of the Land Department of the Illinois Central Railroad, comparing this grant with the Illinois Central Railroad grant, thought it a small estimate to say that if properly managed the Northern Pacific's land would build the entire road connecting the then terminus of the Grand Trunk through to Puget Sound, the head of navigation on the Columbia, fit out an entire fleet of sailing vessels and steamers for the China, East Indian and coasting trade, and leave a surplus that would roll up to millions. He deemed the probable value of the grant $990,000,000, its possible value $1,320,000,000. The Government gained no popularity by a gift so vast. At the Jay Cooke & Co. failure in 1873 a large part of these lands passed to creditors of the road, one of the circumstances which contributed to make bonanza farming so marked a feature in parts of the West.

*In all the Union Pacific received 13,000,100 acres, the Central Pacific, 12,100,100; the Northern Pacific, 47,000,000; the Kansas Pacific, 6,000,000; the Atlantic and Pacific, 42,000,000; the Southern Pacific, 9,520,000. The first transcontinental lines also got subsidies exceeding $60,000,000.

THE LAST QUARTER-CENTURY

In July, 1862, Congress created the Union Pacific Railway Company to build a railroad from the Missouri River to the Pacific Ocean, fixing at $1,000,000,000 the amount of its stock, loaning it a vast sum in government bonds, endowing it with an enormous amount of land along the route, and allowing it till 1876 to complete the enterprise. The shares sold slowly, and it was soon clear that unless Congress gave better terms the undertaking would fail. Accordingly a more liberal act was passed. Even this did not put the road in a way to completion. Contractors, several of whom were besought to do so, hesitated to undertake the building of such a line or any part of it, and but eleven miles of the construction were accomplished up to September, 1865. Most believed either that the road could not be built or that it would never pay.

In March, 1865, the Credit Mobilier of America, a company organized by the Pennsylvania Legislature in 1859 as the "Pennsylvania Fiscal Agency," and in its new form soon amply equipped with capital, contracted with the Union Pacific to go forward with the construction. Two hundred and forty-seven miles of road were thus built, carrying the line to the one-hundreth meridian. Then arose trouble within the Credit Mobilier Company. T. C. Durant, President of this and Vice-President of the Union Pacific, wished the Mobilier to realize at once all possible profits out of the construction, while his opponents, New England parties, believing that the road would pay, were inclined to deal honestly with it, expecting their profits as corporators in the Mobilier to come from the appreciation of the Union Pacific stock, in which, to a great extent, the Mobilier was paid for its work. This party sought to eject Durant from the Mobilier management, and at length did so; but his power in the railway corporation was sufficient to prevent the Mobilier as such from getting a further contract. After much contention, during which the Mobilier was on the verge of failing, Durant consented that Oakes

UNION PACIFIC STOCK SOLD TO CONGRESSMEN

Ames might take a contract to push the construction of the road. Mr. Ames was at the time a Mobilier stockholder and a representative in Congress from Massachusetts.

Ames's contract was dated August 16, 1867, but on the 15th of the next October he made it over to seven trustees, who took Ames's place as contractor. They did all the things which he had agreed to do, and were remunerated just as he was to be. The trustees bound themselves to pay over all the profits of their contract to the Mobilier stockholders in the proportions in which these severally held stock at the date of their contract. This arrangement was fully carried out and the road finished under it. It was an adroit way of circumventing Durant and enabling the Mobilier to build the road in spite of him.

During 1867 and 1868 Ames sold shares of Credit Mobilier stock to many members of Congress. He gave away none, but in a number of cases payment was considerably subsequent to sale. Though worth much more, every share was sold for par and interest, just what it cost Ames himself.

Colonel H. S. McComb, of Delaware, in virtue of a subscription that he said he had made for a friend, claimed of Ames $25,000 in Mobilier stock which he alleged had never been received. Letters passed back and forth between McComb and Ames, in one of which Ames, a blunt, outspoken

EMPEROR WILLIAM I. OF GERMANY

man, declared that he had placed the stock with influential gentlemen (naming several Congressmen) "where it would do the most good." Press and public eagerly took up this phrase. Soon it was in every mouth, all placing upon it the worst construction which the words could bear. McComb pressed his suit and at last the letters were published. The New York *Sun* of September 4, 1872, in the very heat of the Greeley campaign, came out with the heading: "The King of Frauds; How the Credit Mobilier bought its Way through Congress;" stating that Ames had distributed in bribes thirty thousand shares of the stock, worth nine millions of dollars. The scandal ran through the country like wildfire, the allegations being very generally believed, as they probably are still.

But we now know that they comprised partly gross fabrications and partly gross exaggerations. Mr. Ames's motive was laudable—the completion of a great national work, which has long since paid the country many times its cost. He knew that the Pacific Railway had bitter enemies in Congress and outside, most of them not public-spirited, but the blackmailer servants of Durant, who stood ready, should opportunity offer, to work its ruin. He wished to be fortified. His method certainly carried him to the verge of propriety, and perhaps beyond; but, everything considered, the evidence shows little ground for the peculiar execration visited upon him. The Poland Committee of the House, reporting on February 18, 1873, declared that Ames had acted with "intent to influence the votes of members." In the sense that he sought to interest men in the enterprise and to prevent them from sacrificing it through apathy or spite, this was probably true. That it was true in any other sense is at least not proved.

"These, then, are my offences," said Ames, in his defence; "that I have risked reputation, fortune, everything, in an enterprise of incalculable moment to the Government, from which the capital of the world shrank; that I have sought to strengthen the work thus rashly undertaken by invoking the

OAKES AMES'S DEFENCE

charitable judgment of the public upon its obstacles and embarrassments ; that I have had friends, some of them in official life, with whom I have been willing to share advantageous opportunities for investments ; that I have kept to the truth through good and evil report, denying nothing, concealing nothing, reserving nothing. Who will say that I alone am to be offered up a sacrifice to appease a public clamor or expiate the sins of others ?

OAKES AMES

Not until such an offering is made will I believe it possible. But if this body shall so order that it can best be purified by the choice of a single victim, I shall accept its mandate, appealing with unfaltering confidence to the impartial verdict of history for that vindication which it is proposed to deny me here."

The committee recommended his expulsion. "It was useless to point out that no act was before Congress at the time of the alleged bribery, or before or after it, for which Ames was seeking votes. No person whom he had bribed or sought to bribe was produced. Nor was any object he had attempted to accomplish suggested." Hon. B. F. Boyer, one of those who received stock, testified :

" I had no idea of wrong in the matter. Nor do I now see how it concerns the public. No one connected with either the Credit Mobilier or the Union Pacific Railroad ever directly or indirectly expressed, or in any way hinted, that my services as a member of Congress were expected in behalf of either corporation in consideration of the stock I obtained, and certainly no such services were ever rendered. I was much less embarrassed as a member of Congress by the ownership of Credit Mobilier stock than I should have been had I owned stock in a national bank, or in an iron-furnace, or a woollen-mill, or even been a holder of government bonds ; for there

THE LAST QUARTER-CENTURY

was important legislation while I was in Congress affecting all these interests, but no legislation whatever concerning the Credit Mobilier. I can therefore find nothing in my conduct in that regard to regret. It was, in my judgment, both honest and honorable, and consistent with my position as a member of Congress. And, as the investment turned out to be profitable, my only regret is that it was no larger in amount."

The House proceeded to censure Ames, and it would probably have expelled him, had not the alleged offence been committed under a previous Congress. Soon after this censure, which aggravated a disease already upon him, Mr. Ames went home to die. The Wilson Committee reported that the Mobilier had "wronged" the Government, and drafted a bill, which was passed, ordering the Attorney-General to bring suit against its stockholders. He did so, and pushed it to the Supreme Court, but it lamentably failed at every step.

These congressional charges against Oakes Ames have in no wise the weight which has been attached to them. In making them, the House was actuated by a popular clamor against the Credit Mobilier, sedulously worked up by the Democratic press and by Durant. Many members who voted for the censure at once apologized to Ames, saying that they had done so purely for fear of their constituents. That "credit mobilier" was a foreign name rendered men suspicious of the thing named. The French *Crédit Mobilier*, from which the American concern took its title, had got into trouble in 1868 and been wound up. Such as knew of this thought that fraud must of course taint the Credit Mobilier of America as well. Some of those charged with having received Ames's alleged bribes cleared themselves at his expense, falsely denying all knowledge of the Mobilier and declaring that they had never directly or indirectly held any of the stock. Such eagerness to disavow connection with it deepened people's suspicion of it. Pressure was used to force Ames, who himself courted investigation, to support these denials. It availed so far as to

REASONS FOR THE SENTIMENT AGAINST AMES

make him hesitate, telling his story reluctantly and by piecemeal, as if he dreaded the truth. This of course had a further bad effect. In these ways an almost universal impression came to prevail that a fearful crime had been committed, involving most and perhaps all the leaders of the Republican party. Here was rich chance for partisan capital. Democrats and Liberals presented the scandal in the worst possible light and with telling effect. Could anything have defeated Grant, this would assuredly have done so.

CHAPTER V

"CARPET-BAGGER" AND "SCALAWAG" IN DIXIE

GRANT'S RE-ELECTION AND THE SOUTH. —COURT DECISIONS CONFIRMING STATE SOVEREIGNTY. —THE LOUISIANA "SLAUGHTER-HOUSE CASES." —OSBORN VS. NICHOLSON. —WHITE VS. HART. —DESOLATION AT THE SOUTH AFTER THE WAR. —DISCOURAGEMENT. —INTEMPERANCE, IGNORANCE. —SLOW REVIVAL OF INDUSTRY. —SOCIAL AND POLITICAL CONFLICT. —THE "SCALAWAG." —THE "CARPET-BAGGER." —GOOD CARPET-BAGGERS. —THEIR FAILINGS. —RESISTANCE. — NORTHERN SYMPATHY WITH THIS. —THE FREEDMEN. —THEIR VICES. —THEIR IGNORANCE. —FOOLISH AND CORRUPT LEGISLATION —EXTRAVAGANT EXPENDITURES IN VARIOUS STATES. —IN MISSISSIPPI. —IN GEORGIA. —IN SOUTH CAROLINA. —OVERTHROW OF MANY CARPET-BAG GOVERNMENTS. —VIOLENCE STILL, BUT OFTEN EXAGGERATED.

THE re-election of President Grant did not improve the state of feeling at the South. Bitterness toward the powers at Washington and sullen defiance of them were still the temper of most Southern whites. This notwithstanding several facts which might have been expected to produce a contrary effect. Certain important legal decisions of the time should have pleased the South, confirming, as they in a certain way did, the doctrine of State Sovereignty. One such decision was handed down April 14, 1873, in the celebrated Louisiana "Slaughter-House Cases." These arose out of an act passed by the Legislature of Louisiana in 1869, creating the Crescent City Live-Stock Landing and Slaughter House Company, with the exclusive privilege of carrying on the slaughtering business in New Orleans and the adjoining parishes. The butchers of the city contested the act on the ground that it violated the recent constitutional amendments, creating an involuntary servitude, abridging the privileges and

THE LAST QUARTER-CENTURY

immunities of citizens of the United States, denying to the plaintiffs equal protection under the law, and depriving them of their property without due process. In its decision, from which, however, Chief Justice Waite, with Associates Field, Bradley and Swayne, dissented, the Court held that servitude means personal servitude; that "there is a citizenship of the United States and a citizenship of the State, each distinct from the other," that while the amendment placed citizens under federal protection it gave them no new rights as citizens of a State, and finally that the act of the Louisiana Legislature was not a denial of equal protection by the laws or a deprivation of property.

On April 22, 1872, the Court had rendered its decision in the case of Osborn *vs.* Nicholson, confirming the validity of slave contracts entered into before the Emancipation Proclamation. Another important decision of the same date related to the case of White *vs.* Hart. This arose from the attempt of the plaintiff to recover on a promissory note given for the purchase-money of a slave, the defense claiming non-liability on the ground that by the new constitution of Georgia the State courts were forbidden to consider the validity of such contracts. In its decision the Court clearly defined the relation of the seceder States to the Union and held that such a State, having never been out of the Union, was never absolved from the prohibition in the Constitution of the United States against passing laws impairing the obligation of contracts.

On March 22, 1875, the Supreme Court decided that certain corporations created by the Legislature of Georgia while in rebellion were legal. This meant, in effect, that any acts by the *de facto* though unlawful government of that State, so long as they did not tend to aid the rebellion or to abridge the rights of citizens of the United States, were valid.

But Southerners' memories were too sad, their pains too keen, their sufferings of all sorts too terrible, to be assuaged

THE SOUTH AFTER THE WAR

DANIEL H. CHAMBERLAIN

merely by agreeable definitions of points in constitutional law. The war left the South in indescribable desolation. Great numbers of Confederates came home to find their farms sold for unpaid taxes, perhaps mortgaged to ex-slaves. The best Southern land, after the war, was worth but a trifle of its old value. Their ruin rendered many insane; in multitudes more it broke down all energy. The braver spirits—men to whom till now all toil had been strange—set to work as clerks, depot-masters and agents of various business enterprises. High-born ladies, widowed by Northern bullets, became teachers or governesses. In the comparatively few cases where families retained their estates, their effort to keep up appearances was pathetic. One by one domestics were dismissed; dinner parties grew rare; stately coaches lost their paint and became rickety; carriage and saddle-horses were worn out at the plough and replaced by mules. At last the master learned to open his own gates, the mistress to do her own cooking.

In a majority of the Southern cities owners of real estate found it for years after hostilities closed a source of poverty instead of profit. In the heart of Charleston charred ruins of huge blocks or stately churches long lingered as reminders of the horrid past. Many mansions were vacant, vainly flaunting each its placard "for rent." Most of the smaller towns, like Beaufort, threatened permanent decay, their streets silent and empty save for negro policemen here and there in shiny blue uniforms. The cotton plantations were at first largely abandoned owing to the severe foreign competition in cotton-growing occasioned by the war. It was difficult to get help on the plantation, so immersed in politics and so lazy had the field-hands become.

THE LAST QUARTER-CENTURY

Upon the whites in many communities a kind of moral and social stagnation settled down, an unhealthy, hopeless acquiescence in the worst that might come. Politics they long regarded with abhorrence, as the accursed thing that had brought on the war. Whites, as well as negroes, drank recklessly. Few of any class cared much for education. In 1874 Alabama had 380,000 citizens who could neither read nor write, of whom nearly 100,000 were white. Yet the year before the public schools in that State, except in the larger cities, had been closed because the State could not pay the teachers. If, to the Africans, education was freer after the war than before, turmoil and poverty left the young Southerners of paler skin little time or disposition for schooling. The determination, when it came, of the Southern whites to rule, sad as were the atrocities to which it led, was a good sign, marking the end of a lethargy which boded naught save ill to any.

But the end of trouble was not yet. Mere courage would not bring prosperity to a people undergoing a social and political upheaval which amounted to anarchy and promised indefinite continuance. How angry the conflict was will appear when we see that it brought the "scalawag," the "carpet-bagger," and the negro, partly each by himself and partly together, into radical collision with all that was most solid, intelligent and moral in Southern society. "Whatever were the designs or motives of the authors of the reconstruction measures, the work of carrying them out was of necessity committed to those who lived at the South. It is a mild statement to say that those on whom this responsibility fell were not generally well suited or qualified for such work. Sweeping denunciations are seldom just. Those who took part in reconstruction at the South were not all, or nearly all, 'Northern adventurers, Southern renegades and depraved negroes.' Among all the classes so described were worthy and able men; but the crude forces with which they dealt were temporarily

THE "SCALAWAG"

too strong for their control or resistance. Corruption ran riot; dishonesty flourished in shameless effrontery; incompetency became the rule in public offices."*

The South had still, as always, a class of swaggering whites, the kind who earlier said that "the Yankees would back up against the North Pole before they would fight." Once, previous to the war, Hon. John C. Breckenridge, of Kentucky, journeying from New Orleans to Washington, passed through South Carolina. He subsequently related his experience. "But one man," he said, "boarded the cars on the route through that unpopulous piny-wooded land. He was dressed in full regimentals, and entered the smoking-car with the mien of a Cambyses or a Murat. I joined this splendid soldier in the smoking-car. I offered him a fresh cigar to engage him in conversation, and began to question him. 'May I ask,' said I, meekly, 'what is going on in this State?' Tossing his head in proud disdain, he replied 'Going on, suh? We won't stand it no mo,' suh! The Governor has sent for his staff to meet with him and consult about it in Columbia, suh! I am one of his staff, suh! We won't stand it any longer, suh! No, suh! It is intolerable, suh! No, suh!' 'Stand what?' I asked, in surprise, not unmixed with dread. 'What is going on?' He answered: 'Stand the encroachments on our Southern institutions, suh!

*Governor Chamberlain's Administration in South Carolina, Preface, vi.

The abolitionists must be crushed, suh! We will do it, suh! South Carolina is ready, suh!'"*

In reconstruction times Southern heroes of this stamp turned up as "scalawags." Most of the scalawags so hated after the war were the fire-eaters, old slave-traders, and plantation overseers whom decent society had tabooed before the war. They had no social position to lose, and it was but natural, their social superiors being Democrats, that they themselves should become ardent Republicans. Negro voters they now bought and sold, or shot, just as formerly they had bought and sold, or shot, negro slaves. These same men, who, under Republican rule, sought, with too much success, to lead the blacks, reappeared with the restoration of the Democracy in their original character as negro-baiters, hunting and killing their poor victims whenever this met party exigencies better than bribery did. A few old Whigs and perhaps some others joined the Republicans on principle. In the heat of political controversy these might be denounced as scalawags, but they were of a different spirit.

Soon after the reconstruction of his State, at a public meeting in celebration of the event, Wade Hampton advised

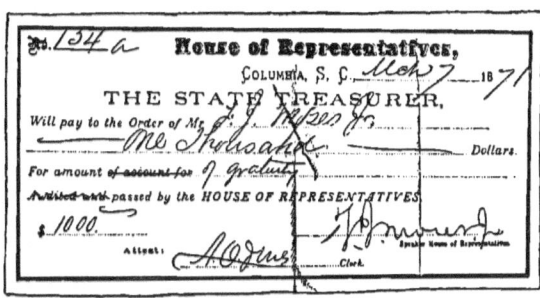

Facsimile of a "Gratuity" Voted to Governor Moses by the South Carolina Legislature in 1871

the blacks to seek political affiliation with the best native whites, as both races equally wished order and prosperity

*S. S. Cox, "Three Decades of Federal Legislation."

THE "CARPET-BAGGER"

restored. Beverly Nash, colored, addressed the meeting, urging the same. "His people," he said, "recognized the Southern white man as their 'true friend,' and he wished all the Confederates re-enfranchised. In this temper colored men formed the Union Republican party of South Carolina, and adopted a platform free from rancor.

Unfortunately, such chance for affiliation was lost. Causes were at work which soon lessened Sambo's respect for "Old Massa," and "Old Massa's" for Sambo. Republicans from the North flocked to the South, whom the blacks, viewing them as representing the emancipation party, naturally welcomed and followed. These "carpet-baggers," as they were called, were made up, in the main, of military officers still or formerly in service, Freedmen's Bureau agents, old Union soldiers who had bought Southern farms, and people who had settled at the South for purposes of trade.

There were, no doubt, many perfectly honest carpet-baggers, and the fullest justice should be done to such. They considered themselves as true missionaries *in partibus*, commissioned by the great Republican party to complete the régime of righteousness which the war and the emancipation proclamation had begun. A prominent Democratic politician, describing a reconstruction Governor of his State, whom he had done his best to overthrow, said: "I regard him as a thoroughly honest man and opposed to corruption and extravagance in office. I think his desire was to make a good Executive and to administer the affairs of the State in the interest of the people, but the want of sympathy between him and the white people of the State, and his failure to appreciate the relations and prejudices of the two races, made it next to impossible for him to succeed."

In the States where the worst evils were suffered the really guilty parties were usually few, the great body of legislators being innocently inspired by some loud and ringing watchword like "internal improvements," or "the development of the

State," to vote for measures devised to enrich cunning sharks and speculators. What history will condemn in connection with the reconstruction governments is not so much individuals as the system which permitted a few individuals to be so banefully influential, not only in spite of their well-meaning associates but by means of these. Moreover, carpet-bagger character differed somewhat with locality. Perhaps the reconstructionists of Mississippi were the best. We have evidence that the majority of the white leaders there were honest, being moved in their public acts by strong convictions of right and justice, which cost many of them their lives.

But even of the honest carpet-baggers many were idealists, little likely to help reconcile the races, nearly certain to be misled by their shrewd but unprincipled colleagues. All were disliked and mistrusted by the local whites, as aliens, as late foes in arms, as champions of an order intolerable to the dominant Anglo-Saxon. The sons of Dixie had been educated to believe in the negro as an inferior being. The Confederacy had been, in a way, based on this principle. To establish a government so founded they had ventured everything and had lost. A power unjust and tyrannical, as they conceived, had filled their States with mourning, beggared them, freed their slaves, and, as a last injury and insult, done its best to make the negro their political equal. They resisted, some passively, others actively. The best of them could not but acquiesce with a certain joy when the younger and more lawless used violence and even murder to remove the curse. The powerful hand of the Federal Government, sometimes itself perpetrating outrages in effort to suppress such, was evaded by excuses and devices of all sorts. When it was withdrawn, the Southerners announced boldly that theirs was a white man's government and that the ex-slaves should never take part in it.

On the race issue the North, including no few Republicans and even carpet-baggers themselves, gradually sided with

BEGINNINGS OF NEGRO SUFFRAGE

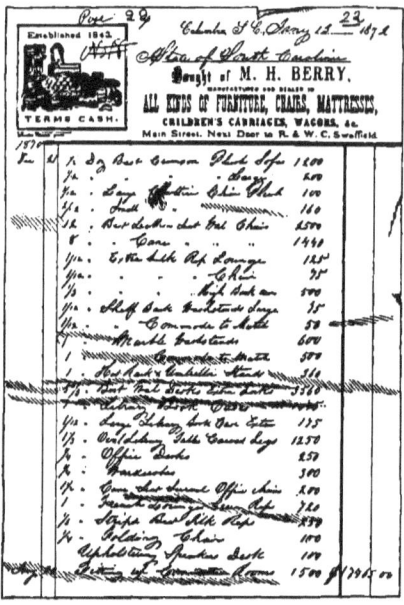

Facsimile of a Bill for Furnishing the State House at Columbia, S. C., in 1872.

the South. Northern Republicans, especially such as had travelled in the South, not seldom regretted that the suffrage had ever been given to the blacks. It is interesting to notice that the idea of colored men's voting did not originate at the North. Till 1834 and 1835 free men of color voted in Tennessee and North Carolina. In some sections "the opposing candidates, for the nonce oblivious of social distinctions and intent only on catching votes, hobnobbed with the men and swung corners all with the dusky damsels at election balls." In 1867 General Wade Hampton, being invited by the colored people to address them at Columbia, S. C., did so, advocating a qualified suffrage for them. After the war Mississippi whites voted unanimously for the Fifteenth Amendment. On the other hand, in the North, at first only Stevens and Sumner were for negro suffrage. So late as 1865 Oliver P. Morton was strenuous against it,* foretelling most of the evils which the system actually brought forth. In 1865 Connecticut rejected a negro suffrage amendment by 6,272 majority; in 1867 Ohio, Kansas and Minnesota did the same by the respective majorities of 50,620, 8,923 and 1,298. In 1868 New York followed their example with a majority of 32,601.

*See *North American Review*, Vol. 123, p. 259 et seq.

THE LAST QUARTER-CENTURY

The experiment being tried, all interests, not least those of the blacks themselves, were found to require that the superior race should rule. It seemed strange that any were ever so dull as to expect the success of the opposite polity. One perfectly honest carpet-bag Governor confessed that while he could give the people of his State "a pretty tolerable government," he could not possibly give them one that would satisfy "the feelings, sentiments, prejudices or what not of the white people generally in that State."

The good carpet-baggers and the bad alike somehow exerted an influence which had the effect of morbidly inflaming the negro's sense of independence and of engaging him in politics. His former wrongs were dwelt upon and the ballot held up as a providential means of righting them. The negro was too apt a pupil, not in the higher politics of principle but in the politics of office and "swag." In 1872 the National Colored Republican Convention adopted a resolution "earnestly praying that the colored Republicans of States where no federal positions were given to colored men might no longer be ignored, but be stimulated by some recognition of federal patronage." The average negro expressed his views on public affairs by the South Carolina catch: " De bottom rail am on de top, and we's gwineter keep it dar." " The reformers complain of taxes being too high," said Beverly Nash in 1874, after he had become State Senator; " I tell you that they are not high enough. I want them taxed until they put those lands back where they belong, into the hands of those who worked for them. You worked for them; you labored for them and were sold to pay for them, and you ought to have them."

The tendency of such exhortation was most vicious. In their days of serfdom the negroes' besetting sin had been thievery. Now that the opportunities for this were multiplied, the fear of punishment gone, and many a carpet-bagger at hand to encourage it, the prevalence of public and private

NEGRO VICES

stealing was not strange. Larceny was nearly universal, burglary painfully common. At night watch had to be kept over property with dogs and guns. It was part, or at least an effect, of the carpet-bag policy to aggravate race jealousies and sectional misunderstandings. The duello, still good form all over the South, induced disregard of law and of human life. "The readiness of white men to use the pistol kept the colored people respectful to some extent, though they fearfully avenged any grievances from whites by applying the torch to out-buildings, gin-houses, and often dwellings. To white children they were at times extremely insolent and threatening. White ladies had to be very prudent with their tongues, for colored domestics gave back word for word, and even followed up words with blows if reprimanded too cuttingly. It was also, after emancipation, notoriously unsafe for white ladies to venture from home without an escort. . . If a white man shot a colored man, an excited mob of blacks would try to lynch him. His friends rallied to the rescue, and a riot often resulted. The conditions were reversed if a white man was shot by a negro." Negro militia at the governors' beck and call alarmed the whites. White companies formed and offered themselves for service, swearing to keep the peace, but were made to disband. To the Union and Loyal Leagues on the reconstructionists' side answered the Ku-Klux Klan, already described, on the other.

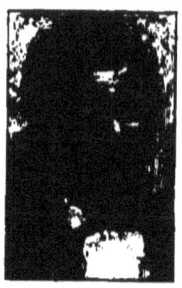

W. BEVERLY NASH

Colored men were quite too unintelligent to make laws or even to elect those who were to do so. At one time dozens of engrossed bills were passed back and forth between the two Houses of the Alabama Legislature that errors in them might be corrected. According to contemporary reports the Lower House expelled one of its clerks for bad orthography and appointed a specialist to rectify the errors. Upon

THE LAST QUARTER-CENTURY

exposure of clerical mistakes the Upper House could not fix the blame, some Senators being unable to write three lines correctly, others wholly ignorant even of reading. One easily imagines how intolerable the doings of such public servants must have been.

The colored legislators of South Carolina furnished the State House with gorgeous clocks at $480 each, mirrors at $750, and chandeliers at $650. Their own apartments were a barbaric display of gewgaws, carpets and upholstery. The minority of a congressional committee recited that "these ebony statesmen" purchased a lot of imported china cuspidors at $8 apiece, while Senators and representatives "at the glorious capital of the nation" had to be "content with a plain earthenware article of domestic manufacture."

Of the Palmetto State Solons in 1873 an eye-witness wrote: "They are as quick as lightning at points of order, and they certainly make incessant and extraordinary use of their knowledge. No one is allowed to talk five minutes without interruption, and one interruption is the signal for another and another, until the original speaker is smothered under an avalanche of them. Forty questions of privilege will be raised in a day. At times nothing goes on but alternating questions of order and of privilege. The inefficient colored friend who sits in the Speaker's chair can not suppress this extraordinary element in the debate. Some of the blackest members exhibit a pertinacity in raising these points of order and questions of privilege that few white men can equal. Their struggles to get the floor, their bellowings and physical contortions, baffle description. The Speaker's hammer plays a perpetual tattoo, all to no purpose. The talking and interruptions from all quarters go on with the utmost license. Everyone esteems himself as good as his neighbor and puts in his oar, apparently as often for love of riot and confusion as for anything else."

Around the State-house, during the session of a Legis-

FREEDMEN AS LEGISLATORS

THE SOUTH CAROLINA LEGISLATURE OF 1873 PASSING AN APPROPRIATION BILL

lature in which were colored representatives, a dense crowd of open-mouthed negroes would stand, rain or shine, and stare at the walls from hour to hour, day after day. In one State election in South Carolina Judge Carpenter, an old South Carolinian and a Republican, ran in opposition to the carpet-bag candidate. Against him it was charged that if he were elected he would re-enslave the blacks, or that, failing in this, he would not allow their wives and daughters to wear hoop-skirts. Another judge was threatened with impeachment and summoned before the Legislature above described, because he had " made improper reflections on a colored woman of doubtful character."

There were said to be in South Carolina alone, in November, 1874, two hundred negro trial justices who could neither read nor write, also negro school commissioners equally ignorant, receiving a thousand a year each, while negro juries, deciding delicate points of legal evidence, settled questions involving lives and property. Property, which had to bear the burden of taxation, had no voice, for the colored man had no property. Taxes were levied ruinously, and money was appropriated with a lavish hand.

The public debt of Alabama was increased between 1868 and 1874 from $8,356,083.51 to $25,503,593.30, including straight and endorsed railroad bonds.* A large part of this went for illegitimate expenses of the Legislature; much more was in the form of help to railroads; much went into the hands of legislators and officials; little was returned to the people in any form. In 1860 the expenses of the Florida Legislature were $17,000; in 1869 they were $67,000.† Bonds to the amount of $4,000,000, which this State issued to subsidize railroads, were marketed with difficulty. For some the best terms obtainable were fifty cents on the dollar.‡ In less than four months the Legislature of North Carolina authorized the issue of more than $25,000,000 in bonds, principally for railroads, $14,000,000 being issued and sold at from nine to forty-five cents on the dollar. The counties began to exploit their credit in the same way, and some of the wealthier

---

*Hilary A. Herbert, "Why the Solid South," p. 62.
†Samuel Pasco, " Why the Solid South, p. 150.
‡Ibid.

EXTRAVAGANT EXPENDITURES

had their scrip hawked about at ten cents on the dollar.* In 1871 the Louisiana Legislature made an over-issue of State warrants to the extent of $200,000, some of which were sold at two and a half cents on the dollar and funded at par.† In 1873 the tax levy in New Orleans was three per cent. Four and a half years of Republican rule cost Louisiana 106 millions, to say nothing of privileges and franchises given away.‡ Clark County, Arkansas, was left with a debt of $300,000 and $500 worth of improvements.¶ Chicot County spent $400,000 with nothing in return; and Pulaski County, including Little Rock, nearly a million. Town, county and school scrip was worth ten to thirty cents on the dollar, and State scrip with five per cent. interest brought only twenty-five cents. The bonded debt of Tennessee, most of it created in aid of railroads and turnpikes, was increased by $16,000,000, and the bonds were sold at from seventeen to forty cents on the dollar for greenbacks.§ In Nashville,** when there was no currency in the treasury, checks were drawn, often in the name of fictitious persons, made payable to bearer, and sold by the ring to note-shavers for what they would bring. Warrants on the Texas treasury brought forty-five cents a dollar, and the bonds of the State were practically valueless.††

In Mississippi during 1875, including $374,119.80, vouchers, etc., not charged on the books, $2,164,928.22 were expended. In 1893 the expenditures were only $1,249,-193.91. In 1870 the State tax rate was $5 on the $1,000. In 1871 it was $4; in 1872, $8.50; in 1873, $12.50; in

---

*S. B. Weeks, Political Science Quarterly, Vol. IX., p. 686 et seq. Cf. "Why the Solid South," pp. 80, 82. Mr. Weeks vouches for the truth of all the above statements relating to North Carolina.

†B. J. Sage, "Why the Solid South," p. 403.   ‡Ibid., 406.

¶W. M. Fishback, "Why the Solid South," p. 309. See ibid. for the other references to Arkansas.

§J. P. Jones, "Why the Solid South," p. 214.   **Ibid, 199.

††Chas. Stewart, "Why the Solid South," p. 378. On all the foregoing debt statements see also S. B. Weeks in Political Science Quarterly, Vol. IX., p. 681 et seq.

THE LAST QUARTER-CENTURY

1874, $14. In 1875 it fell to $9.25. The Democrats came in in 1876, whereupon the rate fell to $6, decreasing continually until it reached $2.50 (1882–1885), after which time it rose once more in, 1894 standing at $6. The average county tax rate also fell from $13.39, in 1874, to $7.68, in 1894. Comparing the average rate between the years 1870 and 1875, inclusive, with that between 1876 and 1894, inclusive, we find that the State tax rate under Republican rule was two and a third times higher than under the Democrats afterward. The county tax rate for the same six years averaged about an eighth higher than for the nineteen years after 1875.

Under the Republicans the annual average of auditor's warrants issued for common schools was $56,184.39. To September, 1895, the Democrats issued an average nearly six times as large. Mississippi's total payable and interest-bearing debt on January 1, 1876, when the Democratic administration succeeded the Republican, amounted to $984,200, besides $414,958.31 in unpaid auditor's warrants. The Republicans' expenditures were as in the following table:

1870 (Beginning March 11)	$ 975,455.65
1871 (For the whole year)	1,729,046.34
1872	1,596,828.64
1873	1,450,632.80
1874	1,319,281.60
1875	1,430,192.83
Total	$8,501,437.86
Average per annum	$1,464,480.00

After the downfall of the Republican order the heaviest expenditures were in 1894—$1,378,752.70; the lightest, $518,709.03, in 1876. The average annual expenditure from 1876 to 1894 was between sixty and seventy per cent. of the average for reconstruction times.*

*The Mississippi figures are vouched for by J. J. Evans, State Treasurer in October, 1895, as from the Mississippi State Treasurer's and Auditor's books and reports. The author begs his readers' pardon for using in the Magazine draft of this History a table of Southern State reconstruction debts which enormously exaggerated the Mississippi and also the Georgia debt.

CORRUPTION IN GEORGIA

When, in July, 1868, Rufus B. Bullock became Governor of Georgia, the debt of that State stood at $5,827,000. All had been created since the war except the Brunswick and Albany debt about to be mentioned. $429,000 of the debt, perhaps more, was paid during Governor Bullock's three years, but the bonded indebtedness of the State was meantime increased by the issue of $3,000,000 in gold bonds for the State's own behoof, and of $1,800,000 gold bonds in payment of a State war debt to the Brunswick and Albany Railroad Company. Considering this sum the State's debt at the end of the war, its actual debt on January 1, 1874, being $8,343,000, we may place the debt incurred during reconstruction at about six and a half millions. The outstanding bonds of defaulted railroads the validity of which was acknowledged by the State, are not included in this amount.

The contingent liabilities of the State were also increased during the Bullock administration by the endorsement of railroad bonds to a total of $6,923,400. The Georgia Air Line returned $240,000, which should be deducted from the above total. On the other hand, the total must be enlarged by $400,000 in bonds of the Macon and Brunswick Railroad Company, endorsed, as it would seem, though no official record was made, by Governor Jenkins. It was charged and almost universally believed, but not proved, that State endorsement was often, if not regularly, secured before the beneficiary roads had built and equipped the required number of miles. The Cartersville and Van Wert secured $275,000 of endorsed bonds; then, changing its name to the Cherokee Railroad and agreeing to withdraw these bonds, obtained a new issue of endorsed bonds to the amount of $300,000. The first issue was not, after all, withdrawn, and color was thus given to insinuations against Governor Bullock's integrity. Such insinuations were also made in the case of the Bainbridge and Columbus road, but fell flat. $240,000 in bonds for this road the Governor endorsed before leaving the State on a temporary visit, but the guarantee could not be valid without the State seal. The Secretary of State was to affix this in case the road complied with the conditions, which was not done, and the bonds were never issued.

CHARLES HAYES
OF ALABAMA

The Georgia railroad bonds were bought partly by Northerners, partly by a German syndicate. At home they were ceaselessly denounced as " bogus " and " fraudulent," on the ground that they had been issued contrary to the conditions of the authorizing statutes, as well as, in some cases, to the Constitution of the State. The State, however, refused to submit the question to her courts, but repudiated the bonds, and, to assure herself against payment, in 1877 embodied the repudiation in her Constitution.*

The first South Carolina Legislature under the reconstructed Constitution, an excellent instrument, by the way, consisted of seventy-two white and eighty-five colored members, containing only twenty-one white Democrats. At that date the State's funded debt amounted to $5,407,306.27. At the close of the four years of Governor R. K. Scott's administration, December, 1872, though no public works of appreciable importance had been begun or completed, that debt, with past-due interest, amounted to $18,515,033.91. This increase represented "only increased, extravagant and profligate current expenditures." In December, 1873, an Act was passed declaring invalid $5,965,000 of the bonds known as "conversion" bonds, recognizing as valid $11,480,033.91 in principal and accrued interest, and providing for refunding the debt in new bonds at 50 per cent. of the par value of the old. Between 1868 and December, 1874, the total cost of sessions of the Legislature, six regular and two special,

---

*The direct gold bonds to the Brunswick and Albany were among the repudiated. The only railroad bonds recognized as valid amounted to $2,688,000 to four different roads, one of which was paying its interest. Tenth Census, Vol. VII., p. 585.

EXAGGERATED STORIES OF VIOLENCE

was $2,147,430.97, to say nothing of bills payable for legislative expenses, amounting to $192,275.15.* The total cost of State printing and advertising during the period named was $1,104,569.91, and during the last three years thereof $918,629.86. Running deficiencies were simply enormous. For the single fiscal year ending October 31, 1874, they were $472,619.54. Warrants, orders and certificates for public money were issued when no funds were on hand to pay them. There was thus, in addition to the bonded debt, a floating indebtedness of nearly or quite a million dollars.†

By 1874, in most of the Southern States, the carpet-bag governments had succumbed. Such States were well on the way to order and prosperity, though breaches of the peace still occurred there with distressing frequency. From Alabama, in particular, came startling reports of terrorism. They had some foundation, but were greatly exaggerated by interested or ill-informed persons. In a letter to Hon. Joseph R. Hawley, Hon. Charles Hayes wrote of one Allen as having been beaten by ruffians and threatened with death if he "didn't keep his mouth shut about that d——d Yankee, Billings," who had been assassinated. To a New York *Tribune* correspondent Allen said he had been assaulted by a solitary gentleman, armed only with the weapons of nature, who scratched his face. Some "massacred" persons denied that they had been hurt at all. Such violence as did occur by no means always proceeded from whites. It is well authenticated that colored Democrats were maltreated by colored Republicans. The blacks were often unfriendly to whites even when these were Republicans. It is quite true that where negroes were thought to be politically dangerous or were otherwise obnoxious to the whites they received little consideration. Sixteen were taken from a jail in Tennessee and shot by a band of masked horsemen, their bodies being left in the road.

*Governor Chamberlain's Administration in South Carolina, p. 17.
†Ibid., p. 18 et seq.

THE LAST QUARTER-CENTURY

The Governor offered a reward for the apprehension of the murderers, when one turned State's evidence and told everything. The others were at once arrested; whether punished does not appear.

CHAPTER VI

DECLINE OF THE TRANSITIONAL GOVERNMENTS IN SOUTH CAROLINA, ARKANSAS, MISSISSIPPI, AND LOUISIANA

GEN. SHERMAN ON THE SOUTHERN PROBLEM.—RECKLESS LEGISLATION IN SOUTH CAROLINA.—APPEAL OF THE TAXPAYERS' UNION.—GOV. CHAMBERLAIN'S REFORMS.—THE CONFLICT IN ARKANSAS.—FACTIONS.—THE STAKE FOUGHT FOR.—A NEW CONSTITUTION.—GOV. GARLAND ELECTED.—REPORT OF THE POLAND COMMITTEE.—THE VICKSBURG "WAR."—MAYOR VERSUS GOVERNOR.—PRESIDENT GRANT WILL NOT INTERFERE.—SENATOR REVELS ON THE SITUATION.—THE MISSISSIPPI RECONSTRUCTIONISTS.—THE KELLOGG-McENERY IMBROGLIO IN LOUISIANA—METROPOLITANS AND WHITE LEAGUERS FIGHT.—THE KELLOGG GOVERNMENT OVERTHROWN BUT RE-ESTABLISHED BY FEDERAL ARMS.—PROTESTS.—THE ELECTION OF NOV. 2, 1874.—METHODS OF THE RETURNING BOARD.—GEN. SHERIDAN IN COMMAND.—LEGISLATURE ORGANIZED AMID BAYONETS.—MEMBERS REMOVED BY FEDERAL SOLDIERS.—SHERIDAN'S VIEWS.—ALLEGATIONS CONTRA.—PUBLIC OPINION AT THE NORTH.—THE "WHEELER ADJUSTMENT."

SOUTH Carolina, Arkansas, Mississippi, and Louisiana were in 1874 still under carpet-bag sway. Their nearly complete deliverance therefrom during this year and the next forms an interesting chapter in the recent history of our country.

In a letter written so early as 1869, after an extended Southern trip, General Sherman said: "I do think some political power might be given to the young men who served in the rebel army, for they are a better class than the adventurers who have gone South purely for office." Again, in 1871, he wrote: "I told Grant plainly that the South would go against him *en masse*, though he counts on South Carolina, Louisiana, and Arkansas. I repeated my conviction that all that was vital in the South was against him; that negroes were generally quiescent and could not be relied on as voters when local questions became mixed up with political matters." This was an exact forecast of the actual event in all the States named. In each a reform faction of white Republicans grew up, disgusted with carpet-bag corruption and unwilling longer to limit their political creed to the single article of negro rights. In the face of this quarrel negroes became bewildered, so that they either scattered, withheld or traded their votes, in a way to replace political power in the hands of the Democrats.

The carpet-bag legislature of South Carolina guaranteed $6,000,000 in railroad bonds to subsidize the Greenville & Columbia and the Blue Ridge Railroads, taking mortgages on the roads to cover the amount. Rings of carpet-baggers and native speculators obtained legislation releasing the mortgages but continuing the State's liabilities. Seven hundred and fifty thousand dollars or more in fraudulent State bank-notes were approved and assumed by the State. Though property in general had lost two-thirds of its ante-bellum value, it paid on the average five times heavier taxes. In 1872, 288,000 acres of land with buildings were said to have been forfeited for the tax of twelve cents an acre. As in Arkansas and in Louisiana, the Governor had dangerously great patronage. Negro felons were pardoned by wholesale for political purposes. Undeserving white convicts could be ransomed for money. Of the three justices on the Supreme Bench one was a carpet-bagger and one a negro. Juries were composed of illiterate and degraded men.

In March, 1874, a committee of the South Carolina Taxpayers' Union waited on President Grant with complaints. He expressed regret at the anarchic condition of South Carolina, but said that as the State government was in complete working order the federal authority was powerless. This appeal, however, favorably affected public opinion. "It shows,"

Painted by W. R. Leigh

THE BEGINNING OF THE CONFLICT IN FRONT OF THE ANTHONY HOUSE, LITTLE ROCK, SUBSEQUENT TO BAXTER'S SPEECH TO THE COLORED REGIMENT

CHAMBERLAIN IN SOUTH CAROLINA

said one journal, "that the South cherishes no sullen hostility." Antipathy toward Southerners slowly changed to sympathy. The doings of the South Carolina Republicans could not but be disapproved by the party in the Nation. Democrats and non-partisans denounced them as travestying free institutions.

ELISHA BAXTER

In 1874 the South Carolina Republicans quarrelled. After a hot contest the regular convention nominated Hon. D. H. Chamberlain for Governor, Moses, his predecessor being set aside. Chamberlain was a native of Massachusetts, a graduate of Yale and of the Harvard Law School. He was a polished gentleman and an able lawyer. During the War he had been First Lieutenant and then Captain in the Fifth Massachusetts Cavalry.

JOSEPH BROOKS

His principal service in the army was in the way of staff duty as Judge-Advocate and as Assistant Adjutant-General. War ended, he became a citizen of South Carolina in time to sit in its Constitutional Convention. The Independent Republicans bolted Chamberlain's nomination and put up for Governor Judge John T. Green, a native South Carolinian, to whose standard rallied the entire "reform" element of the State, whether Conservative or Republican.

CHIEF-JUSTICE
JOHN McCLURE

The Chamberlain ticket was elected. In his inaugural address Governor Chamberlain marked out an able scheme of retrenchment and reform, soon showing, to the astonishment of many and to the dismay of some among his leading supporters that he was in earnest with it. The enormous power given the Executive, apparently that he might abuse it, enabled Chamberlain, spite of his party allies, to effect sweeping improvements. He supplanted dishonest officials with men of integrity, Republicans if such were available, if not, Democrats. He vetoed corrupt jobs and firmly withheld pardons. Ex-Governor Moses and the infamous Whipper, elected by the legislature to the Circuit Bench, he refused to commission. Good jurors were selected, and crime and race hatred wonderfully diminished. Like the English in Ireland, Governor Chamberlain learned that an abstractly good government over a community may fit the community very ill. Carpet-bagger, scalawag, and negro, however well intentioned and wisely led, could not in the nature of the case rule South Carolina well. Nevertheless his praiseworthy effort hastened the advent of order by revealing the nature of the evils which needed reforming.

Arkansas was another of the States where exotic government died extremely hard. Its persistence there was due to the strong Union sentiment which had always existed north of the Arkansas River. The State's colored vote was only a quarter of the whole, but was potent in combination with the large white vote which remained Republican till shamed into change. In this State, so stubborn were the traditions and temper of its citizens, neither faction readily gave way.

The conflict in Arkansas was between the Liberal-Republicans, called "brindle-tails," led by James Brooks, and the Radical-Republicans, headed by Baxter. Chief Justice McClure, nicknamed "Poker Jack," and the United States Senators, Clayton and Dorsey, sided with Baxter. The returns of the 1872 election seemed to make Baxter Governor, but Brooks alleged fraud and sought by every means to change the result. He appealed to the United States Court for a *quo warranto* against Baxter, but it declined to assume jurisdiction in the case. The State Supreme Court also declined. The legislature could have authorized a contest, but refused to do so. Not disheartened, Brooks sued for and secured from the Circuit Court of Pulaski County, April 15, 1874, a judgment of "ouster" against Baxter, took forcible possession of

Painted by Howard Pyle
THE BROOKS FORCES EVACUATING THE STATE-HOUSE AT LITTLE ROCK

BROOKS AND BAXTER IN ARKANSAS

the State-house, and held it with cannon and some hundred and fifty men. Next day Baxter proclaimed martial law, marched two hundred partisans of his into Little Rock and surrounded the State-house. The federal forces, while neutral, enjoined both parties from precipitating an armed collision. Re-inforcements from both sides constantly came in, making Little Rock for the time a military camp.

AUGUSTUS H. GAR-LAND

A body of Baxter's colored supporters, applauding some utterance of his, were fired into—accidentally, as was said. Indiscriminate shooting ensued, with sanguinary results. Federal forces had to quell the disturbance. Excitement was undiminished until the end of April, breaches of the peace being frequent, though no general engagement occurred. On April 30th took place an action in which Brooks suffered the loss of twenty-five men killed and wounded; some accounts say seventy-one. A week later, and again two days later still, there were sharp skirmishes. The streets of Little Rock were barricaded, and communication with the outside world much impeded. Meantime the agents of the two parties in Washington were engaged in legal and diplomatic fencing, but effort after effort at compromise proved abortive.

Neither side had an inspiring cause. In that poverty-stricken State offices were perhaps more numerous and fat than in any other commonwealth of the Union. Each side hungered for these. A cartoon of the period figured Arkansas as a woman gripped between two remorseless brigands with pistols levelled at each other. By the Constitution of 1868 the Governor appointed to five hundred and twenty-six salaried posts, besides creating all the justices of the peace and constables. Public expenditures, which, in six years, had amounted to $17,000,000, might, if properly looked after, be made a rich source of revenue to many. The following instance is well authenticated and where there can be one such there are certain to be many: In Fort Smith in 1873 a widow who made a living by sewing was taxed $60 on a lot fronting in a back alley and a house which could be built for from $300 to $400. It was more money than she ever had at one time in her life. Moved to tears over this woman's deep distress at the prospective loss of her home, a benevolent lady persuaded her husband to pay the taxes as an act of charity.*

The legislature, convened by Baxter on the 11th of May, telegraphed for federal interposition. Grant at once recognized Baxter and his legislature, and ordered " all turbulent and disorderly persons to disperse." But the end was yet remote. The Poland Committee on Arkansas Affairs, appointed by the National House of Representatives, elicited the fact that Baxter and the leaders of his party, notably Clayton and Dorsey, were no longer on good terms. His disappointing integrity had lost Baxter his "pull" with the Senators and with the Arkansas Supreme Court, presided over by McClure. The following is from the evidence laid before the committee during the summer of 1874:

" Q. State what you know in regard to the origin of the difficulties between Governor Baxter and the leaders of the party that elected him.

" A. As I understood it, in the time of it, it originated with an effort made on the part of the Republican party proper to carry through the railroad bill. It originated with his opposition to this bill, or with his declaring that he would defeat the bill.

" Q. What was the nature of the bill?

" A. There had been $5,200,000 State-aid bonds issued, and the object of the bill was for the State to assume that indebtedness and take in lieu of it railroad bonds.

" Q. Was that considered as any fair equivalent?

*W. M. Fishback. "Why the Solid South," p. 308.

ARKANSAS CONSTITUTIONAL CONVENTION

"A. It was considered that that would be of no value at all.

. . . . . .

"Q. What was the general opinion in relation to those bonds; was it that the State had any benefit from them, or the roads, or individuals who pocketed the bonds?

"A. The impression on the public mind is that the bonds were divided up between the managers of the different roads."*

Baxter's new attitude surprisingly quickened the Supreme Court's sense of jurisdiction. Two of its judges were kidnapped, but escaped, and four days before the legislature convened, four of the five, though "feeling some delicacy" in doing so, reversed the former denial of jurisdiction, and on May 7, 1874, affirmed the decision of the Circuit Court. in Brooks's favor.

The legislature provided for a Constitutional Convention to convene on July 14, 1874, an action overwhelmingly indorsed by the people at the next election. The new Constitution, ratified 78,000 to 24,000 in October, swept the Governor's enormous patronage away, as also his power to declare martial law and to suspend *habeas corpus*. The tax-levying and debt-contracting functions of the legislature were strictly hedged about. The number of offices was to be diminished and all were to be elective. Disfranchisements were abolished. The most important of all the changes related to the Returning Board. The old Constitution had vested in this body extraordinary authority, like that given it by statute in Florida, South Carolina, and Louisiana. It designated three officers who were to receive all election returns, compile and count them, reject fraudulent and illegal votes, and in case of irregularities in the election, occasioned by fraud or fear in any county or precinct, to correct the return

*House Committee Reports, 1st Session 43d Congress, Vol. V., Report No. 771, p. 149; Testimony of Ex-Circuit Judge Liberty Bartlett.

THE LAST QUARTER-CENTURY

ADELBERT AMES

or to reject it and order a new election. The judicial part of this fearful sovereignty was now annulled.

The State Democracy endorsed these changes as "just, liberal, and wise," and offered Baxter the nomination for Governor, which he refused. The opposition cried out that the State was betrayed into the hands of the Ku-klux and White Leagues, that Brooks was the true Governor, and that the new Constitution was revolutionary and void. They made no nominations under it, so that at the election Garland, the Democratic nominee, was elected by a majority of 75,000 votes.

Early in 1875 the Poland Committee submitted to the House its report upon the Arkansas imbroglio. It stated that the new Arkansas Constitution was Republican in form and recommended non-interference, saying that while negro citizenship was not relished by the Southern people, few, except certain lawless youths, who should be sternly dealt with, would do aught to disturb it. A minority report was signed by Jasper D. Ward, of Illinois, who had gone to Little Rock in company with Dorsey, and had during his entire stay remained at Dorsey's house, where he met few but Brooksites. The President took issue with the Poland Committee. In a special message, two days after its report, he expressed the opinion that Brooks was the legal Governor of Arkansas and the new Constitution revolutionary. Spite of this, however, the House adopted the Poland report, thus, in effect, ending the long broil and suspense. Governor Garland at once proclaimed Thursday, March 25, 1875, a day of thanksgiving.

Before light one morning in the winter of 1874–75, the white citizens of Vicksburg, Miss., were roused by the news that armed negroes were approaching the city. They sprang to arms and organized. Just outside the city limits a detachment of whites met a body of two hundred negroes and soon

RACE HOSTILITIES IN MISSISSIPPI

THE SCENE OF THE CONFLICT AT THE PEMBERTON MONUMENT, NEAR
VICKSBURG, DECEMBER 7, 1874
The negroes were entrenched in the old federal breastworks at the top of the hill

put them to rout, killing six, wounding several, and taking some prisoners. Almost at the same time a similar engagement was in progress near the monument where Pemberton surrendered to Grant in 1863. The man who headed the citizens said that the conflict lasted only a few minutes. The negroes fled in wild disorder, leaving behind twenty killed and wounded. At still other points negro bands were charged upon and routed. Three whites were killed and three wounded, while of the colored about seventy-five were killed and wounded and thirty or forty made prisoners. By noon the war was over, and on the following day business was resumed amid quiet and order.

The causes of this bloody affair were differently recited. An address published by the citizens of Vicksburg a few days later alleged a series of frauds by certain colored county

THE LAST QUARTER-CENTURY

officials. Some of these had been indicted by a grand jury composed of ten colored and seven white men. Among the accused was George W. Davenport, Clerk of the Court of Chancery and a member of the Board of Supervisors. The citizens further declared that the bonds of Sheriff and Tax Collector Crosby were worthless, and also that he had made away with incriminating records to save comrades of his who were under indictment. A mass-meeting was held, and the accused officials asked to resign. Davenport fled the county; Crosby yielded. Soon, however, by an inflammatory handbill, over Crosby's name, in which the "Taxpayers" were named a mob of ruffians, barbarians and political banditti, the colored people of the county were called upon to support him. It was rumored that a rising of blacks was imminent, though Crosby had disowned the pamphlet and promised to bid his adherents disperse. Governor Ames proclaimed a state of riot and disorder, and invoked the aid of all citizens in upholding the laws. Upon receipt of the Governor's proclamation the Mayor of Vicksburg issued a counter-manifesto asserting that the mass-meeting, which the Governor had denounced as riotous and as having driven the sheriff from his office, was a quiet and orderly gathering of taxpayers who, without arms or violence, had "requested the resignation of irresponsible officials." His Honor continued: "Whereas the Governor's proclamation has excited the citizens of the county, and I have this moment received information that armed bodies of colored men have organized and are now marching on the city," I command such "unlawful assemblages and armed bodies of men to disperse."

Spite of his Honor's denial, Governor Ames ascribed the trouble to violence and intimidation against blacks by whites,

RICHARD O'LEARY
Mayor of Vicksburg in 1874

Drawn by B. W. Clinedinst

THE MISSISSIPPI LEGISLATURE PASSING A RESOLUTION ASKING FOR FEDERAL AID
AFTER THE ATTACK ON VICKSBURG

Scene in the Senate Chamber

FEDERAL INTERVENTION REFUSED

constituting a reign of terror, and convened the legislature in extra session. This body called upon President Grant to awaken what Sumner called "the sleeping giant of the Constitution" and protect the State against domestic violence. Grant was reluctant to interpose. In his annual message hardly a fortnight before he had said: "The whole subject of executive interference with the affairs of a State is repugnant to public opinion." "Unless most clearly on the side of law such interference becomes a crime." He therefore merely issued a proclamation commanding all disorderly bands in Mississippi to disperse. But breaches of the peace continued. At a public meeting in Yazoo City one man was killed and three or four wounded. The speaker of the evening, a Republican office-holder, left the county, professing to believe his life in danger. In Clinton, three days later, at a Republican barbecue, where there was a discussion between a Republican and a Democrat, a personal quarrel sprang up, during which two negroes were shot. This was the signal for a general attack by blacks upon whites, in the course of which three white men were killed and several wounded. Later in the night seven or eight negroes were killed, when the armed men dispersed and quiet was restored. Another outbreak at Friar's Point, a month afterward, was clearly incited by a colored sheriff, who had called together a body of armed negroes to support him in the County Convention.

Ames now renewed his petition for United States troops, but met with a chilling response from the new Attorney-General, Edwards Pierrepont, a Democrat till Seymour's nomination, thereafter a conservative Republican. He declared that the General Government could aid Mississippi only when all the resources of the State Executive had been exhausted. He accompanied this utterance with words from Grant's despatches: "The whole public are tired out with these annual autumnal outbreaks in the South, and the great majority now are ready to condemn any interference on the part of the

Government." Failing to secure assistance from Washington, Governor Ames's party finally made an arrangement with the Conservatives, which assured a peaceable election.

This resulted in Republican defeat, whereupon Mr. Revels, the colored Senator from Mississippi, wrote to the President the following : "Since reconstruction the masses of people have been, as it were, enslaved in mind by unprincipled adventurers. A great portion of them have learned that they were being used as mere tools, and determined, by casting their ballots against these unprincipled adventurers, to overthrow them. The bitterness and hate created by the late civil strife have, in my opinion, been obliterated in this State, except, perhaps, in some localities, and would have long since been entirely effaced were it not for some unprincipled men who would keep alive the bitterness of the past and inculcate a hatred between the races in order that they may aggrandize themselves by office and its emoluments to control my people, the effect of which is to degrade them. If the State administration had advanced patriotic measures, appointed only honest and competent men to office, and sought to restore confidence between the races, bloodshed would have been unknown, peace would have prevailed, federal interference been unthought of, and harmony, friendship, and mutual confidence would have taken the place of the bayonet." This "Yea, yea," as it was called, "of a colored brother who never said nay," was corroborated by testimony from other prominent Republicans, white and black.

On the other hand, it was warmly urged that, as a class, the Northern men in Mississippi were noble ex-soldiers, possessing virtues equal to those of their old associates, worthy sons of the fathers who founded this republic, and that they went to Mississippi with the same commendable motives under which their kinsmen have populated the continent from ocean to ocean—to establish homes and to improve society—taking all their capital and urging others to follow them.

Drawn by C. K. Linson

GENERAL BADGER IN FRONT OF THE GEM SALOON, NEW ORLEANS

On January 10, 1872, General A. S. Badger, under orders from Governor Warmoth, marched to the Gem Saloon in Royal Street, and demanded the surrender of the Carter Legislature which had made its headquarters there.

GOVERNOR AMES'S VIEWS

"The Southern man had a motive in slandering the reconstructionists. He committed crimes upon crimes to prevent the political equality of the negro, and found his justification, before the world, in the conduct of those who were obeying the laws of the land. The debts of South Carolina were made to do duty in Mississippi, where there were no debts. In fact violence began at once, before there was time to contract debts in any of the States.

"At first there was no political question. At first the enmity of a conquered people did not manifest itself. It was left for the Union soldiers practically to solve the problem of reconstruction put upon them by a Union Congress—a Congress whose laws they had always obeyed and the wisdom of whose decisions it never occurred to them to doubt. Their only offense against the State of Mississippi was an honest effort to obey the laws of the United States. They incorporated into the organic laws of the State, to its great benefit, some of the best features found in the constitutions of Northern States. They especially sought to build up, or rehabilitate educational and eleemosynary institutions. They would have liked to help by legislation the material condition of the State in its railroads and levees, but wiser counsels prevailed and the errors of other reconstructed States were avoided.

"The offense of the Northern soldier was in reconstructing at all—in giving (under the law) the negro the ballot. Political equality for the negro meant, to the whites, negro supremacy. Physical resistance followed. The few Union soldiers and their allies in Mississippi soon fell before the Mississippians and their re-inforcements from Louisiana and Alabama."*

Whatever the faults of Republican administration in the State, the only serious assault on the finances of Mississippi during the stormy era of reconstruction was an effort to repay some of the millions which Mississippi had repudiated years before. But this effort was not made by Union soldiers or by

*Ex-Governor Adelbert Ames.

THE LAST QUARTER-CENTURY

Southern unionists, or by freedmen, but by an old Confederate; and the scheme was defeated by a carpet-bagger official. It is well known that while Governor of Mississippi General Ames saved that State in the case of the Confederate General Tucker's railroad about one million dollars, and in the case of the Vicksburg and Ship Island road some seven or eight hundred thousand dollars more. But for General Ames's timely antagonism and the use of counsel to resist the diversion of the State's funds, the State would have lost largely over a million dollars. The intelligent people of Mississippi to this day appreciate Governor Ames's action in this matter.

In Louisiana, because of the peculiarity of its social structure, the color-line was drawn even more sharply than in South Carolina. In South Carolina there were three distinct castes of whites—the aristocracy, the *bourgeoisie*, and the poor whites or "sand-hillers," while the Louisiana white people were a thorough democracy, the only caste division in the State being founded on color. The best families used no coats-of-arms; their coachmen and servants wore no livery. The splendors attending vulgar wealth were eschewed. "There was a nobility in the white skin more sacred and more respected than the one derived from the letters-patent of kings." Such solidarity among the whites rendered the feud precipitated by the negro's enfranchisement peculiarly bitter. White and black children no longer played together as of yore. To avoid seeming inferiority colored servants refused to sleep under the same roofs with their old masters.

It will be remembered that in November, 1872, Kellogg and McEnery each claimed to be elected Governor of Louisiana, that President Grant recognized Kellogg, but that McEnery and his supporters energetically protested. This contest had never been quieted. McEnery's government retained its organization though deprived of all power. Near the close of August, 1874, the troubles grew menacing. The two parties had met in convention, when the country was

Drawn by C. K. Linson

THE MASS-MEETING OF SEPTEMBER 14, 1874, AT THE CLAY STATUE, NEW ORLEANS

KELLOGG AND McENERY IN LOUISIANA

startled by the news of the arrest and deliberate shooting of six Republican officials. As in all such cases the reports were conflicting, one side declaring it a merciless war of whites upon blacks, the other an uprising of the blacks themselves.

The wealth of Louisiana made the State a special temptation to carpet-baggers. Between 1866 and 1872 taxes had risen five hundred per cent. Before the war a session of the legislature cost from $100,000 to $200,000; in 1871 the regular session cost between $800,000 and $900,000. Judge Black considered it "safe to say that a general conflagration, sweeping over all the State from one end to the other and destroying every building and every article of personal property, would have been a visitation of mercy in comparison to the curse of such a government." This statement is not extravagant if his other assertion is correct, that, during the ten years preceding 1876 New Orleans paid, in the form of direct taxes, more than the estimated value of all the property within her limits in the year named, and still had a debt of equal amount unpaid.

Kellogg had a body of Metropolitan Police, mostly colored, paid for by the city of New Orleans but under his personal command, which formed a part of his militia. Over against this was the New Orleans White League, which again is to be distinguished from the White League of the State. On September 14th a mass-meeting was called in New Orleans to protest against the Governor's seizure of arms shipped to private parties. By 11 A. M. the broad sidewalks were filled for several squares, and there was a general suspension of business. A committee was appointed to wait upon the Governor and request him to abdicate. He had fled from the Executive Office to the Custom-house, a great citadel, garrisoned at that time by United States troops. From his retreat he sent word declining to entertain any communication. Their leaders advised the people to get arms and return to assist the White League in executing plans that would be arranged. A large number formed in procession and marched

THE LAST QUARTER-CENTURY

up Poydras Street. By 3 P. M. armed men were posted at street-crossings south of Canal Street. Soon a strong position was taken in Poydras Street, the streets between Poydras and Canal being barricaded with cars turned sideways. General Ogden commanded the citizens and superintended these arrangements. Five hundred Metropolitans, with cavalry and artillery, took their station at the head of Canal Street, while General Longstreet, their leader, rode up and down Canal Street calling upon the armed citizens to disperse. About 4 P. M. the Metropolitans assaulted the citizens' position. A sharp fight ensued. General Ogden's horse was shot under him, as was General Badger's, on the Kellogg side. The colored Metropolitans broke at the first fire, deserting their white comrades. The citizens' victory was soon complete, General Longstreet and others seeking refuge in the Custom-house. Next morning, at seven, the State-house was in the citizens' hands; two hours later the whole Metropolitan force surrendered. The barricades were torn down and street-cars resumed their trips.

Lieutenant-Governor Penn hastened to assure the blacks that no harm was meant toward them, their property or their rights. "We war," said he, "only against the thieves, plunderers and spoilers of the State." All the morning Penn's residence was filled with congratulatory crowds. Throughout Louisiana the *coup-d'état* roused delirious enthusiasm. At the same time leading citizens counseled moderation, especially urging that no violence toward colored people should be permitted. Penn, in a speech, said : " If you have any affection for me, if you have any regard for me, if you have any respect for me, as I believe you have, for God's sake and my sake do nothing to tarnish the fair fame of the State of Louisiana or to diminish the victory you have achieved." The

WILLIAM PITT KELLOGG

FEDERAL AID FOR KELLOGG

JOHN McENERY

Mayor's proclamation ran: "Let me advise extreme moderation; resume your vocations as soon as dismissed. Seek no revenge for past injuries, but leave your fallen enemies to the torture of their own consciences and to the lasting infamy which their acts have wrought for them." No deeds of violence were reported, though McEnery's officials were installed all over the State. About 2 P. M., as three thousand of General Ogden's militia marched past the Custom-house, the United States troops gathered in the windows, took off their hats and gave the citizens three hearty cheers, which were returned. At 3 P. M. ten thousand unarmed citizens, preceded by a band of music, escorted Penn to the State-house.

The triumph was short-lived. The resort to arms displeased President Grant. He commanded the insurgents to disperse in five days—half the time he had allowed in Arkansas and one-fourth the time he had allowed in his Louisiana proclamation of 1873. Troops and men-of-war were ordered to New Orleans, and General Emory was instructed under no circumstances to recognize the Penn government. A Cabinet meeting concluded that "it was important to adopt measures for maintaining, if not the *de jure*, at least the *de facto* government in Louisiana." Attorney-General Williams compared the case with that of Arkansas, where, he confessed, he always believed Brooks had a majority, but said: "The question is not whō ought to be Governor, but who is." Emory received positive directions to recognize the Kellogg government, and on the next day Kellogg was induced to venture

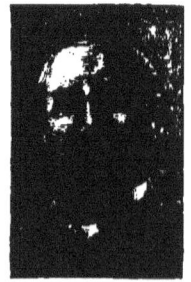

GENERAL DE TRO-
BRIAND

157

from his asylum and resume his office. Not all the McEnery officials were turned out, as several of the Kellogg placemen had fled upon the news of Penn's success and could not be found. The new city police, under Mr. Boylan, a well-known detective, were retained, owing to the demoralization of the Metropolitans. For a time United States soldiers were employed on police duty. On an election day as much as six weeks later, to remove apprehension caused by the inefficiency of the Metropolitans, a detail of the McEnery militia was made to preserve the peace at each polling-place.

McEnery and Penn advised cheerful submission, and while surrendering the State-house to Colonel Brooks showed him every courtesy. The only excess reported was an unsuccessful attack by negroes upon Bayou Sara. In answer to Attorney-General Williams's pronunciamento Penn asserted that the McEnery government had been organized ever since 1872; that McEnery's armed supporters were not insurgents, but militia; that the sole reason why the McEnery government was not *de facto* in function in the whole State was that it was overpowered by the United States forces, but for which it could assert its authority and would be universally obeyed. The Kellogg government, he said, could be placed and kept in power by the United States army, but in no other way whatever. " Is this," he asked, " the Republican form of government guaranteed to every State under the Constitution ? "

Happily the army had no command to repress free speech, which was usefully employed in appeals to the country. Some of these papers were written with unusual clearness and force. Besides describing anew the corruptions already alluded to, they accused the Kellogg faction of altering the registration laws in its own interest. " Many white citizens clearly entitled to registry were refused arbitrarily, while the colored people were furnished registration papers on which, in many instances, they could vote in different wards; and colored crews of steamboats transiently visiting this port were permitted to swell the number of voters." The White League, which, outside New Orleans, seems not to have been an armed body, was declared a necessary measure of defence against a formidable oath-bound order of blacks.

Governor Kellogg sought to explain the uprising. He said: "They first want the offices, and that is the meaning of this outburst. The Governor of Louisiana wields an enormous amount of patronage, for which McEnery and his friends hunger." However, at his instance an Advisory Board, consisting of two men from each party and an umpire chosen by them, was arranged to supervise and carry on the registration for the next election. Though perhaps honestly conceived, this plan amounted to little. About the middle of October the umpire resigned, and the functions of the Board virtually came to an end. Further, the Conservatives were to cause all violence to cease, and were permitted to fill two vacancies on the Returning Board created by resignation for this purpose.

GENERAL PHILIP H. SHERIDAN
From a photograph in the historical collection of
H. W. Fay

The election of November, 1874, was quiet. Indications seemed to point to Democratic success. A break in the colored vote was foreshadowed, among other things, by an address of leading colored men in New Orleans, setting forth that the Republican party in the State had, since reconstruction, been managed and controlled by men in all respects as bad as "the most rampant White Leaguer," that they had shut out the colored wealth and intelligence and put in office "illiterate and unworthy colored men." The colored people, it said, "are ready to adopt any honorable adjustment tending to harmonize the races," to further law and order and a higher standard of administration in public offices.

Of course the Returning Board played an important part in this election. One example will illustrate its methods. The parish of Rapides chose three legislators. The United States Supervisor certified that the election was in all respects full, fair, and free. In the parish itself no one knew that any contest existed. At one of its last sittings the Board, upon an affidavit of its President, Wells, alleging intimidation, counted in all three Republicans. This, like other acts of the kind, was done in secret or "executive" session. The Counsel of the Democratic Committee declared that they had no chance to answer. It came out that Wells was not present at Rapides, and he declined, though given the opportunity, to explain to the Congressional Committee his action. The Rapides change alone sufficed to determine the complexion of the lower house.

After recounting instances of illegal action and fraud on the part of the Returning Board, the Inspecting Committee appealed to the nation: "We, the down-trodden people of once free Louisiana, now call upon the people of the free States of America, if you would yourselves remain free and retain the right of self-government, to demand in tones that cannot be misunderstood or disregarded, that the shackles be stricken from Louisiana, and that the power of the United States army may no longer be used to keep a horde of adventurers in power."

Toward the end of 1874, the Returning Board completed its labors. It gave the treasury to the Republicans, and allowed them a majority of two in the Legislature, five seats being left open. These changes from the face of the returns were made on the ground of alleged fraud, intimidation, or other irregularity at the polls, or in making the returns. The Board dismissed as preposterous all complaints of intimidation

MEETING OF THE LEGISLATURE

by United States soldiery, though at least one case is reported of a federal officer making out affidavits against citizens, and arresting them upon these affidavits. He was stopped later by orders from his superior.

The Congressional Investigating Committee, composed of two Republicans and one Democrat, after citing three or four instances of fraud on the part of the Returning Board, unanimously found itself "constrained to declare that the action of the Returning Board on the whole, was arbitrary, unjust, and illegal; and that this arbitrary, unjust, and illegal action alone prevented the return of a majority of the Conservative members to the lower house."

A few days before the assembling of the legislature one of the Republican members was arrested and confined till after the opening. The Conservatives alleged that this was for embezzlement; the Republicans charged that it was for political purposes, and that their opponents were attempting to kidnap and even threatening to assassinate Republican legislators to wipe out the majority. So threatening an aspect of affairs induced Grant to give Sheridan command of the Military Department of the Gulf in addition to his own. Sheridan started on telegraphic notice.

The legislature convened on January 4th. Suppressed excitement could be seen in every eye. Of the memorable and unprecedented events of this day there are four varying accounts—General Sheridan's statement, two reports to Congress by committees of the two political parties in the Louisiana House of Representatives, and a recital incorporated in the Congressional Committee's report above referred to. The last, of which we give a *résumé*, is the most trustworthy.

The State-house was filled and surrounded by Metropolitans and federal soldiers, and no one permitted to enter save by Governor Kellogg's orders. At noon the clerk of the preceding House, Mr. Vigers, called the Assembly to order and proceeded to call the roll. Fifty Democrats and fifty-two

THE LAST QUARTER-CENTURY

Republicans answered to their names. Instantly a Conservative member, Mr. Billieu, nominated L. A. Wiltz as temporary chairman. The clerk interposed some objection, but Mr. Billieu, disregarding him, hurriedly put the motion and declared it carried upon a *viva voce* vote. Wiltz sprang to the platform, pushed the clerk aside, and seized the gavel. Justice Houston then swore in the members *en bloc*. In the same hurried fashion a new clerk was elected, also a sergeant-at-arms; then, from among gentlemen who had secured entrance under one pretext or another, a number of assistant sergeants-at-arms were appointed. These gentlemen at once opened their coats and discovered each his badge bearing the words "Assistant Sergeant-at-Arms." Protests, points of order, calls for the yeas and nays, were overridden. The five contesting Democrats were admitted and sworn in. The Republicans now adopted their opponents' tactics. Someone nominated Mr. Lowell for temporary chairman, and amid great confusion declared him elected, but he declined to serve. The organization of the House was completed by the election of Wiltz as Speaker. Several Republican members attempting to leave were prevented by the assistant sergeants-at-arms. Pistols were displayed, and the disorder grew so great that the House requested Colonel de Trobriand, commanding the forces at the State-house, to insist upon order in the lobby. This he did, and the House proceeded with the election of minor officers, uninterrupted for an hour. At length de Trobriand received word from Governor Kellogg, which his general orders bound him to obey, to remove the five members sworn in who had not been returned by the Board. Speaker Wiltz refusing to point them out, General Campbell did so, and in spite of protest they were removed by federal soldiers. Wiltz then left the hall at the head of the Conservative members. The Republicans, remaining, organized to suit themselves.

General Sheridan reported the matter somewhat differently. He reached Louisiana in no judicial frame of mind.

Drawn by W. R. Leigh
L. A. WILTZ TAKING POSSESSION OF THE SPEAKER'S CHAIR IN THE LOUISIANA STATE-
HOUSE, JANUARY 4, 1875

SHERIDAN'S ASSERTIONS DENIED

Conservative chagrin and humiliation often took form in foolish threats, which were at once seized upon by the carpet-baggers and scalawags to fan his wrath. The very air seemed to him impregnated with assassination. He suggested that Congress or the President should declare the "ringleaders of the armed White Leagues" banditti; he could then try them by military commission and put an end to such scenes as had occurred. The New Orleans Cotton Exchange, a meeting of Northern and Western residents of New Orleans, and other bodies passed resolutions denying the correctness of Sheridan's impressions. In an appeal to the American people a number of New Orleans clergymen condemned the charges lodged by Sheridan with the Secretary of War as "unmerited, unfounded, and erroneous." General Sheridan reiterated them, and accused Bishop Wilmer, one of the signers of the appeal, of having admitted before the Congressional Committee "that the condition of affairs was substantially as bad as reported." The Bishop agreed that Louisianians were more prone than others to acts of violence, saying "there is a feeling of insecurity here," an expression which he interpreted as meaning, "no security in the courts against theft."

General Sherman commented on the case as follows: "I have all along tried to save our officers and soldiers from the dirty work imposed on them by the city authorities of the South; and may thereby have incurred the suspicion of the President that I did not cordially sustain his forces... I have always thought it wrong to bolster up weak State governments by our troops. We should keep the peace always; but not act as bailiff constables and catch-thieves; that should be beneath a soldier's vocation. I know that our soldiers hate that kind of duty terribly, and not one of those officers but would prefer to go to the plains against the Indians, rather than encounter a street mob or serve a civil process. But in our government it is too hard to stand up in the face of what is apparent, that the present government of Louisiana is not

THE LAST QUARTER-CENTURY

S. S. Marshall G. F. Hoar William A. Wheeler William P. Fry
THE COMMITTEE WHICH FORMULATED THE "WHEELER ADJUSTMENT"

the choice of the people, though in strict technical law it is the State government."

Public opinion at the North sided with the appellants. The press gave a cry of alarm at such military interference in civil affairs. A staunch Republican sheet uttered the sentiment of many when it said, "Unless the Republican party is content to be swept out of existence by the storm of indignant protest arising against the wrongs of Louisiana from all portions of the country, it will see that this most shameful outrage is redressed wholly and at once." Numerous indignation meetings were held in Northern cities. Republicans like William Cullen Bryant, William M. Evarts, Joseph R. Hawley and Carl Schurz openly condemned the use which had been made of the troops. Legislatures passed resolutions denouncing it, and it was understood that Fish, Bristow and Jewell, of the Cabinet, disapproved. Yet patience was urged upon the people of Louisiana. "Whatever injustice," said Carl Schurz, "you may have to suffer, let not a hand of yours be lifted, let no provocation of insolent power, nor any tempting opportunity seduce you into the least demonstration of violence. As your cause is just, trust to its justice, for surely the time cannot be far when every American who truly loves his liberty will recognize the cause of his own rights and liberties in the cause of constitutional government in Louisiana."

THE WHEELER ADJUSTMENT

Under a resolution introduced by Mr. Thurman the Senate called upon President Grant for explanation. A special message was the response, defending the end which had been had in view but really leaving undefended the means employed. Early in 1875 a second committee, George F. Hoar, Chairman, was appointed to investigate Louisiana affairs. The result of their labors was known as the "Wheeler Adjustment," which embraced on the one hand submission to the Kellogg government, and on the other arbitration by the committee of contested seats in the legislature. This arbitration seated twelve of the contestants excluded by the Returning Board. Mr. Hahn vacated the Speaker's chair, Mr. Wiltz withdrew as a candidate therefor, and Mr. Estilette, a Conservative, was elected. This settlement marked the beginning of the end of carpet-baggery in Louisiana.

CHAPTER VII

INDIAN WARS AND THE CUSTER DEATH

CIVILIZED INDIANS IN 1874.—GRANT'S POLICY FOR THE WILD TRIBES.—DIFFICULTIES OF THE INDIAN COMMISSIONERS.—INDIANS' WRONGS AND DISCONTENT.—TROUBLES IN ARIZONA.—GOV. SAFFORD'S DECLARATION.—MASSACRE OF APACHES IN 1871.—REPORT OF FEDERAL GRAND JURY.—THE APACHES SUBDUED.—GRIEVANCES OF THE SIOUX.—THE MODOC WAR AND GEN. CANBY'S DEATH.—TROUBLES IN 1874.—THE MILL RIVER DISASTER IN MASSACHUSETTS.—THE SIOUX REBELLION.—THE ARMY'S PLAN OF CAMPAIGN.—CUSTER'S PART.—HIS DEATH.—HOW THE BATTLE WENT.—"REVENGE OF RAIN-IN-THE-FACE."—CUSTER CRITICISED.—AND DEFENDED.

EARNESTLY as President Grant strove to improve the Indian service it was no credit to the nation during his term. In 1874 the Indian Territory contained not far from 90,000 civilized Indians. The Cherokees, 17,000 strong and increasing, who had moved hither from Alabama, Tennessee, and Georgia, now possessed their own written language, constitution, laws, judges, courts, churches, schools, and academies, including three schools for their former negro slaves. They had 500 frame and 3,500 log-houses. They yearly raised much live-stock, 3,000,000 bushels of corn, with enormous crops of wheat, potatoes and oats—an agricultural roduct greater than New Mexico's and Utah's combined. Similarly advanced were the Choctaws, with 17,000 people and forty-eight schools; the Creeks, with 13,000 people and thirty schools; and the Seminoles, General Jackson's old foes, having 2,500 people and four schools.

These facts inspired the President with a desire to improve the wilder tribes. Deeming clemency and justice, with firmness, certain to effect this, he proposed to transfer the

Indian bureau to the War Department; but Congress, army officers, and the Indians themselves, opposed. He then gave the supervision of Indian affairs to a Commission made up from certain religious bodies. This kindly policy being announced, two powerful Indian delegations, one of them headed by Red Cloud, the Sioux chief, visited the Great Father at Washington, evidently determined henceforth to keep the peace.

Few of the wild Indians did this, however. Perhaps only the Apaches, always our most troublesome wards, have ever pursued murder and rapine out of pure wantonness; yet most of the red men still remained savages, ready for the war-path on slight provocation. If the frontier view—no good Indian but a dead one—is severe, many Eastern people were hardly less extreme in the degree of nobility with which their imagination invested the aborigines. Moreover, despite the Commission's exertions, the Indian service, though its cost increased from three and a quarter million in 1866 to nearly seven million in 1874, sank in character. The Commissioners were partly ignored, partly subjected to needless embarrassment in their work. Members of the Indian Ring secured positions and contracts in preference to people recommended by the Commission, and the Interior Department often paid bills expressly disallowed by the Commission, which was charged with the auditing.

Contractors systematically swindled the Indians. Professor Marsh, of Yale University, wishing to engage in scientific research upon Red Cloud's Reservation, that chief, while protecting his life, forbade him to trespass till he promised to show the Great Father samples of the wretched rations furnished his tribe. "I thought," naively confessed the chief, "that he would throw them away before he got there." But the "man who came to pick up bones" was better than his word. He exhibited the specimens to the President, who was deeply incensed and declared that justice should be done.

DISCONTENT OF THE INDIANS

Marsh drew up ten specific charges, to the effect that the agent was incompetent and guilty of gross frauds, that the number of Indians was overstated to the Department, and that the amount of food and clothing actually furnished them was insufficient and of wretched quality., Army testimony was of like tenor. "The poor wretches," said one officer, "have been several times this winter on the verge of starvation owing to the rascality of the Indian Ring. They have been compelled to eat dogs, wolves, and ponies." It was urged in excuse that the supply-wagons had been delayed by snow. March 18, 1875, General Sherman wrote from St. Louis: "To-morrow Generals Sheridan and Pope will meet here to discuss the Indian troubles. We could settle them in an hour, but Congress wants the patronage of the Indian bureau, and the bureau wants the appropriations without any of the trouble of the Indians themselves."

RED CLOUD
After a photograph by Bell

The Indians' discontent was intensified by the progressive invasion of their preserves by white men, often as lawless as the worst Indians, and invariably bringing intemperance and licentiousness. Frontiersmen looked jealously at the unimproved acres of the reservations as an Eden which they were forbidden to enter, while a horde of thriftless savages were in idle possession. Violence against the red men seemed justifiable and was frequent.

The first troubles were in Arizona. In 1871 the legislature of the Territory, seconded by the California legislature, prayed Congress for protection. Affidavits were submitted declaring that within two years 166 persons had been killed, 801 horses and mules and 2,437 cattle killed or stolen. In

THE LAST QUARTER-CENTURY

November Governor A. P. K. Safford gave out an impassioned letter, of which we reproduce the substance. He said that with natural resources unsurpassed, with gold and silver mines that ought to be yielding annually $20,000,000, the people of his Territory were in poverty, and had undergone for years scenes of death and torture unparalleled in the settlement of our new countries. Instead of receiving sympathy and encouragement from their countrymen they were denounced as border ruffians, though nowhere were the laws more faithfully obeyed or executed than in Arizona. In but one instance had the people taken the law into their own hands. That, as the facts showed, was done under the most aggravating circumstances. In the possession of the Indians killed was found property belonging to men and women who had been murdered while the Indians were fed at Camp Grant. For this attack on the red men the whites were indicted by a grand jury, showing that Arizona courts and judges did not screen any. The Territory was out of debt, and was soon to have a free school in every district, indicating the law-abiding character of the population; yet men who were making money at the cost of the lives and property of the Arizona people denounced them as everything bad, and represented the Apache Indians, who had for four hundred years lived by murder and robbery, as paragons of moral excellence The people of Arizona wanted peace and cared not how it was obtained; but they knew by years of experience that to feed Indians and let them roam over large tracts of lands simply placed them in a secure position to raid the settlers and return to their reservations for safety and rest. Though possessing one of the richest Territories, all the Arizonians felt discouraged. At least five hundred had been killed, a large number of these horribly tortured. Those left, after fighting for years to hold the country, found themselves in poverty and looked upon as barbarians. General Crook struck the keynote when he enlisted Indians against Indians. It threw con-

THE APACHE MASSACRE AND ITS CAUSES

sternation among them such as was never seen before. Had he been allowed to pursue this policy it would have taken but a few months to conquer a lasting peace. But Peace Commissioner Colyer had countermanded the order and millions would have to be expended and hundreds of lives lost before the end could be reached.

The massacre of Indians referred to by Governor Safford occurred in April, 1871. A few hundred Apaches had been gathered at Camp Grant, being fed on condition of keeping the peace, which condition seemed to have been broken. A party of whites with a hundred Papago Indians fell upon the Indian camp, killed eighty-five men and women, and carried away twenty-eight children as prisoners. A Federal grand jury which found indictments against several of the attacking party reported upon a number of important points. They found that the hostile Indians in the Territory, led by many different chiefs, generally adopted the policy of making the point where the Indians were fed the base of their supplies of ammunition, guns, and recruits for their raids, each hostile chief usually drawing warriors from other bands when he undertook an important raid, whether upon Arizona citizens or upon the neighboring state of Sonora, where they were continually making depredations. With few marked exceptions the habit of drunkenness prevailed among the officers at Camps Grant, Goodwin, and Apache, where the Apache Indians were fed. The rations issued to the Indians at these camps were frequently insufficient for their support; also unjustly distributed. Bones were sometimes issued instead of meat. One United States quartermaster acknowledged that he had made a surplus of twelve thousand pounds of corn in issuing rations to the Indians at Camp Goodwin. An officer commanding at Camp Apache, besides giving liquor to the Apache Indians, got beastly drunk with them from whiskey belonging to the United States Hospital Department. Another United States Army officer gave liquor to Indians at the same camp.

THE LAST QUARTER-CENTURY

The Region Occupied by the Modocs, showing the "Lava Beds"

United States Army officers at those camps where the Indians were fed habitually used their official position to break the chastity of the Indian women. The regulations of Camp Grant, with the Apache Indians on the reservation, were such that the whole body of Indians might leave the reservation and be gone many days without the knowledge of the commanding officer. In conclusion this United States grand jury reported that five hundred of their neighbors, friends, and fellow-citizens had fallen by the murdering hand of the Apache Indians, clothing in the garb of mourning family circles in many hamlets, towns and cities of different States. "This blood," they said, " cried from the ground to the American people for justice—justice to all men."

Pacific overtures and presents were made to the Indians by Peace Commissioner Colyer, but his efforts were unpopular and proved futile. By the severer policy which the whites urged and by pitting friendly Indians against them, the Apaches were at last subdued and kept thenceforth under strict registry and surveillance.

During the autumn of 1874 gold was found in the Black Hills Sioux Reservation, between Wyoming and what is now South Dakota. General Sheridan prohibited exploration, but gold-seekers continually evaded his order. Said Red Cloud: " The people from the States who have gone to the Black Hills are stealing gold, digging it out and taking it away, and I don't see why the Great Father don't bring them back. Our Great Father has a great many soldiers, and I never knew

SAVAGES GO UPON THE WARPATH

him, when he wanted to stop anything with his soldiers but he succeeded in it." A still worse grievance was the destruction of buffaloes by hunters and excursionists. Thousands of the animals were slaughtered for their hides, which fell in price from three dollars each to a dollar. In one locality were to be counted six or seven thousand putrefying carcasses. Hunters boasted of having killed two thousand head apiece in one season. Railroads ran excursion trains of amateur hunters, who shot their victims from the car windows. The creatures were at last well-nigh exterminated, so that in 1894 buffalo robes cost in New York from $75 to $175 each.

Rasped to frenzy in so many ways, tribe after tribe of savages resolutely took up arms. The Klamath Indians and the Modocs, hereditary enemies, were shortly after the civil war placed upon a common reservation in Oregon. The Modocs, suffering many annoyances from the Klamaths, and indulging in some retaliation, were at last permitted, leaving their uncongenial corral, to roam abroad. Captain Jack headed the seceders, who were believed by many to have been for the most part inoffensive. Among them, however, eight or ten turbulent spirits, led by Curly-headed Doctor, were accused of such depredations that a new superintendent, appearing in 1872, made unfavorable report of the whole wandering tribe, and recommended what General E. R. S. Canby, commanding the Department of the Columbia, deprecated, a resort to force to bring them back to their reservation. Surprised in camp at gray dawn of November 29, 1872, the chiefs refused to surrender and escaped, leaving eight or nine dead warriors, and killing or wounding about the same number of soldiers, besides three citizen auxiliaries. Curly-headed Doctor's band now went upon the war-path, killing eighteen men, though sparing all women and children. While Captain Jack and his faction had no hand in this, the two chiefs, with about 50 warriors and 175 camp followers, united for defence in the Lava Beds, or "pedregal," of northern California, over which rocks of all shapes and sizes lay where the last ancient volcanic eruption left them, presenting crevices, chasms, and subterranean passages innumerable, with occasional verdant patches of an acre or two. Against these hostiles were sent 400 soldiers and a battery of howitzers. After nearly a month of preparation and skirmishes, on the 17th of January, 1873, 300 soldiers with twenty scouts entered the "pedregal." The stumbling advance exposed not a redskin, but man after man fell as the cracks and crannies of the gray rocks above them kept spitting spiteful puffs of smoke. At night, thirty having been wounded and ten killed, they retreated, and Colonel Wheaton, commanding, asked for 300 more men and four mortars. Meantime the Modocs, by capture or otherwise, secured guns, ammunition, and perhaps some reinforcements.

Now two Peace Commissioners, succeeding each other, endeavored in vain to induce the Indians to remove to a reservation in Arizona or the Indian Territory, far from the persecutions of the Klamaths and from the vengeance of Oregon whites. The eight or ten most desperate Modocs, known as "the murderers," urged the continuance of the war. Lest his tribal kindred should be betrayed to the hangman or some other treachery practiced, Captain Jack wished the soldiers sent away and the Lava Beds made a reservation. Finding that neither of these dangerous boons could be granted, he began to lend ear to his tempters, who surrounded him as he sat despondent on a rock. Hooker Jim said: "You are like an old squaw; you have never done any fighting. You are not fit to be a chief." In like strain George: "What do you want with a gun? You don't shoot anything with it. You don't go any place or do anything. You are sitting around on the rocks." Scar-faced Charley took up the taunt: "I am going with Hooker Jim. I can fight with him. You are nothing but an old squaw." They decked him with a squaw's dress and bonnet and further jeered him. Thus stirred, the savage in Captain Jack triumphed. He turned on them

GEN. CANBY'S CONFERENCE WITH MODOCS

and cried: "I will show you that I am no squaw. We will have war, and Keint-poos will not be the one to ask for peace." It is recorded of Captain Jack that subsequently, with Scarfaced Charley, he all night watched over a white emissary, an old-time friend of the tribe, to prevent his murder by the Indians. Upon returning he assured the Commissioners that the Modocs meant treachery. The interpreter's squaw wife, Toby, also warned them, being herself told by Modoc "Whim" to keep away and to keep the Commissioners away. A parley appointed for April 8th fell through because of the timely discovery of an Indian ambush. Nevertheless, when Bogus Charley came and proposed at the council tent near the edge of the "pedregal" an unarmed conference of the Commissioners and General Canby with an equal number of Modocs, saying that after this they would surrender, General Canby and Dr. Thomas, of the Commission, thought that the importance of the object justified the risk. The scout Riddle, as well as Meacham and Dyar, the other Peace Commissioners, urged that it was a hazardous enterprise, but all three said they would go rather than be chargeable with cowardice. Before starting, Meacham and Dyar provided themselves with pocket pistols, gave up their valuables to a friend, and indicated their last wishes.

The embassy took seats on stones around a small fire of brush. Only Dr. Thomas reclined on the ground. Captain Jack made a speech. As he closed, Hooker Jim took Meacham's overcoat and put it on, insolently remarking, "I am Meacham." Meacham said: "Take my hat, too." "I will, presently," was the response, in Modoc. Perceiving that treachery was contemplated, General Canby told how he had earned the name of "the

GENERAL E. R. S. CANBY

Indian's friend," expressing hope that the Modocs, as others had done, would some day thank him for getting them happy homes. He could not send away the Great Father's soldiers, but what the Commissioners promised should be done, and the citizens should not interfere. Dr. Thomas, too, rising to his knees, with head uncovered and with his hand on Meacham's shoulder, said: "I believe the Great Spirit put it into the heart of the President to send us here to make peace. I have known General Canby fourteen years, Mr. Meacham eighteen years, and Mr. Dyar four years. I know their hearts are good, and I know my own heart. We want no more war. I believe that God sees what we do; that he wishes us all to be at peace; that no more blood should be

THE LAVA BEDS
Looking east, showing the Soldiers' Cemetery in the foreground
From a photograph by Taber

shed." Captain Jack said he did not wish to leave that country for a strange one. "Jack," said Meacham, "let us talk like men and not like children. You are a man that has com-

GEN. CANBY KILLED

mon-sense; isn't there any other place that will do you except Willow Creek and Cottonwood?" Here, while Jack stepped back to the horses, Sconchin broke in: "Give us Hot Creek for a home, and take away your soldiers," repeating, excitedly, "Take away the soldiers and give us Hot Creek, or stop talking." Just then two Indians with three guns apiece came running from their hiding place not far off. Steamboat Frank and a third brave also soon appeared. "What does this mean, Captain Jack?" said some one. The chief, close to Canby, levelled his revolver, said "*Atwe*," "all ready," and pressed the trigger. The cap snapped. In an instant he cocked it again and fired. Canby fell, struck under the eye. Boston Charley shot Dr. Thomas in the left breast. He rose and ran, but Bogus Charley finished the work with a rifle ball. Scon-

THE SCENE OF THE CANBY MASSACRE
The cross indicates the spot where General Canby sat when Captain Jack fired the first shot
From a photograph by Taber

chin missed Meacham, who ran, drew his pistol and fired back, but soon fell senseless with a bullet in his head. General Canby recovered his footing and sought to flee. Ellen's

Man brought him to the earth, while Jack dispatched him with a stab in the neck. Pressed by Hooker Jim, Dyar faced about with his pistol and the redskin fled. Riddle, the interpreter, hounded by three, managed to escape with a mere scratch. His wife, Toby, was struck down, but her life was spared. As the murderers proceeded to the usual savage consummation of their deed, she cried out: "Soldiers! soldiers!" whereat they fled. By this ruse did the faithful squaw save the bodies from mutilation.

At another place Lieutenants Doyle and Sherwood had just before been attacked under a flag of truce, and Sherwood mortally wounded. The camp force, thus apprised of treachery, hastened, too late, to the scene of Canby's death. Only Riddle and Dyar reached their advancing lines. The stripped bodies of Canby and Thomas were first found. Near by lay Meacham, also stripped, shot under his right eye, in the side of the head, and through the right arm. A temple was grazed, a finger lost, an ear cut, while a long gash gaped where Boston Charley had begun to scalp his victim. Meacham still breathed, however, and, after the bullets had been extracted, rapidly recovered.

Attack upon the Indians was now begun in earnest, and their stronghold shelled, but in vain. Not till early summer, when the "murderers" had rebelled and both factions left the lava beds, Jack making for the coveted Willow Creek, seeking, perhaps, a union with disaffected Shoshones, did General Jefferson C. Davis, who took Canby's place, scatter and capture the bloody pack. The Modocs lost a few warriors, besides women and children. Of citizens and the military and Indian allies, sixty-five were killed, sixty-three wounded. The war cost half a million dollars. Captain

GENERAL GEORGE A. CUSTER

TWO VIEWS OF THE MODOC WAR

 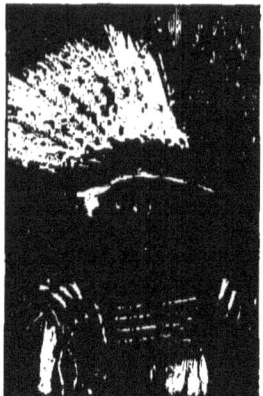

SITTING BULL
After a photograph by Notman

GALL
After a photograph by Barry

TWO FAMOUS SIOUX CHIEFS

Jack, Sconchin, Black Jim, Boston Charley, One-Eyed Jim, and Slolox were tried by a military commission for murder. The first four were hanged, the other two imprisoned for life on Alcatraz Island, San Francisco Harbor.

The above account of the Modoc War is substantially that of those inclined to lay the main guilt of the uprising to the whites and to think well of the Indians. What may in a sense be called the Oregon view differs from it in certain more or less important particulars, mainly (1) in ascribing the provocation to war to the Modocs rather than to the Klamaths or the whites, and to the whole of Jack's band rather than to a turbulent part of it; (2) in setting down as foolish the efforts of peace men to deal with savages, considering these as, practically without exception, heartless and treacherous.

The Cheyennes and allied tribes, in reprisal for the loss of their buffaloes, made many cattle raids. In 1874 the settlers retaliated, but were soon flying from their farms in panic. The Indians, as the papers had it, were at once " handed over to the secular arm," the army being set to deal with them instead of the Peace Commission. Resistance was brief, en-

THE LAST QUARTER-CENTURY

tirely collapsing when at one stroke sixty-nine warriors and two thousand ponies were captured on Elk Creek. In 1874 a massacre by the Sioux was barely averted. The agent at the Red Cloud agency erected a staff, and, on Sunday, unfurled the national flag "to let the Indians know what day it was." Viewing the emblem as meaning hostility, the Sioux beleaguered the agency, and, but for Sitting Bull, would have massacred all the whites there as well as the handful of soldiers sent to their rescue.

While the catastrophes just narrated were occurring a worse horror withdrew public attention for a moment from the Indian hostilities at the remote West to a far Eastern locality over which King Philip's own braves had ranged in the first great Indian war of American history.

GENERAL GEORGE A. CUSTER
After a photograph by Gardner at Falmouth, Va., in 1863

THE WILLIAMSBURG, MASS., FLOOD

On May 16, 1874, the rupture of a reservoir dam in the town of Williamsburg, Mass., caused a disastrous flood, costing 140 lives and the loss of $1,500,000 in property. The basin which collapsed was 300 feet above the level of Williamsburg village, and from three to four miles farther up Mill River. It covered 109 acres to a depth averaging 24 feet, its 650,000,000 gallons of water forming a reserve supply for the factories of Williamsburg, Skinnerville, Haydenville, Leeds, and Florence. The gate-keeper, one George Cheney, made the tour of the premises as usual, early on the fatal morning, but discovered nothing out of order. He went home to breakfast. The meal was just ending when Cheney's father, happening to glance through a window, exclaimed: " For God's sake, George, look there!" A vast block, fifty feet long, was shooting out from the bottom of the dam. Cheney was an old soldier and had presence of mind. Rushing to the gate he opened it to its full width, hoping thus to relieve the pressure at the break. He then made for the barn. Bridling his horse while his father cut him a stick, he mounted, just as the whole dam gave way, and dashed headlong down the valley, warning the population below. He covered the distance to Spellman's button factory, three miles away, in fifteen minutes, the thundering avalanche of waters close behind.

It was about half after seven when the brave herald reached Spellman's, himself spent with excitement and shouting, his horse worsted in the unequal race. D. Collins Graves, a milkman, here took up the news. Saying " If the dam is breaking the folks must know it," he lashed his horse at a breakneck pace to Haydenville, shouting: " The reservoir is right here! Run! It's all you can do!" Spellman's factory, the first building to test the torrent's power, was tossed from its base and dashed in pieces like a child's block-house. The help, heeding Cheney's warning, sped to the hills—too late, for many were caught and borne down to death. The Skinnerville silk operatives had just begun the day's work. When the warning reached them the superintendent was incredulous, and only the roar of the waters, drowning the courier's cry, wrung from him the order to quit. All hands dashed toward the high land, and but three were lost. Of these one had hurried home to save his family, arriving just in time to perish with them. Many other families were hurried to death together, amid noble efforts of the strong to save the weak, whose groans and cries formed an agonizing appeal for aid. The loss of life must have been far greater but for Cheney's and Graves's brave riding.

Many hair-breadth escapes occurred, accounts of which, related afterward, sounded like miracle stories. One man sailed half a mile on the very crest of the deluge, borne upon a raft of *débris*, saving himself at last by grasping a limb of one of the few trees stout enough to stem the flood. Large parts of Williamsburg and Skinnerville, including several mills and factories, were laid in hopeless ruin. The great brass works at Haydenville were totally demolished. A couple of mill-stones, weighing a ton each, were wafted a distance of half a mile. Almost the entire village of Leeds was destroyed. Much damage was done so far down as Florence, where vast fertile tracks were covered beneath feet of sand.

RAIN-IN-THE-FACE
After a photograph by Barry

Relief work for the hundreds left homeless and destitute was at once begun and nobly prosecuted. Supplies came from nearly all parts of Massachusetts and from other States. The Massachusetts legislature was in session and instituted a competent and searching investigation of the accident. Public sorrow turned to public indignation when the calamity was discovered to be due entirely to

BAD CONSTRUCTION OF THE RESERVOIR

THE INDIAN TRADERS' STORE AT STANDING ROCK, DAKOTA*
After a photograph by Barry

culpable negligence on the part of those originating, planning, constructing and approving the reservoir. The wall of the dam was too weak. It was built mainly of irregular instead of cut stone. Save at the middle, where it was re-enforced by about a foot, it was not over 5½ feet thick. Also the earth above the stone was not properly placed or rammed.

*It was here, in the spring of 1875, that Rain-in-the-Face was arrested by Captain Tom Custer, in revenge for which he threatened to eat the latter's heart—a threat said to have been fulfilled at the fight on the Little Big Horn.

THE LAST QUARTER-CENTURY

In 1875 there was pretence of investigating affairs at the Red Cloud post, but with scant result. Much of the testimony was by casual observers or interested parties, and none of it under oath. The Indians did not testify freely, and contradicted each other; Sitting Bull told one story, Red Cloud another. What became clear was that, in Red Cloud's phrase, the Indians were "succeeding backward."

A large portion of the Sioux, under Sitting Bull, had refused to enter into a treaty surrendering certain lands and consenting to confine themselves within a new reservation. Notice was served upon these non-treaty Sioux that, unless they moved to the reservation before January 1, 1876, they would be treated as hostiles. Sitting Bull refused to stir, and early in the spring the army assumed the offensive. The chief chose his position with rare skill, in the wild hunting country of southern Montana, now Custer County, near a quarter-circle of agencies, whence would join him next summer a great troop of discontented and ambitious young " Reservation " braves. The Bad Lands around made defense easy and attack most arduous.

It was determined to close upon the hostiles in three columns, General Gibbon from the west, General Crook from the south, and General Terry, with a somewhat larger body of troops, including the Seventh United States Cavalry, six hundred strong, under Lieutenant-Colonel Custer, from the east. Crook was delayed by unexpected attacks. The other two columns met without interference. Terry followed the Yellowstone up as far as the Rosebud, where he established a supply camp. Here Custer with his cavalry left him, June 22d, to make a detour south, up the Rosebud, get above the Indians, and drive them down the Little Big Horn into the army's slowly closing grip. Three days later, June 25th, Custer struck Sitting Bull's main trail, and eagerly pursued it across the divide into the Little Big Horn Valley. Expecting battle, he detached Major Reno with seven of his twelve companies, to cross the Little Big Horn, descend it, and strike the

THE CUSTER MASSACRE

foe from the west; but Reno was soon attacked and held at bay, being besieged in all more than twenty-four hours. Meantime, suddenly coming upon the lower end of the Indians' immense camp, the gallant Custer and his braves, without an instant's hesitation, advanced into the jaws of death. That death awaited every man was at once evident, but at the awful sensation, the sickening horror attending the realization of that fact, not a soul wavered. Balaklava was pastime to this, for here not one "rode back." "All that was left of them," after perhaps twenty-five minutes, was so many mostly unrecognizable corpses.

"Two hundred and sixty-two were with Custer, and two hundred and sixty-two died overwhelmed. With the last shot was silence. The report might have been written: 'None wounded; none missing; all dead.' No living tongue of all that heroic band was left to tell the story. The miserable half-breed scout, Curley, who might years later be seen hanging around Fort Custer, claimed to have been with Custer when the engagement began, but he pulled a Sioux blanket over his head, mingled with the enemy, and ran away at the first fire. He could only tell that there had been a battle." "Near the high ground and not far from where the Custer monument was erected, the body of Kellogg, special correspondent of the New York *Herald*, was found. He was bravely following the gallant Custer. The guide points out the little wooden slab which marks the spot, for he died like a hero, too, in the line of his duty."

After harrassing Reno, the Indians slipped off under cover of night. Ascending the Big Horn and the Little Big Horn, Gibbon and Terry, on the 27th, discovered the bodies of Custer and his five devoted companies. Custer alone was not mutilated. He had been shot

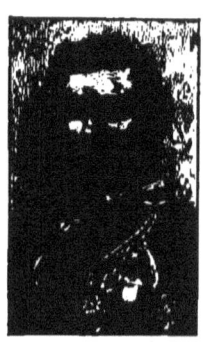

CAPTAIN E. S. GODFREY
After a photograph by Barry

in the left temple, the remainder of his face wearing in death a natural look. Years subsequently a careful survey of the field and talks with savages enabled Captain Godfrey, who was with Reno on the fatal day, to see what course the Custer fight had taken

"Comanche"*
THE ONLY SURVIVORS OF
After a photograph

Finding himself outnumbered twelve or more to one—the Indians mustered about 2,500 warriors, besides a caravan of boys and squaws—Custer had dismounted his heroes, who, planting themselves mainly on two hills some way apart, the advance one held by Custer, the other by Captains Keogh and Calhoun, prepared to sell their lives dearly. The redskins say that had Reno maintained the offensive they should have fled, the chiefs having, at the first sight of Custer, ordered camp broken for this purpose. But when Reno drew back this order was countermanded, and the entire army of the savages was concentrated against the doomed Custer. By waving blankets and uttering their hellish yells, they stampeded many of the cavalry horses, which carried off precious ammunition in their saddle-bags. Lining up just behind a ridge, they would rise quickly, fire at the soldiers, and drop, exposing themselves little, but drawing Custer's fire, so caus-

*Comanche was the horse ridden by Captain Keogh, and was afterward found with seven wounds at a distance of several miles from the battle-field. The Secretary of War subsequently issued an order forbidding any one to ride him, and detailing a soldier to take care of him as long as he lived. Curley, a Crow Indian, was Custer's scout, and is said to have made his escape by wrapping himself in a Sioux blanket when the battle began.

THE REVENGE OF RAIN-IN-THE-FACE

Curley, the Scout
THE CUSTER MASSACRE
by Barry

ing additional loss of sorely needed bullets. The whites' ammunition spent, the dismounted savages rose, fired, and whooped like the demons they were; while the mounted ones, lashing their ponies, charged with infinite venom, overwhelming Calhoun and Keogh, and lastly Custer himself. Indian boys then pranced over the fields on ponies, scalping and re-shooting the dead and dying. At the burial many a stark visage wore a look of horror. "Rain-in-the-Face," who mainly inspired and directed the battle on the Indian side, boasted that he cut out and ate Captain Tom Custer's heart. Most believe that he did so. "Rain-in-the-Face" was badly wounded, and used crutches ever after. Brave Sergeant Butler's body was found by itself, lying on a heap of empty cartridge shells which told what he had been about.

Sergeant Mike Madden had a leg mangled while fighting, tiger-like, near Reno, and for his bravery was promoted on the field. He was always over-fond of grog, but long abstinence had now intensified his thirst. He submitted to amputation without anæsthesia. After the operation the surgeon gave him a stiff horn of brandy. Emptying it eagerly and smacking his lips, he said: "M-eh, Doctor, cut off the other leg."

This distressing catastrophe, which whelmed the country in grief many days, called forth Longfellow's poem, "The Revenge of Rain-in-the-Face," ending with the stanza:

> Whose was the right and the wrong?
> Sing it, O funeral song,
> With a voice that is full of tears,
> And say that our broken faith
> Wrought all this ruin and scathe
> In the Year of a Hundred Years.

THE LAST QUARTER-CENTURY

This poem mistakenly represents "Rain-in-the-Face" as having mutilated General Custer instead of his brother, the Captain. Also it is based on the "ambush" theory of the battle, which at first all shared. We now know, however, that Custer fought in the open, from high ground, not in a ravine. His surprise lay not in finding Indians before him, but in finding them so fatally numerous. Some of General Terry's friends charged Custer with transgressing his orders in fighting as he did. That he was somewhat careless, almost rash, in his preparations to attack can perhaps be maintained, though good authority declares the "battle fought tactically and with intelligence on Custer's part," and calls it unjust "to say that he was reckless or foolish." Bravest of the brave, Custer was always anxious to fight, and, just now in ill favor with President Grant, he was eager to make a record; but that he was guilty of disobedience to his orders is not shown.

THE CUSTER MONUMENT
ERECTED ON THE BATTLEFIELD
After a photograph by Barry

It, indeed, came quite directly from General Terry that had Custer lived to return "he would at once have been put under arrest and court-martialled for disobedience." This might have been the best way to elicit all the facts, and does not prove that even General Terry would have been sure of Custer's conviction.

The present head of the army, General Miles, is strongly of the opinion that Custer was not guilty of disobeying any

DID CUSTER DISOBEY ORDERS?

orders. The late General Fry expressed himself with equal emphasis in the same tenor. Colonel R. P. Hughes, however, who was General Terry's chief of staff during the Sioux campaign, sought, in an able article in the Journal of the Military Service Institution for January, 1896, to defend the contrary proposition. He adduced many interesting considerations, but seemed to the present writer not at all to justify his view.

Custer's expressed hope to "swing clear" of Terry is worked too hard when made to bear the meaning that he deliberately purposed to disregard Terry's orders. To have a superior at his elbow seemed to him queer and unpleasant; he liked, especially in fighting Indians, to be trusted. Had he been minded disobediently to meet the Indians without Gibbon, getting a victory and all its glory for himself alone, he would have marched faster during his first days out from the Rosebud mouth. He in fact moved but 108 miles in four days.

Much turns on the force of Custer's written orders, which, judged by usual military documents of the kind, certainly gave Custer a much larger liberty than Colonel Hughes supposed. There is an affidavit of a witness who heard Terry's and Custer's last conversation together at the mouth of the Rosebud, just before Custer began his fatal ride. Terry said: "Use your own judgment and do what you think best if you strike the trail; and whatever you do, Custer, hold on to your wounded." Even his written orders gave Custer leave to depart from his written orders if he saw reason for doing so, *i. e.*, if, in his judgment, the end of the campaign could be best attained in that way. Hughes argues that because he, Hughes, can see no reason for any such departure, Custer could have seen none. But how can we know this? Custer, who alone could tell, cannot be interrogated; and the purposes and plans that governed his course during his eventful last days men can only surmise.

THE LAST QUARTER-CENTURY

Hughes's contention, in opposition to General Fry, that Terry had and had communicated to Custer a perfectly definite plan of campaign, explicitly involving Gibbon's co-operation in the attack, seems still to lack proof; but the observations here made are little dependent on the decision of that point. A remark or two, however. Colonel Hughes, it seems, wishes us to think that Terry all along knew the exceeding strength of the Indian force, accounting it much too numerous for Custer safely to attack alone. Was it not, then, rash and cruel to send Custer out on that far detour, crowding him so well to the south, where, let Gibbon hurry as he might, the savages would have Custer at their mercy! He could not hope to conceal his march very long. " It is folly to suppose that either a small or a large band of Indians would remain stationary and allow one body of troops to come up on one side of it while another body came up on the other side and engaged it in battle. . . . When Custer's command was ordered to move out as it did it left the Indians, who were acting on interior lines, absolutely free to attack either one of the commands thus separated, or fight them in detail, as might be preferred."

Hughes makes the point that Custer did not report to Gibbon whether he found Indians in Tulloch Creek Valley. General Fry seems justified in calling this a purely formal and immaterial neglect. The valley up and down was completely empty of Indians, and Custer doubtless considered it a needless diminution of his scout force to detach a man to report this. That he did not send word to Gibbon at any later time may seem strange, but he certainly was not commanded to do so.

Hughes charges it as disobedience that Custer did not ride southward when he ascertained that the Indian trail turned toward the Little Big Horn. But his orders did not command him to go southward *the moment he ascertained* the course of the trail, or at any other particular moment. Moreover, what Hughes does not observe, the purpose of veering southward was simply to see that the hostiles did not escape around his

HAD RENO PRESSED FORWARD!

left. The configuration of the country, as Custer saw it, must have assured him that when the hostiles made for the Little Big Horn Valley they gave up all purpose of marching south and were bent upon going down that valley. It would have been foolish for him to have proceeded south after he felt absolutely convinced of the enemy's purpose. He would simply have wasted the strength of his command.

Hughes deems it blameworthy that from the moment when Custer found the trail leading toward the Little Big Horn he quickened his speed. In this he seems to overlook the fact that Custer's discovery may well have led him to fear for Gibbon's command. The redskins had gone to the Little Big Horn on purpose to go down that stream. Custer could not know how far down it they by this time were, or how far up it Gibbon might possibly have come. Had he not made the best of his way on he would certainly have been censurable. At the same time, it obviously would not do for him when he came upon the foe to wait before attacking to ascertain Gibbon's whereabouts. As General Fry observes, had he hesitated, either he would have been attacked himself, or else his foe would have withdrawn to attack Gibbon or to get away entirely.

Small as was Custer's total force, yet had Reno supported him as had been expected, the fight would have been a victory, the enemy killed, captured, driven down upon Gibbon, or so cut to pieces as never to have reappeared as a formidable force. In either of these cases Custer, living or dead, would have emerged from the campaign with undying glory and there would have been no thought of a court-martial or of censure.

OLD SWEDES' CHURCH, PHILADELPHIA, BUILT IN 1700
After a photograph by Rau

CHAPTER VIII

"THE YEAR OF A HUNDRED YEARS"— THE CENTENNIAL EXPOSITION AND THE HAYES-TILDEN IMBROGLIO

ORIGIN OF THE CENTENNIAL EXPOSITION.—PHILADELPHIA LANDMARKS.—THE EXPOSITION BUILDINGS.—THE OPENING.—THE VARIOUS EXHIBITS.—ATTENDANCE.—A POLITICAL CRISIS.—GRANT AND JEWELL.—THE BELKNAP DISGRACE.—ANOTHER REFORM MOVEMENT.—FEAR OF A THIRD TERM FOR GRANT.—ISSUES BETWEEN THE PARTIES.—HAYES AND TILDEN NOMINATED.—THEIR LETTERS OF ACCEPTANCE.—THE CAMPAIGN.—PROPHECY OF TROUBLE OVER THE PRESIDENTIAL COUNT.—THE TWENTY-SECOND JOINT RULE.—RESULT OF THE ELECTION IN DOUBT.—CIPHER DESPATCHES.—QUEER WAYS OF RETURNING BOARDS.—FEARS AND HOPES.—THE ELECTORAL COMMISSION.—THE CASE OF FLORIDA, OF LOUISIANA, OF OREGON, OF SOUTH CAROLINA.—HAYES DECLARED ELECTED.—AN ELECTORAL COUNT LAW.

READERS will rejoice that racial feuds at the South and the West during President Grant's second term did not make up the entire history of these years. Despite those and all its other troubles, the American body politic was

195

THE LAST QUARTER-CENTURY

about to round the first century of its life in satisfactory and increasing vigor.

What could be more fitting than that the hundredth anniversary of the world's greatest Republic should be kept by a monster celebration? Such a question was publicly raised in 1870 by an association of Philadelphia citizens, and it set the entire nation thinking. At first only a United States celebration was proposed, but reflection developed the idea of a Mammoth Fair where the arts and industries of the whole world should be represented. Congress took up the design in 1871–2. In 1873 President Grant formally proclaimed the Exposition, and in 1874 foreign governments were invited to participate in it. Thirty-three cordially responded, including all the civilized nations except Greece, a larger number than had ever before taken part in an event like this.

Philadelphia was naturally chosen as the seat of the Exposition. Here the nation was born, a fact of which much remained to testify. Among the ancient buildings were the "Old Swedes'" Church, built in 1700, Christ Church, begun only twenty-seven years later, still in perfect preservation, St. Peter's, built in 1758–1761, and the sequestered Friends' Meeting-house, built in 1808. The Penn Treaty Monument, unimpressive in appearance, marked the site of the elm under which Penn made his famous treaty with the Indians. Carpenters' Hall, still owned by the Carpenters' Company which built it, had been made to resume the appearance it bore when, in 1774, the first Continental Congress assembled under its roof. In the centre of a line of antique edifices known as State-house Row, stood Independence Hall, erected 1732–1735. The name specifically applied to the large first-floor east room, in which the second Continental Congress adopted the Declaration of Independence. In 1824 Lafayette held a great reception here, and six years later it was consecrated to the past. Revolutionary portraits

THE EXPOSITION BUILDINGS

and relics were placed in it, and the building restored to its original condition. In 1854 the old Liberty Bell was taken down from the tower into the hall and the walls enriched by a large number of portraits from the Peale Gallery. A keeper was then appointed and the hall opened to visitors.

In Fairmount Park, beyond the Schuylkill, a level plat of over 200 acres was inclosed, and appropriate buildings erected. Five enormous structures, the Main Building, with Machinery, Agricultural, Horticultural, and Memorial Halls, towered above all the rest. Several foreign governments built structures of their own. Twenty-six States did the same. Thirty or more buildings were put up by private enterprise in order the better to present industrial processes

STATE-HOUSE ROW, PHILADELPHIA
After a photograph by Rau

and products. In all more than two hundred edifices stood within the inclosure.

The Exposition opened on May 10th, with public exercises, a hundred thousand people being present. Wagner had composed a march for the occasion. Whittier's Centennial Hymn, a noble piece, was sung by a chorus of one thousand voices.

> Our fathers' God ! from out whose hand
> The centuries fall like grains of sand,
> We meet to-day, united, free,
> And loyal to our land and Thee,
> To thank Thee for the era done,
> And trust Thee for the opening one.
>
> Here, where of old, by Thy design,
> The fathers spake that word of Thine,
> Whose echo is the glad refrain
> Of rended bolt and fallen chain,
> To grace our festal time, from all
> The zones of earth our guests we call.

The restored South chanted the praises of the Union in the words of Sidney Lanier, the Georgia poet. President Grant then declared the Exposition open. Further simple but impressive ceremonies were held on July 4th, in the public square at the rear of Independence Hall. On temporary platforms sat 5,000 distinguished guests, and a chorus of 1,000 singers. The square and the neighboring streets were filled with a dense throng. Richard Henry Lee, grandson of the mover of the Declaration of Independence, came to the front with the original document in his hands. At sight of that yellow and wrinkled paper the vast throng burst into prolonged cheering. Mr. Lee read the Declaration, Bayard Taylor recited an ode, and Hon. William M. Evarts delivered an oration.

In the Main Building, erected in a year, at a cost of $1,700,000, manufactures were exhibited, also products of the mine, along with innumerable other evidences of scientific and educational progress. More than a third of the space was reserved for the United States, the rest being divided among foreign countries. The products of all climates, tribes, and times were here. Great Britain, France, and Germany exhib-

THE VARIOUS EXHIBITS

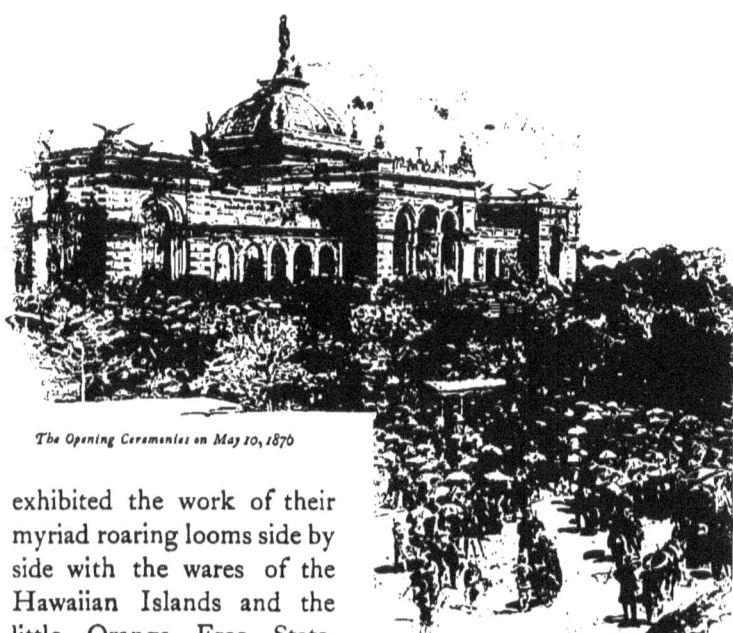

The Opening Ceremonies on May 10, 1876

exhibited the work of their myriad roaring looms side by side with the wares of the Hawaiian Islands and the little Orange Free State. Here were the furs of Russia, with other articles from the frozen North; there the flashing diamonds of Brazil, and the rich shawls and waving plumes of India. At a step one passed from old Egypt to the latest born South American republic. Chinese conservatism and Yankee enterprise confronted each other across the aisle.

From the novelty of the foreign display the American visitor turned proudly to the handiwork of his own land. Textiles, arms, tools, musical instruments, watches, carriages, cutlery, books, furniture—a bewildering display of all things useful and ornamental—made him realize as never before the wealth, intelligence, and enterprise of his native country, and the proud station to which she had risen among the nations of the earth. Three-fourths of the space in Machinery Hall was taken up with American machinery.

THE LAST QUARTER-CENTURY

GENERAL JOSEPH R.
HAWLEY
President of the Centennial Commission

Memorial Hall, a beautiful permanent building of granite, erected by Pennsylvania and Philadelphia at a cost of $1,500,000, was given up to art. This was the poorest feature of the Exposition, though the collection was the largest and most notable ever till then seen this side the Atlantic. America had few art works of the first order to show, while foreign nations, with the exception of England, which contributed a noble lot of paintings, including works by Gainsborough and Reynolds, feared to send their choicest products across the sea. All through the summer and early autumn, spite of the unusual heat that year, thousands of pilgrims from all parts of the country and the world filled the fair grounds and the city. Amid the crowds of visitors Philadelphians became strangers in their own streets. On September 28th, Pennsylvania day, 275,000 persons passed the gates. During October the visitors numbered over two and a half millions. From May 10th to November 10th, the closing day, the total admissions were 9,900,000. The aggregate attendance was larger than at any previous international exhibition, except that of Paris in 1867. The admissions there reached 10,200,000, but the gates were open fifty-one days longer than in Philadelphia. At Vienna, in 1873, there were but 7,255,000 admissions in 186 days, against 159 days at Philadelphia.

Full of peace and promise as was this Philadelphia pageant, in politics these same months saw the United States at a serious crisis. The best interests of the country seemed to depend on the party in power, yet a large and influential section of that party was in all but open revolt. Many base men to whom honest and enterprising public servants were unwelcome were tolerated near the President. Secretary Bristow's

JEWELL AND THE POST-OFFICE DEPARTMENT

noble fight against the Whiskey Ring, his victory, and his resignation from the Cabinet are described in another Chapter. Ex-Governor Marshall Jewell, of Connecticut, was a most efficient Postmaster-General. Upon taking his office he avowed the purpose to conduct it on business principles. He at once began to attack the notorious "straw bids" and other corrupt practices connected with carrying the mails in Texas and Alabama. It was he who introduced the Railway Post-Office System, by which the postal matter for a State, instead of first going to the capital or to one or two central cities and being slowly distributed thence, was sent to its destination directly, by the shortest routes and in the most expeditious manner. Yet in 1876, two years from the time of his appointment, much to the surprise of the public, Jewell left the Cabinet. An officeholder explained that "they didn't care much for Jewell in Washington; why, he ran the Post-Office as though it was a factory!" The ring politicians were a unit against him, and finally succeeded in displacing him. In a speech before the Senate during the impeachment trial of Belknap, Grant's War Secretary, Hon. George F. Hoar declared that he had heard the taunt from friendliest lips that "the only product of the United States' institutions in which she surpassed all other nations beyond question was her corruption."

The Sherman Letters threw much light on the Belknap disgrace. July 8, 1871, General Sherman wrote: "My office has been by law stript of all the influence and prestige it possessed under Grant (as General), and even in matters of discipline and army control I am neglected, overlooked, or snubbed." Later, Sherman wrote: "Belknap has acted badly by me ever since he reached Washington. General Grant promised me often to arrange and divide our functions, but he never did, but left the Secretary to do all those things of which he himself, as General, had complained to Stanton." "The President and Belknap both gradually withdrew from me all the powers which Grant had exercised in the same

THE LAST QUARTER-CENTURY

office, and Congress capped the climax by repealing that law which required all orders to the army to go through the General." " I have no hesitation in saying that if the Secretary of War has the right to command the army through the Adjutant-General, then my office is a sinecure and should be abolished."

Why the General of the Army had been thus extruded from the authority and functions properly attending his office, was clear when, on February 29th, 1876, Caleb P. Marsh, one of a firm of contractors in New York City, testified before a Congressional Committee that, in 1870, Belknap had offered him the control of the post-tradership at Fort Sill, Indian Territory, for the purpose of enabling him to extort from the actual holder of the place, one John S. Evans, $3,000 four times a year as the price of continuing in it. The Secretary and his family appeared to have received $24,450 in this way. Belknap's resignation was offered and accepted a few hours before the House passed a unanimous vote to impeach him. Other dubious acts of Belknap's came to light, notably a contract for erecting tombstones in national cemeteries, from which, as was charged, he realized $90,000. In the fall of 1874, General Sherman actually transferred his headquarters to St. Louis, to remove himself from official contact with Belknap, who was issuing orders and making appointments without Sherman's knowledge. Two years later, after Belknap's resignation, the office of General of the Army was re-invested with the powers which had formerly belonged to it. Then the General moved back to Washington.

Belknap demurred to the Senate's jurisdiction, but on May 29th the Senate affirmed this, 37 to 29, Morton and Conkling voting nay, Cameron, Edmunds, Morrill and Sherman aye. Thurman moved the resolution of impeachment. Belknap's counsel refused to let him plead, urging that the vote to assume jurisdiction, not being a two-thirds vote, was equivalent to an acquittal. The Senate, however, proceeded,

VIEW FROM PHOTOGRAPHIC HALL LOOKING TOWARD MACHINERY HALL.

THE NEW REFORM MOVEMENT

as on a plea of " not guilty," to try him. He was acquitted, one Democrat voting for acquittal. Morton was among the Republicans who voted for conviction.

After the above recitals one is not surprised that in April, 1876, over the signatures of William Cullen Bryant, Theodore D. Woolsey, Alexander H. Bullock, Horace White, and Carl Schurz, was issued a circular call for a conference of Republicans dissatisfied at the "wide-spread corruption" with which machine politics had infected our public service. The conference organized about five weeks later, electing Theodore D. Woolsey for president, and for secretaries, among others, Henry Cabot Lodge, Francis A. Walker and Henry Armitt Brown. A Committee on Business next reported "An Address to the American people," by which the assemblage, after recounting the threatening growth of official corruption hand in hand with the spoils system, invoked all good citizens to join them in a pledge to support no presidential aspirant not known " to possess the moral courage and sturdy resolution to grapple with abuses which had acquired the strength of established customs, and to this end firmly to resist the pressure even of his party friends."

The New York *Herald* had in 1874 started a cry that Grant would not be averse to breaking the canon set by Washington against a third presidential term. Democratic journals took up the alarm and soon the press all over the land was vocal with denunciations of " Grantism," " Cæsarism," " Third Termism ! " So nervous did the din make Republicans, that in 1875 the Pennsylvania Republican Convention passed a resolution of unalterable " opposition to the election to the presidency of any person for a third term." Grant had thus far been almost alone in keeping silence, but he at last felt called to express himself. He wrote a letter to the chairman of the convention. " Now for the third term," said he, " I do not want it any more than I did the first." Yet he remarked that the Constitution did not re-

THE LAST QUARTER-CENTURY

Exterior of Horticultural Hall

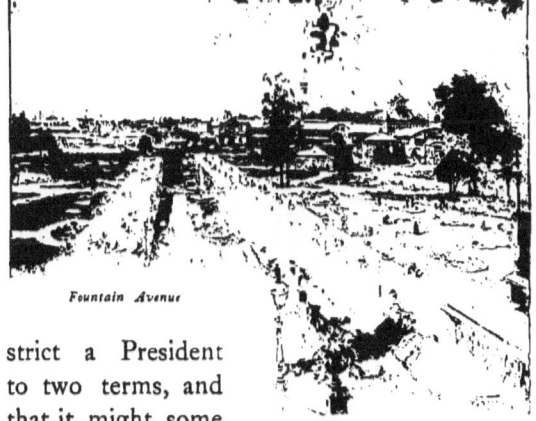

Fountain Avenue

VIEWS AT THE PHILADELPHIA CENTENNIAL

strict a President to two terms, and that it might some time be unfortunate to dismiss one so soon. However, he would not accept a nomination unless "under such circumstances as to make it an imperative duty—circumstances not likely to arise." This was too equivocal. The National House of Representatives therefore passed a resolution, 234 to 18, seventy Republicans voting for it:

"That in the opinion of this House the precedent established by Washington and other Presidents of the United

PARTY PLATFORMS IN 1876

States after their second term, has become, by universal concurrence, a part of our Republican system of government, and that any departure from this time-honored custom would be unwise, unpatriotic, and fraught with peril to our free institutions."

The issues with a view to which, in 1876, the two great parties constructed their platforms, were mainly three: The "Southern question," specie resumption, and civil service reform. The Republican party endorsed its own civil rights and force legislation, but called for better administration. The Democracy had at last, to use J. Q. Adams's phrase, "sneaked up to its inevitable position." It reaffirmed its faith in the Union, and its devotion to the Constitution, with its amendments, universally accepted, as a final settlement of the controversy which engendered civil war. This was a re-emergence of Vallandigham's New Departure for the party. The Democratic platform rang with the cry of "Reform," which had been so effectual in New York State in the election of Tilden as Governor. The catalogue of shocking Republican scandals was gone over to prove the futility of attempting "reform within party lines." "President, Vice-President, Judges, Senators, Representatives, Cabinet Officers—these and all others in authority are the people's servants. Their offices are not a private perquisite; they are a

Interior of Horticultural Hall

public trust." This was the origin of an expression, afterward usually referred to President Cleveland, which bade fair to be immortal.

While the Republicans favored a "continuous and steady progress to specie payments," the hard-money men failed to get the Convention to endorse the Resumption Clause of the Act of 1875. The Democrats denounced that clause as a hindrance to resumption, but their Convention would not commit itself to a condemnation of the resumption policy. The Republicans favored a revenue tariff with incidental protection. The Democrats repudiated protection, and demanded "that all custom-house taxation should be only for revenue."

The Republican Convention met in Cincinnati on June 14th. "Third-termers" saw no hope for Grant. James G. Blaine was thought the man most likely to receive the nomination. His name was placed before the Convention by Colonel Robert G. Ingersoll, in one of the most eloquent addresses ever heard on such an occasion. When in the roll-call of States Maine was reached, boundless enthusiasm reigned, with cheering that died away only to be renewed, closing with three cheers for James G. Blaine. Mr. Ingersoll mounted the platform. As he was then comparatively unknown, the epigrammatic force and the fervor of his words took his hearers by surprise. His concluding periods were not soon forgotten, and the title of " Plumed Knight" with which he dubbed his hero adhered to Mr. Blaine through life.

"This is a grand year," he said: "a year filled with the recollections of the Revolution; filled with proud and tender memories of the sacred past; . . the span is too long filled with legends of liberty;—a year in which the sons of freedom will drink from the fountain of enthusiasm; a year in which the people call for the man who has preserved in Congress what their soldiers won upon the field; a year in which they call for the man who has torn from the throat of treason the tongue of slander; the man who has snatched the mask of Democracy

THE MAIN BUILDING AT PHILADELPHIA

THE LAST QUARTER-CENTURY

from the hideous face of the rebellion; the man who, like the intellectual athlete, has stood in the arena of debate, challenging all comers, and who, up to the present moment, is a total stranger to defeat. Like an armed warrior, like a plumed knight, James G. Blaine marched down the halls of the American Congress, and threw his shining lance full and fair against the brazen forehead of every traitor to his country and every maligner of his fair reputation. For the Republican party to desert that gallant man now is as though an army should desert its general upon the field of battle. . . James G. Blaine is now and has been for years the bearer of the sacred standard of the Republican party. I call it sacred because no human being can stand beneath its folds without becoming and without remaining free.

W. W. BELKNAP

"Gentlemen of the Convention: In the name of the great Republic, the only Republic that ever existed upon the face of the earth; in the name of all her defenders and of all her supporters; in the name of all her soldiers living; in the name of all her soldiers that died upon the field of battle; and in the name of those that perished in the skeleton clutch of famine at Andersonville and Libby, whose sufferings he so vividly remembers—Illinois—Illinois—nominates for the next President of this country that prince of parliamentarians, that leader of leaders, James G. Blaine."

Blaine was indeed a brilliant parliamentarian, but his prospects were weakened by alleged questionable proceedings, the nature of which we shall exhibit later. Most of the Southern delegates were for Oliver P. Morton, of Indiana. Conkling, of New York, in addition to the potent support of his State, enjoyed the favor of the Administration. The reform and anti-Grant delegates were enthusiastic for the gallant destroyer of the Whiskey Ring, ex-Secretary Bristow, of Kentucky.

GOVERNOR HAYES

MARSHALL JEWELL

George William Curtis said that at the Attorney-General's table he asked Jewell whom the party—not the managers— would make the candidate, and that Jewell instantly answered, " Bristow." Pennsylvania, Connecticut and Ohio all appeared with favorite sons in their arms: Hartranft, Jewell and Hayes, respectively. The names familiar enough to evoke cheers from one faction drew "curses not loud but deep" from other cliques. Upon the seventh ballot, therefore, the Convention united upon Governor Rutherford B. Hayes, of Ohio, a man who, though little known, awakened no antagonism and had no embarrassing past, while he had made a most creditable record both as a soldier and as the chief magistrate of his State.

When Hayes was nominated for Governor in 1875 inflation was popular all over the West. Both parties were infected, though the Democrats the worse. The Ohio Democracy was led that year by William Allen and Samuel F. Carey, two of the ablest campaigners ever heard upon the stump in this country. Hayes dared them to the issue. Spite of protests from timid Republicans, he came out boldly for resumption and the re-establishment of the specie standard, turned the tide against the inflationist hosts, and carried the State. From that moment the Ohio Governor was seen by many to be of presidential stature. John Sherman was the first to name him for the higher office. In a letter dated January 21, 1876, he had written : " Considering all things I believe the nomination of Governor Hayes would give us more strength, taking the whole country at large, than that of any other man."

The Democratic Convention convened at St. Louis on June 28th, nominating Samuel J. Tilden on the second ballot. Tilden was born in New Lebanon, N. Y., February 9, 1814. In 1845 he was elected to the New York Assembly; in 1846 and again in 1867 to the State Constitutional Convention. He was a keen lawyer. By his famous analysis of the Broadway Bank accounts during the prosecution of the Tammany Ring he rendered an invaluable service to the cause of reform. As Governor, in 1875, he waged relentless and triumphant war against the Canal Ring, "the country thieves," as they were called to distinguish them from Tweed and his coterie.

In accepting the nomination Tilden reiterated his protests against "the magnificent and oppressive centralism into which our government was being converted." He also commended reform in the Civil Service, deprecating the notion that this service existed for office-holders, and bewailing the organization of the official class into a body of political mercenaries. Hayes's letter emphasized Civil Service reform even more strongly. He zealously descanted upon the evils of the spoils system, and pledged himself, if elected, to employ all the constitutional powers vested in the President to secure reform, returning to the "old rule, the true rule, that honesty, capacity and fidelity constitute the only real qualifications for office." Both candidates wished the Executive to be relieved of the temptation to use patronage for his own re-election. Mr. Hayes made "the noble pledge" that in no case would he be a candidate again. Mr. Tilden disparaged self-imposed restrictions, but recommended that the chief magistrate be constitutionally disqualified for re-election.

Hayes's ambiguity touching the Southern question gave hope that, even if the Republicans succeeded, a milder Southern policy would be introduced. Tilden, while crying out against the insupportable misgovernment imposed upon reconstructed States, frankly accepted the Democrats' new departure. Before the end of the canvass he published a pledge that, if elected, he would enforce the constitutional amendments and resist Southern claims.

The campaign was tame. The fact that both candidates were of blameless character muffled partisan eloquence. Great

MORTON A PROPHET

efforts were made to discredit Tilden for connection with certain railroad enterprises, and he was sued for an income tax alleged to be due. Retorting, the Democrats sneered at Hayes as an "obscure" man, and roundly denounced the extortion practiced upon office-holders under Secretary Chandler's eye. This chatter amounted to little. All signs pointed to a close election.

So early as May, 1874, Mr. Morton of Indiana had proposed in the Senate an amendment to the Constitution making the President eligible by the people directly. The proposal was committed and, the next January, debated. Each State was to have as many presidential as congressional districts. The presidential candidate successful in any district would receive therefrom one presidential vote, while two special presidential votes would fall to the candidate receiving the greatest number of district votes in the State.

In reviewing the need of some such change Morton spoke like a prophet. "No State," he declared "has provided any method of contesting the election of electors. Though this election may be distinguished by fraud, notorious fraud, by violence, by tumult, yet there is no method of contesting it." Again, "It seems never to have occurred to the members of the Convention that there could be two sets of electors; it seems never to have occurred to them that there would be fraud and corruption, or any reason why the votes of electors should be set aside. It is clearly a *casus omissus*, a thing overlooked by the framers of the Constitution." The subject was, however, laid aside, and never taken up again till the dangers

SAMUEL J. TILDEN

THE LAST QUARTER-CENTURY

which Morton had so faithfully foretold were actually shaking the pillars of our government.

Morton also sought to amend and render of service the twenty-second joint rule, the substance of which was that in counting the electoral votes no question should be decided affirmatively and no vote objected to be counted, "except by the concurrent votes of the two houses." This rule had been passed in 1865, being meant to enable the radicals to reject electoral votes from Mr. Lincoln's "ten per cent. States," viz., those reconstructed on the presidential plan. Morton proposed to modify this rule so that no vote could be *rejected* save by concurrent vote of the two houses. A bill providing for such change passed the Senate, six Republicans opposing. It was never taken up in the House. Morton introduced the bill again in the next Congress, only to see it killed by delays.

The election of 1876 passed off quietly, troops being stationed at the polls in turbulent quarters. "The result was doubtful up to the day of election; it was doubtful after the election was over, and to this day the question, Was Tilden or Hayes duly elected? is an open one. The first reports received in New York were so decidedly in favor of the Democratic ticket that the leading Republican journals admitted its success." The *Times* alone stood out, persistently declaring that Hayes was elected, which caused intense excitement among the huge crowd gathered in the square fronting the *Times* office. The next day different reports were received, and both sides claimed the victory. Hon. Hugh McCulloch, a Republican, but eminently free from partisan bias, was of the opinion at the time, and so long as he lived, that if the distinguished Northern men who visited those States had stayed at home, and there had been no outside pressure upon the returning boards, their certificates would

"I DON'T KNOW."

1900!
A Ku-Klux Notice Posted Up in Mississippi During the Election of 1876

THE CIPHER DESPATCHES

have been in favor of the Democratic electors. This opinion was confirmed by a remark of the President of the Union Telegraph Company at the annual meeting of the Union League Club of New York, in 1878. In a conversation with that gentleman Mr. McCulloch happened to speak of the election of Mr. Hayes, when he interrupted by saying: "'But he was not elected.' 'If he was not, the emanations of your office failed to show it,' McCulloch replied. 'Oh, yes,' he rejoined; 'but that was because the examiners did not know where to look.' . . . 'Mr. Tilden,' said a prominent Republican, 'was, I suppose, legally elected, but not fairly.'" This was doubtless the conclusion of a great many other Republicans, as well as of practically all the Democrats.

Pending the meeting of the State electoral colleges, some of Tilden's warmest supporters undertook negotiations to secure for him one or more electoral votes from South Carolina or Florida. As their apologists put it, "they seem to have feared that the corrupt canvassers would declare" those States for Hayes, "and being convinced that the popular vote had been cast for Tilden, to have been willing to submit to the payment of moneys which they were informed some of the canvassers demanded by way of blackmail." One Hardy Solomon, pretending to represent the South Carolina Canvassing Board, went to Baltimore expecting to receive $60,000 or $80,000 in this interest; but, upon applying to Mr. Tilden for the sum, he was peremptorily refused. These negotiations were authorized neither by Mr. Tilden, who, under oath, denied all knowledge of them, nor by the Democratic National Committee. The Republican members of the Clarkson investigating committee thought them traceable to Tilden's secretary, Colonel Pelton, with Smith M. Weed and Manton Marble; but the responsibility for them was never really fixed upon anyone. The despatches went back and forth in cipher. Under a subpœna from the Senate Committee on Privileges and Elections, the Western Union Telegraph Company delivered

THE LAST QUARTER-CENTURY

them to that Committee, and on January 25, 1877, they were locked in a trunk in its room. When this trunk was returned to New York City on the following March 13th it was discovered that a large number of the cipher despatches had been abstracted. Of those missing, some seven hundred were, in May, 1878, in possession of G. E. Bullock, messenger of the committee last named. Part of these subsequently found their way into the office of the New York *Tribune*, where they were translated and published, causing much excitement and comment. There is some evidence that Republican cipher despatches no less compromising than these and used for the same purpose, had been filched from the trunk and destroyed.

Tilden carried New York, New Jersey, Indiana, and Connecticut. With a solid South he had won the day. But the returning boards of Louisiana, Florida, and South Carolina, throwing out the votes of several Democratic districts on the ground of fraud or intimidation, decided that those States had gone Republican, giving Hayes a majority of one in the electoral college. The Democrats raised the cry of fraud. Threats were muttered that Hayes would never be inaugurted. Excitement thrilled the country. Grant strengthened the military force in and about Washington. However, the people looked to Congress for a peaceful solution, and not in vain.

The Constitution provides that the " President of the Senate shall, in presence of the Senate and House of Representatives, open all the (electoral) certificates, and the votes shall then be counted." Attending to the most obvious meaning of these words, a good many Republicans held that the power to count the votes lay with the President of the Senate, the House and Senate being mere spectators. The Democrats objected to this construction, since, according to it, Mr. Ferry, the Republican President of the Senate, could count the votes of the disputed States for Hayes, and was practically certain to do so.

THE ELECTORAL COMMISSION

"I shall decide every point in the case of post-office elector in favor of the highest democratic elector, and grant the certificate accordingly on morning of the 6th inst. Confidential."—CONGRESSIONAL RECORD.

One of the "Cipher Despatches," sent During the Election Deadlock, with Translation, as Put in Evidence Before the Congressional Committee

The twenty-second joint rule had, when passed, been attacked as grossly unconstitutional. Republicans now admitted that it was so, and the Senate, since the House was Democratic, voted to rescind it. As it stood, electoral certificates were liable to be thrown out on the most frivolous objections, as that of Arkansas had once been, simply because it bore the wrong seal. But now the Democrats insisted that Congress should enforce this old rule. That done, the House, rejecting the vote of one State, would elect Tilden.

Only a compromise could break the deadlock. A joint committee reported the famous Electoral Commission Bill, which passed House and Senate by large majorities. The main faith in the plan was on the Democratic side. In a Senate speech, February 2, 1881, Blaine spoke of the commission as "a rickety makeshift." One hundred and eighty-six Democrats voted for it and eighteen against, while the Republican vote stood fifty-two for, seventy-five against. With regard to single returns the bill reversed the Rule of 1865, suffering none to be rejected save by concurrent action of the two houses. Double or multiple returns were, in cases of dispute, to be referred to a commission of five Senators, five Representatives, and five Justices of the United States Supreme Court, the fifth justice being selected by the four appointed in the bill. Previous to this choice the Commission contained seven Democrats and seven Republicans. The five Senators on the Commission were George F. Edmunds, Oliver P. Morton, Frederick T. Frelinghuysen, Republicans; and Allan G. Thurman and Thomas F. Bayard, Democrats. The members of the House were Henry B. Payne, Eppa Hunton and Josiah G. Abbott, Democrats; and James A. Garfield and George F. Hoar, Republicans. Four Justices of the Supreme Court were designated in the Act by the circuits to which they belonged. These were Nathan Clifford and Stephen J. Field, Democrats, and William Strong and Samuel F. Miller, Republicans. These four Justices were by the Act to select the fifth. It was expected that the fifth Justice would be Hon. David Davis, of Illinois, a neutral with Democratic leanings, who had been a warm friend of President Lincoln's but an opponent of Grant. Mr. Davis's unexpected election as Senator from his State made Justice Bradley the decisive umpire.

The Commission met on the last day of January, 1877. The cases of Florida, Louisiana, Oregon, and South Carolina were in succession submitted to it, eminent counsel appearing for each side. There were double or multiple sets of returns from each State named. Three returns from Florida were passed in. One contained four votes for Hayes, certified by the late Republican Governor, Stearns. One return gave four votes for Tilden, bearing the certificate of the Attorney-General, a member of the returning board. Third was the same return reinforced with the certificate of the new Democratic Governor, Drew, under a State law passed a few days before, directing a re-canvass of the votes. Democratic counsel urged that the first return should be rejected as the result of fraud

THE FLORIDA CASE

and conspiracy by the returning board, whose action the State Supreme Court had held to be *ultra vires* and illegal.

In Baker County, which was decisive of the result in Florida, the canvassers were the county judge, the county clerk, and a justice of the peace to be called in by them. The judge refusing to join the clerk in the canvass, the latter summoned a justice and with him made the canvass, which all admitted to be a true one. The same night the judge called in the sheriff and another justice, and together they surreptitiously entered the clerk's office, lit it up, and took out the returns from a drawer in his desk. There were only four precincts in the county, and of the four returns from these, confessedly without the slightest evidence of fraud or intimidation, they threw out two. The other two they certified.

RUTHERFORD B. HAYES

The Republican counsel maintained that the issue was not which set of Florida electors received an actual majority, but which had received the legal sanction of State authority; in short, that the business of the Commission was not to go behind the returns, which, they argued, would be physically, legally and constitutionally impossible. This view the Commission espoused, which sufficed to decide not only the case of Florida, but also that of Louisiana, whence came three sets of certificates, and that of South Carolina, whence came two. The first and third Louisiana returns were duplicates, signed by Governor Kellogg, in favor of the Hayes electors. The second was certified by McEnery, who claimed to be Governor, and was based not upon the return as made by the board, but upon the popular vote. The return of the Tilden electors in South Carolina was not certified. They alleged that they had been counted out by the State

Board in defiance of the State Supreme Court and of the popular will.

In Oregon the Democratic Governor declared one of the Hayes electors ineligible because an office-holder, giving a certificate to Cronin, the highest Tilden elector, instead. The other two Hayes electors refused to recognize Cronin, and, associating with them the rejected Republican elector, presented a certificate signed by the Secretary of State. Cronin, as the Republican papers had it, "flocked all by himself," appointed two new electors to act with him, and cast his vote for Tilden, though his associates voted for Hayes. The Cronin certificate was signed by the Governor and attested by the Secretary of State.

After deciding not to go behind any returns that were formally lawful the Commission, by a strict party vote of eight to seven, decided for the Hayes electors in every case. Whether the result would have been different if Justice Davis had been the fifth justice in the Commission is a question that must always remain open. By no utterance of Mr. Davis was there ever an indication of what his action would have been, but he had a high opinion of Mr. Tilden, and his political sympathies were known by his intimate friends to have been on the side of the Democrats. The Commission adjourned March 2d. The same day, "the counting of the votes having been concluded, Senator William B. Allison, one of the tellers on the part of the Senate, in the presence of both Houses of Congress, announced, as a result of the footings, that Rutherford B. Hayes had received 185 votes for President, and William A. Wheeler 185 votes for Vice-President; and thereupon the presiding officer of the Convention of the two Houses declared Rutherford B. Hayes to have been elected President, and William A. Wheeler Vice-President of the United States for four years from the 4th day of March, 1877." Hayes was inaugurated without disturbance.

For this outcome, owing to the determining position

AN ELECTORAL COUNT ACT

which he held on the Commission, Mr. Justice Bradley was made to bear wholly unmerited censure. The fault lay not in him but elsewhere. Vicious State laws were to blame for giving judicial powers to partisan returning boards, and for otherwise opening the door to confusion and fraud; but Congress was the worst sinner, failing to pass a law to forestall the difficulty of rival certificates.

The Commission having decided, the whole country heaved a sigh of relief; but all agreed that provision must be made against such peril in the future. An Electoral Count Bill was passed late in 1886, and signed by the President, February 3, 1887. It aimed to throw upon each State, so far as possible, the responsibility of determining its own vote. The President of the Senate opens the electoral certificates in the presence of both houses, and hands them to tellers, two from each House, who read them aloud and record the votes. If there is no dispute touching the list of electors from a State, such list, being certified in due form, is accepted as a matter of course. In case of dispute, the procedure is somewhat complex, but quite thorough. It will be set forth with some detail in Chapter XIII.

CHAPTER IX

HAYES AND THE CIVIL SERVICE

HAYES'S CHARACTER. — HIS CABINET. — END OF BAYONET RULE AT THE SOUTH. — THIS THE RESULT OF A "DEAL." — "VISITING STATESMEN" AT THE LOUISIANA COUNT. — HAYES FAVORS HONESTY. — HIS RECORD. — HAYES AND GARFIELD COMPARED. — THE SPOILS SYSTEM. — EARLY PROTESTS. — A CIVIL SERVICE COMMISSION. — ITS RULES. — RETROGRESSION UNDER GRANT. — JEWELL'S EXIT FROM THE CABINET. — HOAR'S. — BUTLER'S "PULL" ON GRANT. — COLLECTOR SIMMONS. — THE SANBORN CONTRACTS. — BRISTOW A REFORMER. — THE WHISKEY RING. — MYRON COLONY'S WORK — PLOT AND COUNTER-PLOT. — "LET NO GUILTY MAN ESCAPE." — REFORMERS OUSTED. — GOOD WORK BY THE PRESS. — THE "PRESS-GAG." — FIRST DEMOCRATIC HOUSE SINCE THE WAR. — HAYES RENEWS REFORM. — OPPOSED BY CONKLING. — FIGHT OVER THE NEW YORK COLLECTORSHIP. — THE PRESIDENT FIRM AND VICTORIOUS.

PARTLY the mode of his accession to office and partly the rage of selfish placemen who could no longer have their way, made it fashionable for a time to speak of President Hayes as a "weak man." This was an entire error. His administration was in every way one of the most creditable in all our history. He had a resolute will, irreproachable integrity, and a comprehensive and remarkably healthy view of public affairs. Moreover, he was free from that "last infirmity," the consuming ambition which has snared so many able statesmen. He voluntarily banished the alluring prospect of a second term, and rose above all jealousy of his distinguished associates. Never have our foreign affairs been more ably handled than by his State Secretary. His Secretary of the Treasury triumphantly steered our bark into the safe harbor of resumption, breakers roaring this side and that, near at hand. In his appointments as well as his other official duties Hayes acted for himself, with becoming independence even of his Cabinet. On

THE LAST QUARTER-CENTURY

one occasion, as he was announcing certain appointments connected with the State Department, Secretary Evarts looked up in surprise, evidently hearing the names for the first time. " Mr. President," said he, with veiled irony, " I have never had the good fortune to see the 'great western reserve' of Ohio, of which we have heard so much." That Hayes was such men's real and not their mere nominal chief, in naught dims their fame, though heightening his.

True to his avowed principles, President Hayes had made up his Cabinet of the ablest men, disregarding party so far as to select for Postmaster-General a Democrat, David M. Key, of Tennessee. William M. Evarts was Secretary of State; John Sherman, Secretary of the Treasury; Carl Schurz, Secretary of the Interior. The first important act of his administration was to invite the rival Governors of South Carolina, Hampton and Chamberlain, to a conference at Washington. It will be remembered that when Chamberlain became Governor his integrity awakened the hate of his old supporters, while his former antagonists smothered him with embraces. The hate was more enduring than the love. Good government was restored, but this was purely an executive reform, which the vulgar majority ridiculed as a weakness. Race antipathy still rankled, for Governor Chamberlain would not yield an inch as a defender of the negro's political and civil rights. The Democratic successes of 1874 in the country at large inspired the South Carolina Democrats with the wildest zeal. Wade Hampton, "the Murat of the Confederacy," dashing, fervid, eloquent, the Confederate veterans' idol, was nominated for Governor. The party which elected Chamberlain was forced to re-nominate him. The pressure of

WADE HAMPTON

official patronage was used to this end, and it was known that he alone among Republicans could preserve the State from a reign of terror.

The whites rallied to Hampton with delirious enthusiasm. "South Carolina for South Carolinians!" was their cry. White rifle clubs were organized in many localities, but the Governor disbanded them as unsafe and called in United States troops to preserve order. In the white counties the negroes were cowed, but elsewhere they displayed fanatical activity. If the white could shoot, the black could set fire to property. Thus crime and race hostility increased once more to an appalling extent. The Hamburg massacre, where helpless negro prisoners were murdered, was offset by the Charleston riot, where black savages shot or beat every white man who appeared on the streets. The course of events in Louisiana had been similar, though marked by less violence. Nichols was the Democratic aspirant, and S. B. Packard the Republican. Both were in earnest, and, if federal forces were to be kept in use as a Southern police, the conflict bade fair to last forever. But this was not to be. Even President Grant had now changed his view of the Southern situation, stating frankly "that he did not believe public opinion would longer support the maintenance of State governments in Louisiana by the use of the military, and that he must concur in this manifest feeling."

President Hayes withdrew federal support from the South Carolina and Louisiana governments, and they at once fell. Many Republicans fiercely criticised this policy. Some said that by failing to support the governments based upon the canvass of the very returning boards that gave him the electoral delegations in the two States named, he impeached his own title. This was untrue. With regard to State officers, the judicial powers of the returning boards were clearly usurpations, contrary to the State constitutions, while, as to federal officers, such as electors, the power of the boards to

THE LAST QUARTER-CENTURY

FRANCIS T. NICHOLS

modify or reject returns was independent of the State constitutions, yet not forbidden by any federal law. .

As the old *Cincinnati Commercial* once expressed it, Hayes was "good, but not goody-good." He was no mere idealist, no doctrinaire, but a practical though honorable man of affairs. The new "deal" in the South was probably due to an understanding arrived at before the electoral count, and shared by the President-elect, though F. H. Wines and others among Hayes's warmest friends denied that he was privy to it. In the Charleston *News and Courier* under date of June 20, 1893, Hon. D. H. Chamberlain showed that, while the proceeding was not necessarily corrupt, and was probably the part of good politics and even of statesmanship, Hayes was certainly party to a "bargain," agreeing to remove troops from South Carolina in case he was permitted to be seated. Chamberlain said: "While Hayes did not expressly promise to remove the troops, he did by speech or by failing to speak give sufficient assurance to the 'shrewd, long-headed men' with whom he was dealing to warrant them in supporting his claim to the Presidency on so tremendous an issue to the South." "Hayes's friends assembled, met the 'shrewd, long-headed men' of the South, negotiated, winked and nodded, and finally gave the express promise which the South demanded. Hayes knew it all. He did not contradict his friends. He accepted his seat, secured to him by the attitude of the South. He removed the troops. Here was a bargain in all its elements."

Unless this understanding may be considered such, Mr. Hayes had no part in any of the devices by which he was placed in the presidential chair. When Senator Edmunds introduced the Electoral Commission Bill, Hayes viewed it with no favor. He did not regard the Commission as constitutional, but considered the duty of Congress in reference to counting the electoral ballots to be purely ministerial. The same as to post-election proceedings in the South. The prominent Republicans who visited New Orleans to witness the canvass of the Louisiana presidential vote did so solely at the instance of President Grant. From Ohio went John Sherman, Stanley Matthews, J. A. Garfield and Job E. Stevenson. From Iowa went J. M. Tuttle, J. W. Chapman, W. R. Smith and W. A. McGrew; from Illinois, C. B. Farwell, Abner Taylor, S. R. Haven and J. M. Beardsley; from New York, E. W. Stoughton and J. H. Van Alen; from Indiana, John Coburn and Will Cumback; from Pennsylvania, William D. Kelley; from Kansas, Sidney Clarke; from Maryland, C. Irving Ditty; from Maine, Eugene Hale.

Not only had Governor Hayes nothing to do with the origination of this ambassage, but when it was in function he urged that it should be guilty of no abuse. From Columbus, O., November 27, 1876, he wrote: "A fair election would have given us about forty electoral votes at the South—at least that many. But we are not to allow our friends to defeat one outrage and fraud by another. There must be nothing crooked on our part. Let Mr. Tilden have the place by violence, intimidation and fraud, rather than undertake to prevent it by means that will not bear the severest scrutiny." Even had Mr. Hayes wished fraud it is hard to see how, under the circumstances, he could have procured or induced such; for watchers for the Democratic party were also at the count: from Indiana, J. E. McDonald, George W. Julian, M. D. Manson and John Love; from Illinois, John M. Palmer, Lyman Trumbull and William R. Morrison; from Pennsylvania, Samuel J. Randall, A. G. Curtin and William Bigler; from Kentucky, Henry Watterson, J. W. Stevenson and Henry D. McHenry;

S. B. PACKARD
From a photograph by Vandyke, lent by Charles W. Boothby.

THE LAST QUARTER-CENTURY

from Wisconsin, J. R. Doolittle and George B. Smith; from Ohio, J. B. Stallo and P. H. Watson; from New York, Oswald Ottendorfer and F. R. Coudert; from Missouri, Louis V. Bogy, James O. Brodhead and C. Gibson; from Maryland, John Lee Carroll and William T. Hamilton; from Connecticut, Professor W. G. Sumner. Upon invitation of the Returning Board, five of the Democratic "visitors," as well as a like number of the Republicans, attended the several sessions of the Board to watch. The proceedings were thrice reported, once for the Board itself and once for each body of the Northern guests. The evidence taken and the acts performed were published by Congress. Senator Sherman felt "bound, after a long lapse of time, to repeat what was reported to General Grant by the Republican visitors, that the Returning Board in Louisiana made a fair, honest and impartial return of the result of the election." Sherman wrote Hayes at the time: "That you would have received, at a fair election, a large majority in Louisiana, no honest man can question; that you did not receive a majority is equally clear."* Some pretended to think that if Hayes had the slightest doubt touching the legitimacy of any proceedings resorted to for the purpose of seating him he ought not to have accepted the presidency. Such failed to bear in mind that the country was then at a crisis, and that Mr. Hayes's refusal of the presidency would in all probability have resulted in anarchy and war. His acceptance, under the circumstances, was therefore clearly his duty, whatever he thought of antecedent procedure.

Mr. Sherman believed "that the nomination of Hayes was not only the safest, but the strongest that could be made. The long possession of power by the Republicans naturally produced rivalries that greatly affected the election of any one who had been constantly prominent in public life, like Blaine, Conkling and Morton. Hayes had growing qualities, and in every respect was worthy of the high position of President. He

*John Sherman's Recollections, p. 557.

HAYES'S RECORD

An Incident of the State Election of 1876 in South Carolina, when both Hampton and Chamberlain claimed to have been elected Governor.

had been a soldier, a member of Congress, thrice elected as Governor of Ohio, an admirable executive officer, and his public and private record was beyond question. He was not an aggressive man, although firm in his opinions and faithful in his friendships. Among all the public men with whom I have been brought in contact, I have known none who was freer from personal objection, whose character was more stainless, who was better adapted for a high executive office."

" There was a striking contrast between the personal qualities of Garfield and Hayes. Hayes was a modest man, but a very able one. He had none of the brilliant qualities of his successor, but his judgment was always sound, and his opinion, when once formed, was stable and consistent. . . During his entire term, our official and personal relations were not only cordial, but as close and intimate as those of brothers could be. I never took an important step in the process of resumption and refunding . . without consulting him. . . Early in his administration we formed the habit of taking long drives on each Sunday afternoon in the environs of Washington. He was a regular attendant with Mrs. Hayes, every Sunday morning, at the Methodist Episcopal Church, of which she was a member. This duty being done, we felt justified in seeking the seclusion of the country for long talks about current measures and policy."*

Mr. Hayes came to the presidency at a very critical time. The financial situation of the country, the still unsettled state of affairs at the South, faction, rebellion, and greed for official spoils within his own party, called upon the new Chief Magistrate for skill and resolution such as few men in his place could have supplied. Mr. Hayes responded nobly and successfully. He triumphed in a task which ablest and purest political leaders have always found so hard: he repressed corruption in his own party. Under President Hayes the systematic prostitution of our public offices for partisan and private purposes was, if not definitively ended, so discouraged that it has never since recovered its old shamelessness. In this those years form an epoch in the Nation's history.

Ever since the days of President Jackson, in 1829, appointments to the minor federal offices had been used for the payment of party debts and to keep up partisan interest. Though this practice had incurred the deep condemnation of Webster, Clay, Calhoun, and all the best men in public life, it did not cease, but prevailed more and more. So early as 1853 pass examinations had been made prerequisite to entering the civil service, but the regulation had amounted to

*John Sherman's Recollections, pp. 550, 551, 807.

CIVIL SERVICE REFORM

nothing. President Lincoln once inquired where he could get the small-pox. "For," said he, "then I should have something I could give to everybody." The honor of being the first to make a systematic endeavor against the spoils abuse belongs to the Hon. Thomas A. Jenckes, a representative in Congress from Rhode Island between March, 1863, and March, 1871. Beginning in 1865, Mr. Jenckes, so long as he continued in Congress, annually introduced in the House a bill "to regulate the civil service of the United States." Early in 1866 Senator B. Gratz Brown, of Missouri, also undertook to get the "spoils system" superseded by the "merit system." No success attended these efforts.

In 1870–1871 reform in the civil service almost became an issue. It was one of the three cardinal principles of the Liberal Republicans, was an item in the "New Departure" made by the Democrats that year, received compliments, more or less sincere, from politicians of all stripes, and in 1872 was recognized for the first time in all the party platforms. On March 3, 1871, an act was passed authorizing the President, through a commission to be appointed by himself, to ascertain "the fitness of candidates as to age, health, character, knowledge and ability, by examination," and to prescribe regulations for the conduct of appointees. The President that year appointed a commission, George William Curtis its chairman. On December 19th he sent a message to Congress, transmitting the report of the commissioners, together with the rules submitted by them in relation to the appointment, promotion and conduct of persons filling the offices covered by the law.

These rules provided that each applicant should furnish evidence as to his character, health and age, and should pass a satisfactory examination in speaking, reading and writing the English language. Positions were to be grouped and graded according to the nature of the work, admission to the civil service always introducing the candidate to the lowest group.

Public competitive examinations were to be instituted, and a list of examinees made up and kept on record, with the order of their excellence. Each appointment was to be made from the three leading eligibles. Admission to a group above the lowest could be had only by one of three candidates from the next lower grade who stood highest in a competitive examination. An applicant for a place of trust where another officer was responsible for his fidelity could not be appointed without the approval of such officer; and postmasterships yielding less than two hundred dollars a year were not placed under the rule. With some exceptions, notably of postmasters and consuls, appointments were to be probationary for a term of six months. Best of all the regulations presented was the following: "No head of a department or any subordinate officer of the Government shall, as such officer, authorize or assist in levying any assessment of money for political purposes, under the form of voluntary contributions or otherwise, upon any person employed under his control, nor shall any such person pay any money so assessed." Higher officials and some others were, however, excepted from the operation of this rule.

President Grant reported that the new methods "had given persons of superior capacity to the service"; yet Congress, always niggardly in its appropriations for the Commission's work, in 1875 made no appropriation at all, so that the rules were perforce suspended. Ardor for spoils was not the sole cause of this. Many friends of reform thought the new system, as it had been begun, too stiff and bookish, too little practical; nor could such a view be declared wholly mistaken. Intelligent labor-leaders, it was found, usually opposed the reform in that shape, as it would exclude themselves and all but the most favored of their children from public office.

Unfortunately, the President cared as little as Congress for a pure civil service. This was everywhere apparent. It cannot be ignored that Grant's second administration was

William M. Evarts, State   *Carl Schurz, Interior*   *Richard W. Thompson, Navy*

David M. Key, Post.-Gen.   *George W. McCrary, War*   *John Sherman, Treasury*   *Charles Devens, Attorney-Gen.*

PRESIDENT HAYES'S CABINET

GRANT'S SECOND TERM

shamefully weak and corrupt. "The very obstinacy of temper which made him so formidable in the field, now, when combined with the self-confidence bred by his re-election and the flattery of his adherents, not only made him impervious to public opinion but made all criticism of him seem an act of insolent hostility, to be punished or defied." Charles Francis Adams quoted it as the opinion of a Republican, he thought Evarts, during Grant's second four years, that "the Republican party was like an army the term of enlistment of which had expired." It was a happy simile. Straggling was common, complaints were numerous, and mutiny had begun. Summary, worse than military methods of appointment and dismissal were employed.

BENJAMIN F. BUTLER

In respect to the manner of Jewell's resignation, the story went—believed to be on the authority of Vice-President Wilson—that Grant and Jewell were alone together, talking over matters, when, without any previous suggestion of the subject, the President said: "Jewell, how do you suppose your resignation would look written out?" Thinking or affecting to think the question a joke of Grant's, Jewell said he would write it and see. "All right," said Grant, "you just take some paper and write it down and see how it looks." Jewell wrote and handed the paper to Grant. The President eyed it a moment and then remarked: "That looks well. I will accept that." He was in earnest, and on July 11, 1876, Jewell was out of the Cabinet. Verisimilitude is lent this account by the known abruptness with which Judge Hoar was ejected from the office of Attorney-General. He was sitting in his room, bent upon the business of his office, absolutely without a hint of what was coming, when a messenger entered with a letter from Grant. It contained the naked statement that the President found himself under the necessity of asking for Mr. Hoar's resignation. "No explanation of any kind was given, nor reason assigned. The request was as curt and as direct as possible. A thunderclap could not have been more startling."

Benjamin F. Butler obtained great power with Grant, which immensely aided him in "capturing" the Massachusetts governorship. Patronage was liberally accorded him. "In every town and village a circle was formed round the postmaster, the collector, or some other government officer, who was moved by the hope of personal gain. Not a man who wished for place or had a job on hand but added to their numbers." Foiled at two elections, Butler was not in the least daunted, but spurred to renewed exertion, sure that the powers at Washington would deny him nothing. At last "Mr. Simmons, who, in a subordinate position, had particularly distinguished himself in the management of the last canvass, was promoted by the President to the Collectorship of Boston, in the hope that the most important national office in New England might offer a fitting sphere of action for his peculiar abilities." Even a Republican Convention had rebuked this man for his unendurable officiousness as a political boss. *Harper's Weekly* for March 21, 1874, said: "No recent political event is comparable in the excitement it has caused to the appointment of the Boston Collector. The situation every day forces upon the most unwavering Republicans the question, When will it be necessary for our honor as men and patriots to oppose the party?"

In 1874 public wrath was aroused by the exposure of the "Sanborn Contracts," made in 1872, between the Hon. William A. Richardson, then Acting Secretary of the Treasury, subsequently promoted to Mr. Boutwell's seat in the Cabinet, and Mr. John D. Sanborn, giving Sanborn the right to collect

BRISTOW IN THE TREASURY

for the Treasury, "share and share alike," taxes which were already collected by regular officers of the Government. Such officers were not only directed not to interfere with Mr. Sanborn, but bidden to co-operate with him. By March, 1874, less than two years, this profitable arrangement had paid Sanborn over $200,000. Morally indefensible as it was, it seems to have been legal. The House Committee of Ways and Means examined into the case. Unable, on the evidence adduced, exactly to fix the responsibility of making the contracts, the committee could not "in justice to itself ignore the fact" that three persons, Richardson, Secretary of the Treasury, the Assistant Secretary, and the Solicitor of the Treasury, "deserved severe condemnation for the manner in which they permitted this law to be administered." The committee, however, found no fact on which to base a belief that any of these officers had acted from wrong motives. It recommended repealing the law and the annulment of all contracts made under it. Mr. Richardson's resignation was soon after reluctantly accepted by the President, and his nomination to the Court of Claims confirmed with equal reluctance by the Senate. Hon. B. H. Bristow, of Kentucky, succeeded him in the Treasury.

The new Secretary at once bent his attention to reorganizing and improving the customs and internal revenue service. His fearless removals and searching investigations soon stirred the venomous hostility of various corrupt cliques which had been basking on the sunny side of the Treasury. There were the instigators of the Safe-Burglary frauds, of the Seal-Lock frauds, and of the Subsidy frauds, besides jealous, chagrined and corrupt officials; but most formidable of all, and in a sense, at the head of all, was the Whiskey Ring. It was patent from statistics that the United States had, by 1874, in St. Louis alone, lost at least $1,200,000 of the revenue which it should have received from whiskey, yet special agents of the Treasury set to work from time to time had failed to do more than cause an occasional flurry among the thieves. The

THE LAST QUARTER-CENTURY

ORVILLE E. BABCOCK

guilty parties were somehow always effectively forewarned and forearmed against any effort to punish or identify them. The Ring seemed to have eyes, ears and hands in every room of the Internal Revenue Department, in the Secretary's office, and even in the Executive Mansion.

The Whiskey Ring was organized in St. Louis, when the Liberal Republicans there achieved their first success. It occurred to certain politicians to have the revenue officers raise a campaign fund among the distillers. This idea the officers modified later, raising money in the same way for themselves, and in return conniving at the grossest thievery. As it became necessary to hide the frauds, newspapers and higher officials were hushed, till the Ring assumed national dimensions. Its headquarters were at St. Louis, but it had branches at Milwaukee, Chicago, Peoria, Cincinnati, and New Orleans. It had an agent at Washington. A huge corruption fund was distributed among gaugers, storekeepers, collectors, and other officials, according to a fixed schedule of prices. Subordinate officers were not merely tempted to become parties, but were even obliged to do so on penalty of losing their places. Honest distillers and rectifiers were hounded with false accusations and caught in technical frauds, till their choice seemed to lie between ruin and alliance with the Ring. One or two inquirers peculiarly persistent were assaulted and left for dead. They besought the Government for speedy relief, threatening, unless it was granted them, to expose the corrupt intimacy between the Internal Revenue Bureau and the Ring. So potent had the organization grown that the politicians persuaded Grant, "for the party's sake," to countermand, though he had at first approved, Bristow's order directing a general transfer of supervisors, as such transfer would have thrown the thieves' machine out of adjustment.

At length, upon the recommendation of Mr. George Fishback, editor of the St. Louis *Democrat*, the reform Secretary appointed Mr. Myron Colony, of St. Louis, a special agent to unearth the frauds, with the co-operation of Bluford Wilson, the Solicitor of the Treasury. One of the conditions upon which Mr. Colony accepted his grave and difficult charge was that of perfect secrecy. The first plan was to ascertain by means of detectives the amount of grain carted into the distilleries, with the amount of whiskey shipped to rectifying-houses or elsewhere, and to establish the fact of illegal nocturnal distillation—for the law allowed but one distillation every seventy-two hours. This effort the guilty parties discovered and opposed, midnight combats taking place between the burly detectives and ruffians hired to fight them. That line of attack was finally abandoned, but not till valuable evidence had been secured.

The next move was as follows: Under pretext of gathering commercial statistics, a work which, as financial editor of the *Democrat* and as Secretary of the St. Louis Board of Trade, Mr. Colony had often done, and could, of course, do without suspicion, he obtained, at landings and freight depots, copies of bills of lading that showed all the shipments of staple articles, including whiskey, to or from St. Louis, Chicago, and Milwaukee. The record gave the names of the shippers and the consignees, the number of gallons and the serial number—never duplicated—of the revenue stamps on each and every package. The discrepancies between these way-bills and the official records furnished to the Internal Revenue Office showed conclusively the extent of the frauds and the identity of the culprits. From July 1, 1874, to May 1, 1875, no less than $1,650,000 had been diverted from the government till.

The illicit distillers lay quite still while the toils were woven around them. They were aware of the Secretary's enmity and cordially reciprocated it, but their suspicions had been lulled by his first retreat. Moreover, they felt that news of any proposed investigation would be sure to reach them from their official correspondents. They were not prepared for an investigation conducted in the main by private citizens, and kept secret from the Department, which was in more intimate alliance with them than with its own chief or with the people whom he was serving. When little remained but to unmask the batteries, a vague sense of uneasiness began to express itself in Congressional and other queries at the Internal Revenue Office—which was as blissfully ignorant as the Ring itself—and later at the White House, where it was learned that investigation was indeed on foot. The investigators, too, were startled, after they had fixed Monday, May 10th, as the date for the *coup*, by learning of a telegram to St. Louis running, " Lightning will strike Monday ! Warn your friends in the country ! " It turned out that this telegram was from a gentleman who had been informed of the purpose to strike on that day, and had communicated it to a distilling firm in St. Louis hostile to the Ring.

Its torpid writhings availed the monster naught. Equally vain the pious preparations at once made against a mere raid. The traps set with secrecy and patience were sprung simultaneously in St. Louis, Chicago and Milwaukee. Records seized justified numerous arrests in nearly every leading city. Indictments were found against one hundred and fifty-two liquor men and other private parties, and against eighty-six Government officials, among them the chief clerk in the Treasury Department, and President Grant's Private Secretary, General O. E. Babcock. On the back of a letter from St. Louis, making a charge or suggestion against Babcock, Grant had indorsed, " Let no guilty man escape." Five or six times in the progress of the case he said: " If Babcock is guilty there is no man who wants him proven guilty as I do, for it is the greatest piece of traitorism to me that a man could possibly practise."

THE REFORMERS OUT

Still, Babcock's prosecutors complained that efforts were made to transfer the case to a military court, to deprive them of papers incriminating the Private Secretary, and to prevent important testimony being given by informers on promise of immunity. All the prominent defendants were convicted save Babcock, but three of them were pardoned six months later. After his acquittal Babcock was dismissed by the President.

In the spring of 1876 the dauntless Secretary Bristow assaulted the California Whiskey Ring, but here at last he was foiled. When the temperature rose to an uncomfortable degree a Senator demanded, and in spite of the Secretary secured, the removal of the more active government prosecutors in that section. The retirement of Secretary Bristow followed soon after. With him went Solicitor Wilson, Commissioner Pratt, Mr. Yaryan, chief of revenue agents, and District-Attorney Dyer. The Treasurer and the First and Fifth Auditors of the Treasury also resigned. The whole course of proceedings was embarrassed by misunderstandings with the President, who was misled into the belief that his own ruin and that of his family was sought by the investigators, especially by Bristow, who, it was whispered, had designs upon the Presidency. The President broke from these maligners more than once, but there was enough in the press, in the popular applause with which the prosecution was hailed, and in the conduct of the trials, to renew his suspicions, to hinder the prosecution of the St. Louis Ring, and finally to unseat the anti-machine Secretary himself. This officer's retirement occurred not quite a month before that of Postmaster-General Jewell.

A. B. CORNELL

Great credit was due to the press for its assistance in discovering and

THE LAST QUARTER-CENTURY

exposing the whiskey frauds. Notwithstanding exaggerations and errors here and there, laying faults at wrong doors, its work was praiseworthy in the extreme. As the New York *Times* had exposed the "Tweed Ring," so to the St. Louis newspaper men was due, in large part, the glory of bringing to light the whiskey iniquity. As in so many other instances, the press proved the terror of unclean politicians and the reliance of the people. In those times and in the course of such complicated investigations, it was inevitable that libels should occur and do harm. Naturally, and perhaps justifiably, Congress undertook to remedy this ill by amending the law of libel. The debate over the measure was in great part composed of philippics against "the licentious newspaper." The licentious newspaper retorted in the teeth of the law, which was christened the " Press-Gag Law." The enactment, too much resembling the old "Sedition Law," was universally unpopular, contributing not a little to the Democratic victories of 1874. Judge Poland, of Vermont, the chief sponsor for it, was defeated in this election. As a further consequence of it, in the Forty-fourth Congress, first session, meeting in 1875, the National House of Representatives, for the first time since the Civil War, had a Democratic majority. It was seventy strong, and elected Hon. Michael C. Kerr Speaker.

These paragraphs perhaps afford the reader sufficient insight into the condition of Republican politics when Mr. Hayes became President; they indicate the strength of the evil tide which he so resolutely set himself to turn. Even from a party point of view the plunder system of party politics had failed to justify itself. Yet, while his efforts for reform were endorsed by thousands of the rank and file Hayes found himself strenuously opposed by a large and powerful Republican faction. As the head and front of this, championing all that Grant had stood for, his sins of omission and his sins of commission alike, towered Senator Roscoe Conkling, of New

HAYES AND THE NEW YORK CUSTOM-HOUSE

THEODORE ROOSEVELT

York, one of the most formidable personal leaders in the grand old party Though knowing of this gentleman's sure and potent antagonism, the President did not hesitate, but early and firmly took the bull by the horns.

He touched the danger-line in removing Chester A. Arthur from the office of Collector of the Port of New York, A. B. Cornell from that of Naval Officer, and George H. Sharpe from that of Surveyor. Over two-thirds of the nation's customs revenue was received at that port, and its administration could not but be important. Numerous complaints having been made concerning affairs and methods at the port, a Commission was appointed in April, 1877, to make an examination. Its first report, dwelling on the evils of appointments for political reasons without due regard to efficiency, was rendered May 24th, and it recommended considerably sweeping changes. President Hayes concurred in these recommendations. He wrote Secretary Sherman: " It is my wish that the collection of the revenues should be free from partisan control, and organized on a strictly business basis, with the same guarantees for efficiency and fidelity in the selection of the chief and subordinate officers that would be required by a prudent merchant. Party leaders should have no more influence in appointments than other equally respectable citizens. No assessments for political purposes on officers or subordinates should be allowed. No useless officer or employé should be retained. No officer should be required or permitted to take part in the management of political organizations, caucuses, conventions, or election campaigns. Their right to vote, and to express their views on public questions, either orally or through the press, is not denied, provided it does not interfere with the discharge of their official duties."

THE LAST QUARTER-CENTURY

Five more reports were made, exhibiting in all their gravity the evils then prevalent in the business of the port. Twenty per cent. of the persons employed needed to be dropped. Ignorance, inefficiency, neglect of duty, dishonesty, inebriety, bribery, and various other forms of improper conduct were all common. At first there was no thought of removing Arthur or Cornell, but they were seen to be so bound up with the unbusiness-like system that they must fall with it. The Commissioners "found that for many years past the view had obtained with some political leaders that the friends of the Administration in power had a right to control the customs appointments; and this view, which seemed to have been acquiesced in by successive administrations, had of late been recognized to what the commission deemed an undue extent by the chief officer of the service. These gentlemen, on the ground that they were compelled to surrender to personal and partisan dictation, appeared to have assumed that they were relieved, in part at least, from the responsibilities that belonged to the appointing power." The Administration became convinced "that new officers would be more likely to make the radical reforms required," that in order to accomplish any thorough reform of the Government's business methods at the New York port, the Collector, the Naval Officer and the Surveyor must either resign or be removed. On September 6, 1877, Secretary Sherman wrote his Assistant Secretary:

"After a very full consideration and a very kindly one, the President, with the cordial assent of his Cabinet, came to the conclusion that the public interests demanded a change in the three leading offices in New York, and a public announcement of that character was authorized. I am quite sure that this will, on the whole, be considered to be a wise result. The manner of making the changes and the persons to be appointed will be a subject of careful and full consideration, but it is better to know that it is determined upon and ended. This made it unnecessary to consider the telegrams in regard

ARTHUR, CORNELL, AND SHARPE REMOVED

to Mr. Cornell. It is probable that no special point would have been made upon his holding his position as Chairman of the State Committee for a limited time, but even that was not the thing, the real question being that, whether he resigned or not, it was better that he and Arthur and Sharpe should all give way to new men, to try definitely a new policy in the conduct of the New York Custom-house. I have no doubt, unless these gentlemen should make it impossible by their conduct hereafter, that they will be treated with the utmost consideration, and, for one, I have no hesitation in saying that I hope General Arthur will be recognized in a most complimentary way."

JUSTIN S. MORRILL
of Vermont

A great fight was now on. Arthur was offered the eligible post of Consul-General at Paris, thought likely to be highly agreeable to him, but he declined it. None of the officials would resign. On the contrary, pushed by Senator Conkling, all three preferred to make an issue against the proposed reform. On October 24, 1877, the President nominated for Collector Theodore Roosevelt, for Surveyor Edward A. Merritt, and for Naval Officer L. B. Prince. Five days later the Senate rejected them. Conkling was in high feather. On December 6th, during the following session, the three were again nominated, but only the last, ten days later, confirmed. "No doubt," said Sherman, "the Democratic majority in the Senate might defend themselves with political reasons, but the motive of Mr. Conkling was hostility to President Hayes and his inborn desire to domineer." After the session closed, in 1878, the President temporarily placed Edwin A. Merritt in the office of Collector, and Silas W. Burt in that of Naval Officer. With the opening of the next

Senate it became necessary to submit the nominations to that body for confirmation. The Secretary of the Treasury, so interested in the case that he had determined to resign should the Senate reject again, wrote Senator Allison:

"I would not bother you with this personal matter, but that I feel the deepest interest in the confirmation of General Merritt, which I know will be beneficial to us as a party, and still more so to the public service. Personally I have the deepest interest in it because I have been unjustly assailed in regard to it in the most offensive manner. I feel free to appeal to you and Windom, representing as you do Western States, and being old friends and acquaintances, to take into consideration this personal aspect of the case. If the restoration of Arthur is insisted upon, the whole liberal element will be against us and it will lose us tens of thousands of votes without doing a particle of good. No man could be a more earnest Republican than I, and I feel this political loss as much as anyone can. It will be a personal reproach to me, and merely to gratify the insane hate of Conkling, who in this respect disregards the express wishes of the Republican members from New York, of the great body of Republicans, and as I personally know, runs in antagonism to his nearest and best friends in the Senate."

To Senator Justin S. Morrill Sherman wrote a much longer letter, giving reasons in detail in favor of confirming the new men, and containing specific charges of neglect of duty on the part of Arthur and Cornell. After seven hours of struggle in the Senate Conkling was decisively defeated, Merritt being confirmed 33 to 24, and Burt 31 to 19. Four-fifths of the Democrats and two-fifths of the Republicans voted for confirmation.

While temper over this controversy was at its hottest George William Curtis supported in the New York State Republican Convention a resolution commending Hayes's Administration, and especially his course with regard to the civil service. This aroused Conkling to make a fierce personal attack upon Curtis. Curtis wrote: " It was the saddest sight I ever knew, that man glaring at me in a fury of hate and storming out his foolish blackguardism. It was all pity. I had not thought him great, but I had not suspected how small he was. His friends, the best, were confounded. One of them said to me next day, ' It was not amazement that I felt, but consternation.' Conkling's speech was carefully written out, and therefore you do not get all the venom, and no one can imagine the Mephistophelian leer and spite."

After all, strange as it may seem, Hayes's bold independence did not seriously divide his party. Few stalwarts dared call him a traitor. Democratic opposition fortified him against this. The House, Democratic throughout his term, fought nearly all his wishes, as did the Senate, now also Democratic, during his last two years. To balk him, appropriation bills were laden with riders involving legislation which he could not approve, but he firmly applied the veto. The futile attempt to "right" the alleged "fraud of 1877" by ripping up the Electoral Commission's work, kept Hayes before the country as the Republicans' man, incidentally doing much to advertise his sterling character. Refreshing decency marked all of Mr. Hayes's public doings. The men placed in office by him were as a rule the best available, chosen with the least possible regard to political influence, and, like all others in the civil service, they were required to abstain from active participation in political affairs. This policy enraged politicians, but, by immensely relieving the party from the odium into which it had fallen, aided to put it in condition for the campaign of 1880.

CHAPTER X

"THE UNITED STATES WILL PAY"

BACK TO HARD MONEY.—ACT TO STRENGTHEN THE PUBLIC CREDIT.
—DIFFICULTY OF CONTRACTION.—IGNORANCE OF FINANCE.—DEBTORS PINCHED.—THE PANIC OF 1873.—CAUSES.—FAILURE OF JAY COOKE & CO., AND OF FISKE & HATCH.—BLACK FRIDAY NO. 2.—ON CHANGE AND ON THE STREET.—BULLS, BEARS AND BANKS.—CRITICISM OF SECRETARY RICHARDSON.—FIRST USE OF CLEARING-HOUSE CERTIFICATES.—EFFECTS AND DURATION OF THE PANIC.—AN IMPORTANT GOOD RESULT.—RESUMPTION AND POLITICS.—THE RESUMPTION ACT.—SHERMAN'S QUALIFICATIONS FOR EXECUTING IT.—HIS FIRMNESS.—RESUMPTION ACTUALLY BEGUN.—MAGNITUDE AND MEANING OF THIS POLICY.—OUR BONDED DEBT RAPIDLY REDUCED.
—LEGAL TENDER QUESTIONS AND DECISIONS.—JUILLIARD VS. GREENMAN.—THE "FIAT-GREENBACK" HERESY.—" DOLLAR OF THE FATHERS" DEMONETIZED.—NOT BY FRAUD BUT WITHOUT DUE REFLECTION.—THE BLAND BILL AND THE "ALLISON TIP."—THE AMENDED BILL VETOED, BUT PASSED.—SUBSEQUENT SILVER LEGISLATION.

THE most momentous single deed of Mr. Hayes's Administration was the restoration of the country's finances, public and private, to a hard-money basis. On January 1, 1879, the United States began again the payment, suspended for more than sixteen years, of specie in liquidation of its greenback promises. The familiar legend upon our Treasury notes, "The United States will pay," became true at last. Our paper dollar had begun to sink below par so early as December 28, 1861, after which date it underwent the most painful fluctuations. On July 11, 1864, it was sixty-five per cent. below par, thenceforward sinking and rising fitfully, but never reaching gold value again till the month of December, 1878.

The difficulties of replacing the country's business on a solid monetary platform had been foreseen as soon as the subject loomed into view. Senator Sherman, upon whom finally fell the main burden of carrying the operation through, wrote

THE LAST QUARTER-CENTURY

in 1868: "I am in real embarrassment about questions that I must now act upon. My conviction is that specie payments must be resumed, and I have my own theories as to the mode of resumption, but the process is a very hard one and will endanger the popularity of any man or administration that is compelled to adopt it."

The very first act of the Forty-first Congress was one entitled "An Act to strengthen the public credit." Introduced in the House by General Schenck on March 12, 1869, it there passed on that day, reaching the Senate on the 15th, where also it speedily passed. On the 19th this memorable bill became law. It ran:

"That, in order to remove any doubt as to the purpose of the Government to discharge all just obligations to the public creditors, and to settle conflicting questions and interpretations of the laws by virtue of which said obligations have been contracted, it is hereby provided and declared that the faith of the United States is solemnly pledged to the payment in coin, or its equivalent, of all obligations of the United States not bearing interest, known as United States notes, and of all interest-bearing obligations of the United States, except in cases where the law authorizing the issue of such obligations has expressly provided that the same may be paid in lawful money or other currency than gold or silver. . . And the United States also solemnly pledges its faith to make provision, at the earliest practicable period, for the redemption of the United States notes in coin."

However necessary to final prosperity, the contraction of our currency was a sore process, and it encountered at every stage the most bitter opposition. The war left us, as it found us, with painfully little grasp on the principles of money. Men of one type felt that low or falling prices, however caused, meant prosperity; another class attached this meaning to high prices, however caused. Few reflected enough to see that great and solid prosperity may attend rising prices, as

G. F. Edmunds   John Sherman   W. B. Allison
O. P. Morton   John A. Logan

Painted by W. R. Leigh
T. W. Ferry   F. T. Frelinghuysen   T. O. Howe
Roscoe Conkling   G. S. Boutwell
                                              A. A. Sargent

THE REPUBLICAN CAUCUS COMMITTEE WHICH FORMULATED THE RESUMPTION ACT
IN DECEMBER, 1874

between 1850 and 1870, or that, on the other hand, prices may be going down and yet greater and greater effort be required to obtain the necessaries of life. The generally conceded desirableness of replacing business upon a precious-metal basis, whatever hardship in lowered values this might cost those whose property consisted of goods or lands and not of money, misled many, even after the gold platform was reached, to hail each drop in general prices with hallelujahs. Eastern people and the creditor class elsewhere were usually in this frame of mind.

Far different felt those, so numerous throughout the West, who had run in debt when rank inflation was on, and who, tied to their mortgaged farms, were compelled to produce against a constantly falling market. They writhed under the pinch, and more or less correctly understood the philosophy of it. A Montgomery County, Pa., farmer once went into a store in Norristown and bought a suit of clothes. The storekeeper said: "That is the cheapest suit of clothes you ever bought." "Oh, no," said the farmer, "this suit cost me twenty bushels of wheat. I have never paid over fifteen bushels of wheat for a suit of clothes before."

The panic of 1873, so far as it resulted from contraction, had its main origin abroad, not in America, so that its subordinate causes were generally looked upon as its sole occasion; yet these bye causes were important. The shocking destruction of wealth by fires and by reckless speculation, of course had a baneful effect. During 1872 the balance of trade was strongly against the United States. The circulation of depreciated paper money had brought to many an apparent prosperity which was not real, leading to the free creation of debts by individuals, corporations, towns, cities and States. An unprecedented mileage of railways had been constructed. Much supposed wealth consisted in the bonds of these railroads and of other new concerns, like mining and manufacturing corporations. Thus the entire business of the country was on a basis of inflation, and when contraction came disaster was inevitable.

In the course of the summer solid values began to be hoarded and interest rates consequently to rise. In August there was a partial corner in gold, broken by a government sale of $6,000,000. In September panic came, with suspension of several large banking-houses in New York. Jay Cooke & Co., who had invested heavily in the construction of the Northern Pacific Railway, suspended on September 18th. When authoritative news of this event was made known in the Stock Exchange a perfect stampede of the brokers ensued. They surged out of the Exchange, tumbling pell-mell over each other in the general confusion, hastening to notify their respective houses. Next day, September 19th, Fiske & Hatch, very conservative people, went down.

September 19th was a second Black Friday. Never since the original Black Friday had the street and the Stock Exchange been so frantic. The weather, dark and rainy, seemed to sympathize with the gloom which clouded the financial situation. Wall, Broad and Nassau Streets were thronged with people. From the corner of Wall Street and Broadway down to the corner of Hanover Street a solid mass of men filled both sidewalks. From the Post-office along Nassau Street down Broad Street to Exchange Place another dense throng moved slowly, aimlessly, hither and thither. Sections of Broadway itself were packed. Weaving in and out like the shuttles in a loom were brokers and brokers' clerks making the best speed they could from point to point. All faces wore a bewildered and foreboding look. To help them seem cool, moneyed men talked about the weather, but their incoherent words and nervous motions betrayed their anxiety. The part of Wall Street at the corner of Broad Street held a specially interested mass of men. They seemed like an assemblage anxiously awaiting the appearance of a great spectacle. High up on the stone balustrade of the Sub-Treasury were numerous

Painted by Howard Pyle
THE RUSH FROM THE NEW YORK STOCK EXCHANGE ON SEPTEMBER 18, 1873

SECOND BLACK FRIDAY

spectators, umbrellas sheltering them from the pelting rain as they gazed with rapt attention on the scene below. All the brokers' offices were filled. In each, at the first click of the indicator, everybody present was breathless, showing an interest more and more intense as the figures telegraphed were read off.

It was half-past ten in the morning when the Fiske & Hatch failure was announced in the Stock Exchange. For a moment there was silence; then a hoarse murmur broke out from bulls and bears alike, followed by yells and cries indescribable, clearly audible on the street. Even the heartless bear, in glee over the havoc he was making, paused to utter a growl of sorrow that gentlemen so honorable should become ursine prey. The news of the failure ran like a prairie fire, spreading dismay that showed itself on all faces. Annotators of values in the various offices made known in doleful ticks the depreciation of stocks and securities. Old *habitués* of the exchanges, each usually placid as a moonlit lake, were wrought up till they acted like wild men.

At the corner of Broad Street and Exchange Place a delirious crowd of money-lenders and borrowers collected and tried to fix a rate for loans. The matter hung in the balance for some time until the extent of the panic became known. Then they bid until the price of money touched one-half of one per cent. a day and legal interest. One man, after lending $30,000 at three-eighths per cent., said that he had $20,000 left, but that he thought he would not lend it. As he said this, he turned toward his office, but was immediately surrounded by about twenty borrowers who hung on to his arms and coat-tails till he had agreed to lend the $20,000.

The Stock Exchange witnessed the chief tragedy and the chief farce of the day. Such tumult, push and bellowing had never been known there even in the wildest moments of the war. The interior of the Exchange was of noble altitude, with a vaulting top, brilliantly colored in Renaissance design, that

THE LAST QUARTER-CENTURY

sprang upward with a strength and grace seldom so happily united. A cluster of gas-jets, hanging high, well illuminated the enclosure. On the capacious floor, unobstructed by pillars or by furniture, save one small table whereon a large basket of flowers rested, a mob of brokers and brokers' clerks surged back and forth, filling the immense space above with roars and screams. The floor was portioned off to some twenty different groups. Here was one tossing " New York Central " up and down; near by another playing ball with " Wabash ; " " Northwestern " jumped and sank as if afflicted with St. Vitus's dance. In the middle of the floor " Rock Island " cut up similar capers. In a remote corner " Pacific Mail " was beaten with clubs, while " Harlem " rose like a balloon filled with pure hydrogen. The uninitiated expected every instant to see the mob fight. Jobbers squared off at each other and screamed and yelled violently, flinging their arms around and producing a scene which Bedlam itself could not equal.

Behind the raised desk, in snowy shirt-front and necktie, stood the President of the Exchange, his strong tenor voice every now and then ringing out over the Babel of sounds beneath. The gallery opposite him contained an eager throng of spectators bending forward and craning their necks to view the pandemonium on the floor. The rush for this gallery was fearful, and apparently, but for the utmost effort of the police, must have proved fatal to some. Excitement in Wall Street not infrequently drew crowds to the main front of the Exchange; but hardly ever, if ever before, had the vicinity been so packed as now. Two large blackboards exhibited in chalk figures the incessantly fluctuating quotations. Telegraph wires connected the Exchange with a thousand indicators throughout the city, whence the quotations, big with meaning to many, were flashed over the land.

The first Black Friday was a bull Friday; the second was a bear Friday. Early in the panic powerful brokers began

STOCK EXCHANGE CLOSED

to sell short, and they succeeded in hammering down from ten to forty per cent. many of the finest stocks like " New York Central," " Erie," " Wabash," " Northwestern," " Rock Island" and " Western Union." They then bought to cover their sales. Bull brokers, unable to pay their contracts, shrieked for margin money, which their principals would not or could not put up. They also sought relief from the banks, but in vain. It had long been the practice of certain banks, though contrary to law, early each day to certify checks to enormous amounts in favor of brokers who had not a cent on deposit to their credit, the understanding in each case being that before three o'clock the broker would hand in enough cash or securities to cancel his debt. The banks now refused this accommodation. In the Exchange, eighteen names were read off of brokers who could not fulfill their contracts. As fast as the failures were announced the news was carried out on to the street. In spite of the rain hundreds of people gathered about the offices of fallen reputation, and gazed curiously through the windows trying to make out how the broken brokers were behaving. Toward evening, as the clouds lifted over Trinity spire, showing a ruddy flush in the west, everybody, save some reluctant bears, said, " The worst is over," and breathed a sigh of relief. The crowd melted, one by one the tiny little Broadway coupés rattled off, one by one the newsboys ceased shrieking, and night closed over the wet street.

In deference to a general wish that dealings in stocks should cease, the Exchange was shut on Saturday, September 20th, and not opened again till the 30th. Such closure had never occurred before. On Sunday morning President Grant and Secretary Richardson, of the Treasury, came to New York, spending the day in anxious consultation with Vanderbilt, Clews, and other prominent business men.

Had the Secretary of the Treasury acted promptly and firmly he might have relieved the situation much; but he vacillated. Some $13,500,000 in five-twenty bonds were bought, and a few millions of the greenbacks which Secretary McCulloch had called in for cancellation were set free. But as Mr. Richardson announced no policy on which the public could depend, most of the cash let loose was instantly hoarded in vaults or used in the purchase of other bonds then temporarily depressed, so doing nothing whatever to allay the distress. On the 25th the Treasury ceased buying bonds. The person who, at the worst, sustained the market and kept it from breaking to a point where half of the street would have been inevitably ruined, was Jay Gould, mischief itself on the first Black Friday, but on this one a blessing. He bought during the low prices several hundred thousand shares of railroad stocks, principally of the Vanderbilt stripe, and in this way put a check on the ruinous decline.

The national banks of New York weathered this cyclone by a novel device of the Clearing-house or associated banks. These pooled their cash and collaterals into a common fund, placed this in the hands of a trusty committee, and issued against it loan certificates that were receivable at the Clearing-house, just like cash, in payment of debit balances. Ten million dollars worth of these certificates was issued at first, a sum subsequently doubled. This Clearing-house paper served its purpose admirably. By October 3d confidence was so restored that $1,000,000 of it was called in and cancelled, followed next day by $1,500,000 more. None of it was long outstanding. The Clearing-house febrifuge was successfully applied also in Boston, Philadelphia, Pittsburg and other cities, but not in Chicago.

The panic overspread the country. Credit in business was refused, debtors were pressed for payment, securities were rushed into the market and fell greatly in price. Even United States bonds went down from five to ten per cent. There was a run upon savings banks, many of which succumbed. Manufactured goods were little salable, and the prices of agricultural products painfully sank. Factories began to run on

W. A. Richardson, Massachusetts, March 17, 1873–June 2, 1874

B. H. Bristow, Kentucky, June 2, 1874–June 21, 1876

L. M. Morrill, Maine, June 21, 1876–March 8, 1877

John Sherman, Ohio, March 8, 1877–March 5, 1881

William Windom, Minnesota, March 5, 1881–October 27, 1881

C. J. Folger, New York, October 27, 1881–October 24, 1884

W. Q. Gresham, Indiana, October 24, 1884–October 28, 1884

Hugh McCulloch, Indiana, October 28, 1884–March 6, 1885

Daniel Manning, New York, March 6, 1885–April 1, 1887

C. S. Fairchild, New York, April 1, 1887–March 5, 1889

Charles Foster, Ohio, February 24, 1891–March 6, 1893

James G. Carlisle, Kentucky, March 6, 1893–

THE SECRETARIES OF THE TREASURY DURING THE LAST QUARTER-CENTURY*

*For G. S. Boutwell, March 11, 1869–March 17, 1873, see page 35.

RESUMPTION AND THE POLITICAL PARTIES

short time, many closed entirely, many corporations failed. The peculiarity of this crisis was the slowness with which it abated, though fortunately its acute phase was of brief duration. No date could be set as its term, its evil effects dragging on through years.

In convincing multitudes, as it did, of the imperative necessity of replacing our national finances on a coin foundation, this panic was worth all it cost. It was influential in uniting the friends of sound finance and of national honesty upon the resumption policy. Men saw that this policy, however hard to enter upon, however disastrous in the execution, however sure of terrible opposition at every step, must succeed, and could not but bring lasting credit to the political party bold enough to espouse and push it. At first the resumption plan divided both parties; but, little by little, the Republicans came generally to favor it, the Democrats, some in one way and some in another, to gainsay.

The policy and the details of resumption were hotly debated all through the presidential campaign of 1876. Many opposed return to specie from ignorance of its meaning. Some thought that after resumption no paper money of any kind would be in circulation, or at least that all greenbacks would be gone. Most, even of such as favored it, probably expected that resumption would involve paying out by the Government of almost unlimited sums in gold. Few, comparatively, could see that it consisted merely in bringing United States notes to gold par and keeping them there. Mr. Tilden would assign this work to the domain of "practical administrative statesmanship." Like all other Democrats, he urged "a system of preparation" for resumption in place of the Republican Resumption Act. "A system of preparation without the promise of a day, for the worthless promise of a day without a system of preparation would be the gain of the substance of resumption in exchange for its shadow." In reply it was maintained that "the way to resume was to resume." This

THE LAST QUARTER-CENTURY

thought fortunately determined the policy of the country and was justified by the event.

The Resumption Act, passed January 14, 1875, had set a date for resumption—four years ahead, January 1, 1879. The first section provided for the immediate coinage of subsidiary silver to redeem the fractional currency. This was practicable, as the now low gold price of that metal rendered possible its circulation concurrently with greenbacks. The master-clause of the act authorized the Secretary to buy "coin" with any of his surplus revenues, and for the same purpose "to issue, sell, and dispose of bonds of the United States." It was fortunate for the country that Mr. Sherman, who, as Senator, had drafted the measure, was, as Secretary of the Treasury in the Hayes Cabinet, called to execute it.

Ever since 1859 his connection with the Committee of Ways and Means in the House and with the Committee on Finance in the Senate had brought him into close official relations with the Treasury Department. This legislative training gave him a full knowledge of the several laws that were to be executed in relation to public revenue, to all forms of taxation, to coinage and currency and to the public debt. The entire system of national finance then existing grew out of the Civil War, and Mr. Sherman had participated in the passage of all the laws relating to this subject. His intimate association with Secretaries Chase, Fessenden, and McCulloch, and his friendly relations with Secretaries Boutwell and Richardson, led him, as Chairman of the Senate committee on finance, to have free and confidential intercourse with them as to legislation affecting the Treasury. Though a good lawyer and an able man, Secretary Bristow had not had the benefit of experience either in Congress or in the Department. He doubted whether resumption would be effective without a gradual retirement of United States notes, a measure to which Congress would not agree, repealing even the limited retirement of such notes provided for by the resumption act. Secretary Morrill,

SHERMAN AND RESUMPTION

Sherman's immediate predecessor, was in hearty sympathy with the policy of resumption, but his failing health had kept him from that efficiency as Secretary which he would otherwise have displayed. For some time before the end of his term in the Treasury, illness had confined him to his lodgings. The Treasury Department was, however, well organized, most of its chief officers having been long in service. But few changes here were made under Hayes, and only as vacancies occurred or incompetency was demonstrated.*

In resolutely preparing for Resumption, spite of cries that it was impossible, or, if possible, certain to be ruinous and deadly, Sherman, whom many had thought timid and vacillating, evinced the utmost strength of will. The Democracy was for the most part adverse to all effort for immediate resumption, favoring, rather, an enlarged issue of Treasury notes. The elections of 1877 and 1878, generally either Democratic or Republican by lowered majorities, would have made many an administration retreat or pause. Opposition to the party in power was of course due in part to the wide belief that Hayes had been jockeyed into the presidency, and in part to the great railway strikes, where the President had promptly suppressed criminal disorder by the use of federal arms. Clearly, however, very much of it arose from the Administration's avowal that the resumption act "could be, ought to be, and would be executed if not repealed."

In the advertising and placing of his loans, Mr. Sherman showed himself a master in big finance. By the sale of four-and-a-half per cent. bonds, callable in 1891, he had, before the appointed day, accumulated an aggregate of $140,000,000 gold coin and bullion, being forty per cent. of the then outstanding greenbacks. Partly owing to several abundant harvests, throwing the balance of European trade in our favor and crowding gold this way, resumption proved easier than any anticipated. The greenbacks rose to par thirteen days before

*John Sherman's Recollections, pp. 565, 566.

THE LAST QUARTER-CENTURY

The Telegram Announcing the Result of the First Day's "Resumption" at the New York Sub-Treasury

the date fixed for beginning gold payments. Rumors were rife of a conspiracy to "corner" gold, and to make a run on the Sub-Treasury New Year's day, 1879, the day for beginning resumption. On the 30th of December, 1878, the president of the National Bank of Commerce and chairman of the Clearing-house committee, begged for $5,000,000 in gold in exchange for a like amount of United States notes on the following day, a proposition which was forthwith declined. "The year closed with no unpleasant excitement, but with unpleasant forebodings. The first day of January was Sunday and no business was transacted. On Monday anxiety reigned in the office of the Secretary. Hour after hour passed; no news came from New York. Inquiry by wire showed that all was quiet. At the close of business came this message: '$135,000 of notes presented for coin—$400,000 of gold for notes.' That was all. Resumption was accomplished with no disturbance. By five o'clock the news was all over the land, and the New York bankers were sipping their tea in absolute safety. The prediction of the Secretary had become history. When gold could with certainty be obtained for notes, nobody wanted it. The experiment of maintaining a limited amount of United States notes in circulation, based upon a reasonable reserve in the Treasury pledged for that purpose, and supported also by the credit of the Government, proved generally satisfactory, and the exclusive use of these notes for circulation may become, in time, the fixed financial policy of the Government."*

The straggling applications for coin made when resumption day arrived were less in amount than was asked for in greenbacks by bondholders, who could in any event have demanded coin. During the entire year 1879 only $11,456,536 in greenbacks were offered for redemption, while over $250,000,000 were paid out in coin obligations. It was found that people preferred paper to metal money, and had no wish for gold instead of notes when assured that the exchange could be made at their option. Notwithstanding our acceptance of greenbacks for customs—$109,467,456 during 1879—the Treasury at the end of that year experienced a dearth of these and a plethora of coin, having actually to force debtors to receive hard money.

The magnitude and meaning of the financial policy thus launched can hardly be over-estimated. The Nation had piled up a war debt amounting to the enormous sum of $2,844,649,626. This figure, the highest which the debt ever attained, was reached in August, 1865. Many people at home and in other countries thought that amounts so vast as were called for could never possibly be paid. When we began borrowing, the London *Economist* declared it "utterly out of the question for the Americans to obtain the extravagant sums they asked," saying: "Europe *won't* lend them; Americans *cannot.*" The Washington agent of the London bankers through whom our Government did foreign business, after the battle of Bull Run called at the Treasury on Sunday to get his "little bill" settled, having the effrontery to ask the acting Secretary, Mr. George Harrington, to give security

*J. K. Upton, in Scribner's Magazine, July, 1892.

that the balance, about $40,000, would be paid. Mr. Harrington directed the anxious Englishman to wait, as the Government would probably not break up before business hours next day. The London *Times* declared: " No pressure that ever threatened is equal to that which now hangs over the United States, and it may safely be said that if in future generations they faithfully meet their liabilities, they will fairly earn a fame which will shine throughout the world." In March, 1863, concluding an article on Secretary Chase's stupendous operations, the same newspaper exclaimed: " What strength, what resources, what vitality, what energy there must be in a nation that is able to ruin itself on a scale so transcendent!"*

No nation ever took a braver course than did the United States in deliberately beginning the reduction of that enormous war debt. The will to reduce it opened the way, and the payment went on by leaps and bounds. The policy was to call in high-rate bonds as soon as callable, and replace them by others bearing lower rates. So immense was the Government's income that to have set so late a date as 1891 for the time when the four-and-a-halfs could be cancelled proved unfortunate. To fix for the maturity of the fours so remote a date as 1907 was worse still. The three-per-cents of 1882, which supplanted earlier issues, were wisely made payable at the Government's option. For the twenty-three years beginning with August, 1865, the reduction proceeded at an average rate of a little under $63,000,000 yearly, which would be $5,250,000 each month, $175,000 each day, $7,291 each hour, and $121 each minute.

An act of Congress passed February 25, 1862, had authorized the issue of $150,000,000 in non-interest-bearing Treasury notes. These notes had no precedent with us since colonial times. Neither receivable for duties nor payable for interest on the public debt, they were yet legal tender for all

*Shuckers, Life of S. P. Chase, pp. 225, 226.

CONSTITUTIONALITY OF THE GREENBACK

other payments, public and private. As the Government paid its own debts with them they amounted to a forced loan.

The legal-tender clause of the 1862 law roused bitterest antagonism. The press ridiculed it, in some cases being refused the use of the mails for that reason. "The financial fabric of the Union totters to its base," said a leading journal. Secretary Chase himself, the father of

ELBRIDGE G. SPAULDING*

the greenback, afterward, as Chief-Justice, pronounced the law unconstitutional. This was his judgment from the first, and he overrode it, after painful deliberation, only because such a course seemed absolutely necessary to save the nation. Mr. Lincoln is said to have aided his Secretary at this crisis by the parable of the captain who, his ship aleak, worse and worse in spite of his prayers to the Virgin, threw her image overboard, and, having successfully made port and docked his vessel for repairs, found the image neatly filling the hole where the water had come in. Both deemed it patriotic to make jetsam of the Constitution if thereby they might bring safe into port the leaky ship of state, in danger of being engulfed in the mad ocean of civil war.

Thus the issue of legal-tenders began under the pressure of urgent necessity. From first to last $450,000,000 of this paper had been voted, whereof, on January 3, 1864, $449,338,902 was outstanding. Specie payments were suspended two days before the introduction of the legal-tender act. Gold went to a premium while that act was under discussion, remaining so till just before resumption, January 1, 1879. Even the subsidiary silver coinage disappeared, and Congress was obliged to issue fractional paper currency, "shin-plasters," in its stead.

*One of the chief promoters of the Legal Tender Act.

THE LAST QUARTER-CENTURY

Several constitutional questions were connected with the greenback. In Hepburn vs. Griswold (8 Wall., 603) the Court held, four* Justices against three, that, while the act of February 25, 1862, might, as a war measure, be valid, making greenbacks legal tender for debts contracted after its passage, yet, so far as its provisions related to pre-existing debts, it was inconsistent with the Constitution, not being a "necessary" or "proper" means to any end therein authorized. In Parker vs. Davis (12 Wall., 457), the *personnel* of the Court having been changed by the resignation of Justice Grier and the appointment of Justices Bradley and Strong, though Chase, Clifford, and Field strenuously maintained their former views, the Hepburn vs. Griswold decision was reversed. That case, the Court now said, "was decided by a divided Court," having fewer Judges "than the law then in existence provided that this Court shall have. These cases have been heard before a full Court, and they have received our most careful consideration." Justice Bradley, whom in the judgment of Senator Hoar, "the general voice of the profession and of his brethren of the bench would place at the head of all then living American jurists," concurred with the majority in a separate opinion of his own, at once elaborate and emphatic. In the famous case of Juilliard vs. Greenman (110 U. S. Reports, 421) a third question was tried out, namely, whether Congress has the constitutional power to make United States Treasury notes legal tender for private debts in peace as well as in war. The decision was again in favor of the greenback, Field being the only Justice to register dissent.

Though this was the first decision of the question arrived at by strictly legal reasoning, it evoked much hostile criticism. *The Financial Chronicle* said: "All reliance upon constitutional inhibition to do anything with the currency which Congress may have a whim to do must be aban-

---
*Or five if Grier be counted. He agreed with the majority, but resigned before the opinion was announced.

Field Miller Clifford Nelson Chase Grier Swayne Davis

CHIEF-JUSTICE CHASE ANNOUNCING THE DECISION OF THE SUPREME COURT IN THE FIRST "LEGAL-TENDER" TRIAL: HEPBURN VS. GRISWOLD

doned henceforth and forever." The historian Bancroft vented a formidable brochure, richer in learning than in law, entitled "The Constitution Wounded in the House of its Friends." The Court's logic, however, was not easily controverted. It closely followed John Marshall's reasoning in McCulloch vs. Maryland.* An enactment by Congress the Supreme Court presumes to be constitutional unless it is certainly unconstitutional. If there is doubt upon the point there is no doubt. Congress is right. The authority " to emit bills of credit" as legal tender was not expressly delegated to the Federal Government, but it may well claim place in the goodly family of "implied powers," apparently being implied by its prohibition to the States, or involved in the power to borrow money, or in that to regulate commerce. Again, if Congress could pass such a law to meet an exigency, as held in Parker vs. Davis, Congress must be left to determine when the exigency exists. The intention of the Fathers to inhibit bills of credit cannot be conclusively shown. Even if it were certain it would be inconclusive; the question being not what they intended to do, but what they actually did in framing and ratifying the Constitution.

The wisdom of the legal tender law is a different question, but, like the other, should not be pronounced upon without reflection. It was easy to condemn it after the event. No doubt, had conditions favored, more might have been done, saving millions of debt and half the other financial evils of war, to keep the dollar at gold par, as by not compelling gold payment of the seven-thirty bonds, by heavier tax levies, by earlier resort to large loans, even at high rates, instead of emitting legal-tenders, and also by forcing national banks, created on purpose to help market bonds, to purchase new ones directly from the Government. Yet, under the circumstances, such defects in our policy early in the war could hardly have been avoided, so uncertain were national spirit and credit then,

*4 Wheaton, p. 421.

THE LAST QUARTER-CENTURY

and so little were the magnitude and duration of the war foreseen. When the old demand notes were issued, more than one professedly loyal railroad corporation refused them in payment of fares and freight. Hotels were shy of them. A leading New York bank refused to receive them save as a special deposit, though these notes, being receivable for customs, like coin, went to a premium along with gold. One depositor in the bank just referred to found on withdrawing his deposit that his notes as reckoned in legal tender* had advanced in value nearly or quite one hundred and fifty per cent. People being so shy of the demand notes, what wonder that the greenbacks, which bore no interest, were long in ill repute.

The Nation's resolute purpose to reduce its debt changed this. When equal to gold, greenbacks were glorified, and all thoughts of retiring them gave way. In 1865 Secretary McCulloch had boldly recommended the calling in of greenback notes in preparation for the restoration of specie. The people were then willing to submit to this. The act of March 12, 1866, authorized the cancellation of $10,000,000 or less within six months, and thereafter of $4,000,000 or less each month. By this method the amount was by the end of 1867 cut down to $356,000,000, but the act of February 4, 1868, forbade any further decrease. Between March 17, 1872, and January 15, 1874, the amount was raised some $25,000,000, but a bill passed in 1874, known as the "inflation bill," still further to increase it, was vetoed by President Grant. June 20, 1874, the maximum greenback circulation was placed at $382,000,000, which the operation of the Resumption Act in 1875 brought down to $346,681,000, letting the gap be filled by national bank notes. All further retirement or cancellation of legal-tenders was forbidden by the act approved May 31, 1878, which provided, in part, that "it shall not be lawful . . to cancel or retire any more of the United States legal-tender

*Shuckers, Life of S. P. Chase, p. 225.

THE "FIAT-GREENBACK" THEORY

notes. And when . . redeemed or received into the Treasury . . they shall be reissued and paid out again and kept in circulation." Secretary Sherman recommended the passage of this law, as he believed that the retirement of greenbacks pending the preparation for resumption, by reducing the volume of the currency, increased the difficulties of resumption.

This popularity of the greenbacks stimulated to fresh life the "fiat-greenback" theory, whose pith lay in the proposition that money requires in its material no· labor-cost value, its purchasing power coming from the decree of the public authority issuing it, so that paper money put forth by a financially responsible government, though involving no promise whatever, will be the peer of gold. People who held this view opposed all resumption, proximate or remote, wishing to print United States dollar notes each bearing the legend " This is a Dollar," and notes of other denominations similarly, not allowing any of them to *promise* payment or to have any other relation whatever to coin. This idea was long very influential throughout States so conservative as Illinois, Indiana, and Ohio, where, in several campaigns, the able stump addresses of men like Garfield, Schurz, and Stanley Matthews laid it pretty well to rest. It was, however, the rallying thought of the National Labor Greenback Party, organized at Indianapolis, May 17, 1876, when it nominated Peter Cooper for the Presidency. On the very day that resumption went into effect a Greenbacker Convention in New England declared it the paramount issue of their party to substitue greenbacks for national bank notes.

The old silver dollar, "the Dollar of the Fathers," had never ceased to be full legal tender until 1873, although it had since 1853 been, as compared with the gold dollar, too valuable to circulate much. In 1873 a law was unobservedly passed demonetizing it, and making gold the exclusive form of United States full-tender hard money.

THE LAST QUARTER-CENTURY

RICHARD P. BLAND

WILLIAM B. ALLISON

That legislation of such importance should have passed without general debate, either in Congress or by the public, was unfortunate; but, contrary to a very prevalent view, there is no evidence that a single Congressional vote for it was secured by fraud. Little silver had been coined by the United States since 1834. The monetary problem of 1873 was not that of subsequent years. Then, simplicity of monetary system was considered the great desideratum, whereas, with discussion, authorities came to agree that adequacy in volume is the most important trait in a hard-money system. In 1873 gold had been for twenty years pouring out of the earth in immense sums, rendering not unnatural the expectation that it alone, without silver, would soon suffice for the world's hard-money stock. Such was then the judgment of the leaders of public opinion in all lands. It was the view of the Paris Conference in 1867, which recommended the general demonetization of silver—a recommendation extremely influential in determining to a gold policy the German Empire, whose course toward silver in 1873 was identical with ours.

European opinion on the subject was known and concurred in here. At intervals ever since 1816 representative Americans had suggested that we should adopt Great Britain's metallic money system. In his report of November 29, 1851, the Director of our Mint declared the "main features" of that system "eminently worthy of adoption into the monetary

RASHNESS OF DEMONETIZING SILVER

policy of our own country." Hon. Thomas Corwin, of Ohio, then Secretary of the Treasury, whom no one will charge with obsequiousness to England or to the Money Power at home, in his Report of January 6, 1852, seconded the recommendation of the Director of the Mint, carefully setting forth the argument for adopting it. To the Act of 1873 the Senators from Oregon, California, and Nevada unanimously agreed. At the 1867 Paris Conference the United States was (by delegates) present as a gold country, Mr. Seward, then Secretary of State, being responsible for this, though no one protested. Inspired by such example and by the recommendation of the Conference, the Secretary of our Treasury, in 1870, drafted the bill discontinuing the silver dollar, which passed the Senate early in 1871 and became a law in 1873.

But, while one must thus discredit the allegation of fraud and of sinister motive in this legislation, it nevertheless seems clear that the silver people and the entire country had a grievance in connection with it. "No man in a position of trust has a right to allow a measure of such importance to pass without calling attention sharply to it, and making sure that its bearings are fully comprehended. And no man who did not know that the demonetization of silver by the United States was a measure of transcendent importance had any right to be on such a committee or to put his hand to a bill which touched the coinage of a great country. Everyone knows that but few members upon the floor of Congress read the text of one in twenty of the bills they have to pass upon; and it is the duty of the committees dealing with any class of subjects to see to it that every proposed change is fully explained, and that the attention of the House and of the country is fairly called to it. They are not discharged of their obligations simply by giving members an opportunity to find it out for themselves. If this be a requirement of ordinary political honesty, much more is it the dictate of political prudence. An important change in the money or in the industrial system of a nation,

THE LAST QUARTER-CENTURY

if effected without full and free and thorough discussion, even though no surprise or concealment be used, is almost certain to be subsequently challenged. 'Things,' says Bacon, 'will have their first or second agitation : If they be not tossed upon the waves of counsel, they will be tossed upon the waves of fortune, and be full of inconstancy, doing and undoing, like the reeling of a drunken man.' The unwisdom of a few people assuming to be wise for the whole of a great people, was never more conspicuously shown than in the demonetization of the silver dollar."*

An increased value attaching to gold was soon apparent, or, what is the same thing, a general fall in prices. This began so soon as silver full money had been laid aside, silver falling in gold price almost exactly as products at large fell. In view of this movement, since all Government bonds outstanding in 1873 were payable in "coin," it was a nearly universal belief in most sections of the country that the annulment of the right to pay debts in silver would, if persisted in, be very unjust to taxpayers in liquidating the national debt. The Bland Bill was therefore brought forward, and in 1878 passed, restoring silver again to its ancient legal equality with gold as debt-paying money. A clause of it read: "Any owner of silver bullion may deposit the same at any coinage mint or assay office to be coined into dollars, for his benefit, upon the same terms and conditions as gold bullion is deposited for coinage under existing laws." In the act as finally passed, however, so great was now the disparity in value between gold and silver at the ratio of 16 to 1, Congress did not venture to give back to the white metal the right of free coinage. In the Senate, at the urgent request of Secretary Sherman, the "Allison tip," as it was called, was incorporated in the bill, requiring the Secretary of the Treasury to purchase monthly not less than two million dollars' worth of silver, or more than four million dollars' worth, and to coin

*Francis A. Walker.

END OF SILVER PURCHASES

it into dollars. This amendment was concurred in by the House. Spite of Secretary Sherman's attitude in favor of it the Bland-Allison Act was disapproved by President Hayes, but immediately passed over his veto by both Houses of Congress on the same day, February 28, 1878. The Senate vote was 46 yeas to 19 nays; that of the House 196 to 73.

The advocates of gold mono-metallism believed that the issue of these dollars would speedily drive gold from the country. Owing to the limitation of the new coinage no such effect was experienced, and the silver dollars or the certificates representing them floated at par with gold, which, indeed, far from leaving the country, was imported in vast amounts nearly every year. After 1880 the money in circulation in the United States was gold coin, silver coin, gold certificates, greenbacks or United States notes, and the notes of the national banks. The so-called Sherman Law, of 1890, added a new category, the Treasury notes issued in payment for silver bullion. It stopped the compulsory coinage of full-tender silver, though continuing and much increasing the purchase of silver bullion by the Government. The repeal of the purchase clause of this law, in 1893, put an end to the acquisition of silver by the United States.

CHAPTER XI

AGRARIAN AND LABOR MOVEMENTS IN THE SEVENTIES

THE "GRANGERS."—THEIR AIMS.—ORIGIN OF THE INTER-STATE COMMERCE ACT.—DEMAND FOR CHEAP TRANSPORTATION.—ILLINOIS'S "THREE-CENT WAR."—COURT DECISIONS.—LAND-GRANT COLLEGES.—THEIR SIGNIFICANCE.—VARIOUS LABOR CONGRESSES AND PLATFORMS.—RISE OF LABOR BUREAUS.—THE NATIONAL DEPARTMENT OF LABOR.—ITS WORK, METHODS, AND INFLUENCE.—VALUE OF THE STATE BUREAUS.—CONTRACT-LABOR LAW.—THE GREENBACK PARTY.—PETER COOPER AND GEN. BUTLER.—VIOLENCE IN THE LABOR CONFLICT.—CAUSES.—COMBINATIONS OF CAPITAL.— OF LABORERS.—BLACK LIST AND BOYCOTT.—LABOR WAR IN PENNSYLVANIA.—METHODS OF INTIMIDATION.—THE "MOLLY MAGUIRES."—MURDER OF ALEXANDER REA.—POWER AND IMMUNITY OF THE MOLLIES.—PLAN FOR EXPOSING THEM.—GOWEN AND McPARLAN.—ASSASSINATION OF THOMAS SANGER.—GOWEN'S TRIUMPH AND THE COLLAPSE OF THE CONSPIRACY.—GREAT RAILWAY STRIKE IN 1877.—RIOT AT PITTSBURG.—DEATH AND DESTRUCTION.—SCENES AT READING AND OTHER PLACES.—STRIKES COMMON FROM THIS TIME ON.

THE complaints evoked by industrial depression were in due time echoed in politics. Agrarian movements and labor movements in great numbers—social phenomena at first, but rapidly evolving political significance—marked the times. One of these, the California Sand Lot Campaign, because of its close connection with the Chinese Question, is deferred for discussion to Chapter XIII. The "Grangers," or "Patrons of Husbandry," was a secret organization for the promotion of farmers' interests. It was founded at Washington, December 4, 1867, women as well as men being members. In 1868 there were but 11 granges. The total membership of the order by 1875, six years from the time when local granges began to

THE LAST QUARTER-CENTURY

be formed, was 1,500,000, distributed throughout nearly all the States, though most numerous in the West and South.

The central aim of Granger agitation at first was to secure better transportation and lower freight rates, particularly from the West to the East. After waiting for railway facilities to be developed the shippers of grain and beef found themselves, when railways were at last supplied, hardly better off than before. The vast demand for transportation sent freight charges up to appalling figures. All sorts of relief devices were considered, among them a project for opening canal and slack-water navigation between the Mississippi and the Atlantic coast. This was earnestly urged by the Southern Commercial Convention at Cincinnati in 1870.

The difficulties of freight transportation between the States was discussed at length by Congress, spite of railway attorneys' insistence that the subject was beyond Congressional control. In the House of Representatives, during January, 1874, Hon. G. W. McCrary, Chairman of the Committee on Railroads and Canals, made an exhaustive report affirming the constitutional power of Congress to regulate interstate commerce. This valuable paper laid bare, in Section 8, Article I., of the Constitution, a depth of meaning which, till then, few had suspected, a discovery that prepared the way for the Interstate Commerce Act, passed on February 4, 1887.

A National Cheap Transportation Association was organized in New York on May 6, 1873, which also demanded lower transportation rates and an increase of avenues for commerce by water and rail. Its manifesto to the public asserted that cheap transportation for persons and property is essential to the public welfare

G. W. McCRARY

AGRICULTURAL AND MECHANICAL COLLEGES

and to the maintenance of a homogeneous and harmonious population. Another Cheap Transportation Convention was held in Richmond, December 1–4, 1874, which petitioned Congress in this interest.

Discrimination in freight charges was a fruitful source of discontent. In Illinois a dispute known as the "Three-Cent War" intensified feeling against railroads. This particular trouble was the outgrowth of the Illinois Central's disregard of an order issued by the Illinois Railroad Commissioners, limiting passenger fares to three cents per mile. The Commissioners' decree having been found contrary to the State Constitution, the legislature passed a law to limit fares. This the railroads fought with all energy in both State and Federal Courts. In November, 1875, in the case of the people against the Chicago and Alton Railroad Company, the United States Circuit Court handed down a decision sustaining the constitutionality of the law. Several "Granger" cases went to the national Supreme Court, which affirmed a State's right to fix maximum railway charges.

An interesting line of educational development, though originating otherwise, at length became connected with the general agrarian movement here under review. On July 2, 1862, President Lincoln put his signature to an act which had just passed Congress, donating public land to the several States and Territories which might provide colleges for instruction in branches of learning bearing on agriculture and the mechanic arts. By this act every State became entitled to 30,000 acres of government land for each senator and representative falling to it by the apportionment under the census of 1860. States containing no United States land received land scrip, entitling them, not directly but through their assignees, to locate and sell the amounts of land respectively due them. All the States and Territories in the Union, without a single exception, in the course of time, provided themselves with educational institutions on this basis. Some States

THE LAST QUARTER-CENTURY

sold the scrip early and realized little. Others carefully husbanded the scrip and became possessed of large sums, founding and sustaining educational institutions of vast usefulness and importance.

No State proceeded in this matter more discreetly than New York. Her share amounted to a million acres less ten thousand. Seventy-five thousand acres of this were sold at about eighty-five cents an acre. In the fall of 1863 Ezra Cornell purchased a hundred thousand acres for fifty thousand dollars, upon condition that all the profits accruing from the sale should be paid to Cornell University. Next year the rest was purchased at thirty cents an acre, with thirty cents more contingent upon Mr. Cornell's realizing that sum upon sale of the land. In 1874 Cornell University was subrogated to Mr. Cornell's place in dealing with the State, and from the lands handed over by him the Board of Trustees had in 1894–95 realized a net return of nearly four million dollars.

On March 2, 1887, there was approved by the President of the United States another piece of land-grant legislation, known as the Hatch Act. This act was intended to diffuse "useful and practical information on subjects connected with agriculture, and to promote scientific investigation and experiment respecting the principles and applications of agricultural science." For these purposes each State received from the United States, by virtue of this act, the sum of $15,000 a year, which was expended in connection with some agricultural experiment station or stations. The act presupposed that these stations would, as a rule, be established in conjunction with the institutions receiving the benefit of the act of 1862, and most of them were so associated; but the Hatch Act, in its 8th Section, provided that States electing so to do might join their experiment stations to agricultural schools separate from the colleges erected under the act of 1862, and this was done in a few States. By a third act of Congress, approved August 30, 1890, entitled "An Act to apply a portion of the proceeds

THE SECOND MORRILL ACT

of the public lands to the more complete endowment and support of the colleges for the benefit of agriculture and the mechanic arts established under the provisions of an act of Congress approved July 2, 1862," each of the States became entitled to $15,000 for the year ending June 30, 1890, $16,000 for the United States fiscal year 1890–91, $17,000 for the next fiscal year, and so on, the sum increasing by $1,000 each year, till it reached $25,000 a year, which was the permanent annual appropriation. A good endowment in itself!

In the more fortunate sections of the country these government grants simply made welcome additions to the excellent educational facilities in existence already. In the South and the far West they meant, educationally, life from the dead. Good schools rose even upon the frontiers, where the children of poorest farmers and mechanics might, at a nominal cost, fit themselves for high stations in life. Large and fruitful experimentation, especially in agriculture, was made possible. In turn these colleges of agriculture and the mechanic arts became rallying centres for agrarian and populist interest, which involved them in politics, and at least in certain instances much hindered their usefulness.

In 1865 a Labor " Congress " was held at Louisville, with but twenty-five or thirty delegates. A second sat at Baltimore in August, the next year, whose proceedings attracted some attention. Labor agitation had by this time assumed considerable proportions, most, perhaps, in Massachusetts, where the Knights of St. Crispin throve so early as 1868. Able men and influential newspapers began to espouse the labor cause. The Congress of 1867 was held in Chicago, and it mooted a scheme of labor unions, city, county and State. The Congress of 1868 was in New York, that of 1869 in Philadelphia. These marked little progress; but the National Labor Congress which met in Cincinnati August 15, 1870, was said to represent four hundred thousand people. It demanded Treasury notes not based on coin, an eight-hour work-day, the exclusion of Chinese laborers from the country, and the creation of a National Department of Labor.

Till now the movement was non-political, but the Chicago Congress, by a close vote, adopted a resolution creating an independent political organization to be known as the National Labor Reform Party. The party at once began to have influence. In the Massachusetts election of 1870 it fused with the Prohibitionists, making Wendell Phillips the candidate for Governor, who received nearly twenty-two thousand of the about one hundred and fifty-two thousand votes which were cast. One labor reformer was elected to the Massachusetts Senate, and eleven to the House. In 1871 the Congress met at St. Louis, August 10th. Little was done here beyond adopting a platform on which it was proposed to appeal to the country in the presidential election of 1872.

WENDELL PHILLIPS

This platform, slightly modified, was launched at the Columbus Convention, which met on February 21, 1872. Twelve States were represented. The Convention demanded as the nation's money, greenbacks not based on coin. A tariff taxing luxuries and protecting home industries, a law for an eight-hour labor-day, and the governmental control of railways and telegraphs were also insisted on. Hon. David Davis was nominated for the Presidency, but declined to run. Subsequently Charles O'Conor was named. The Forty-Second Congress, second session, discussed at length some of the Labor Party's proposals, but did nothing to realize any of them. An attempt was made to erect a Labor Commission, but for the present in vain. The first State Bureau of Labor Statistics had been established in 1869 in Massachusetts, where, as we have seen, the Labor Party showed exceptional strength.

U. S. DEPARTMENT OF LABOR

Pennsylvania followed in 1872, Connecticut in 1873-75. By the end of 1884 eleven other States had bureaus. From 1884 to 1894 thirteen more were erected. At last, by an Act of Congress, approved June 13, 1888, an independent Department of Labor was established by the Federal Government, a bureau with similar functions having existed in connection with the Interior Department since 1884.

The act of 1888 provided that the design and duty of the new department should be " to acquire and diffuse among the people of the United States useful information on subjects connected with labor, in the most general and comprehensive sense of that word, and especially upon its relation to capital, the hours of labor, the earnings of laboring men and women, and the means of promoting their material, social, intellectual, and moral prosperity."*

Clothed with these powers the Commissioner undertook investigations into such matters as industrial depressions, convict labor, strikes and lockouts, the condition of working women in large cities, railroad labor, cost of production, wages

* Section 7 of the act provides more specifically, that the Commissioner "is specially charged to ascertain, at as early a date as possible, and whenever industrial changes shall make it essential, the cost of producing articles at the time dutiable in the United States, in leading countries where such articles are produced, by fully specified units of production, and under a classification showing the different elements of cost, or approximate cost, of such articles of production, including the wages paid in such industries per day, week, month or year, or by the piece; and hours employed per day; and the profits of the manufacturers and producers of such articles; and the comparative cost of living, and the kind of living. 'It shall be the duty of the Commissioner also to ascertain and report as to the effect of the customs laws, and the effect thereon of the state of the currency in the United States, on the agricultural industry, especially as to its effects on mortgage indebtedness on farmers;' and what articles are controlled by trusts, or other combinations of capital, business operations or labor, and what effect said trusts or other combinations of capital, business operations or labor have on production and prices. He shall also establish a system of reports by which, at intervals of not less than two years, he can report the general condition, so far as production is concerned, of the leading industries of the country. The Commissioner of Labor is also specially charged to investigate the causes of, and facts relating to, all controversies and disputes between employers and employés as they may occur, and which may tend to interfere with the welfare of the people of the different States, and report thereon to Congress. The Commissioner of Labor shall also obtain such information upon the various subjects committed to him as he may deem desirable from different foreign nations, and what, if any, convict-made goods are imported into this country, and if so, from whence."

and cost of living abroad and in this country, prices, marriage and divorce. The results of these investigations were rigidly verified both in copy and in proof, and scrutinized for internal discrepancies. The information was collected through personal interviews and statements directly from parties cognizant of the ultimate facts. The Department's special agents were generally accorded a kind reception, and more and more as it appeared that no person's name was betrayed, were by manufacturers in this and in other countries given access to books and accounts. Estimates, hearsay and opinions were wholly excluded from consideration, and the returns made upon carefully prepared schedules of inquiry in the hands of experts.

The American Department of Labor established its standing by its first report upon "Industrial Depressions," made with experienced help and in face of many difficulties. After experience, the Department maintaining a non-partisan and a non-propagandist attitude, its reports came to be looked upon at home and abroad as the highest attainable evidence in their line. They were quoted in Parliament, in the Reichstag, and in the Chamber of Deputies. Foreign countries, notably England, France, Germany and Belgium, established similar bureaus.

The State Labor Bureaus also well served the public, though the spoils system and the changeable gusts of local public opinion hindered their usefulness. One New York Commissioner was at one time thought to have used his office for partisan ends, but no other functionary of his class fell under such suspicion. On the contrary, practical good of the most pronounced sort was traceable in greater or less degree to these bureaus. The tenement-house evil and the sweat-shop, if not banished, were thoroughly advertised by them. Child labor laws, laws prescribing maximum hours of labor, and employers' liability laws were placed upon many statute books mainly through the bureaus' influence. Though not banished, the "truck" or "pluck-me" store, whereby

THE CONTRACT-LABOR LAW

the employer-store-owner, forcing his employés' patronage, left them hardly a driblet of wages, was rendered far less common than it had been. Weekly in place of monthly wage payments were made more common. Frauds upon laboring men and false labor statistics were exposed. Thus when in 1878 complaint was made that Massachusetts had from 200,000 to 300,000 unemployed in her borders, the State bureau showed this estimate to be exaggerated from seven to ten times. Similarly State labor statistics, subsequently corroborated by the census, in effect bisected certain wild estimates of mortgage indebtedness, pointing out that nine-tenths of this indebtedness indicated prosperity rather than poverty.

All welcomed the Act of Congress, approved August 3, 1882, forbidding convicts, lunatics, idiots and paupers to enter the United States from other lands. Under this act, up to January 30, 1893, an average of about eleven hundred persons per annum, mostly paupers, were shipped back across the ocean. February 18, 1885, a stringent contract-labor law was passed, making it unlawful for any person, company or corporation to assist or encourage the immigration into the United States of any alien under contract or agreement previously made, every such contract to be void, and each violation of the law finable in the sum of $1,000. An amendment passed in 1885 excepted professional actors, artists, lecturers, singers, persons employed strictly as domestic servants, and even skilled workmen for a new industry which could not be established without such. Also the law did not forbid a person from assisting to this country members of his or her family intending to settle here. The amendment referred to provided for the return of persons who had come to the United States on labor contracts before the law was passed. Under this provision nearly eight thousand persons had been up to 1888 sent back to Europe. During the fiscal year ending June 30, 1893, 464 persons were thus returned. New York State having voted a tax of fifty cents upon each immigrant

THE LAST QUARTER-CENTURY

landing in its ports, the money to be for the maintenance of an Immigration Commission, the United States Supreme Court declared the act unconstitutional, whereupon Congress passed an act levying the same impost as a federal tax, its proceeds to go for the support of State Immigration Commissions in the States where most immigrants arrived. The New York Commission wrought incalculable good in preventing frauds upon immigrants, and in assisting them to their destination.

After the passage of the Resumption Act, January 14, 1875, the forces of labor reform were quite generally directed against the policy of contraction. A convention of anti-contractionists met in Detroit, on August 23, 1875. Protesting that they were not inflationists, they yet earnestly depre-

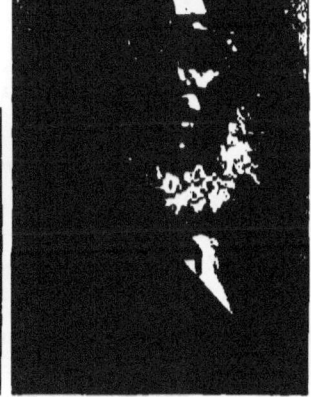

SAMUEL F. CARY PETER COOPER NEWTON BOOTH

cated any diminution in the volume of currency, which they would maintain by greenbacks redeemable only in bonds, these, in turn, being convertible into greenbacks.

The Independents, known as the National Greenback Party, assembled at Indianapolis, Ind., on May 17, 1876. Two hundred and thirty-nine delegates were present from nineteen States. The platform was essentially a demand for the immediate and unconditional repeal of the Resumption

NATIONAL GREENBACK-LABOR PARTY

Act and for the issue of United States notes convertible on demand into Government obligations bearing a low rate of interest, such notes to form our circulating medium, and such bonds, re-exchangeable for notes at the option of the holder, to render needless any further sales of bonds payable in coin. Peter Cooper was the nominee for President, Newton Booth for Vice-President. Mr. Booth declining, Samuel F. Cary, of Ohio, was chosen in his stead. Mr. Cooper accepted the nomination conditionally, expressing the hope that the Independents might attain their aims through either the Republican or the Democratic party, permitting him "to step aside and remain in that quiet which was" he declared "most congenial to his nature and time of life." Cooper ran, however, receiving 82,640 votes. The next year his party polled 187,095 votes, and in 1878, 1,000,365. The Greenback or National Greenback-Labor Party entered actively into the canvass of 1880, running General J. B. Weaver for President, who polled 307,740 votes. Four years later General B. F. Butler was the presidential candidate both of this party and of the "Anti-monopoly" party. He received 133,825 votes.

Happy had it been for the country could we have diverted the entire force of the labor agitation into political channels. But this was impossible. The worst labor troubles of these years had to be settled not at the polls but by force. This was mainly due to the large number of immigrants now arriving, among them Hungarians, Poles, Italians and Portuguese, usually ignorant clay for the hand of the first unscrupulous demagogue. Another cause of the labor wars was the wide and sedulous inculcation in this country of the social-democratic, communist and anarchist doctrines long prevalent in Europe. Influences concurrent with both these were the actual injustice and the haughty and overbearing manner of many employers. Capital had been mismanaged and wasted. The war had brought unearned fortunes to many, sudden wealth to a much larger number, while the unexampled prosperity of the country raised up in a perfectly normal manner a wealthy class, the like of which, in number and power, our country had never known before. As, therefore, immigration, along with much else, multiplied the poor, the eternal angry strife of wealth with poverty, of high with low, of classes with masses, crossed over from Europe and began on our shores.

The rise of trusts and gigantic corporations was connected with this struggle. Corporations worth nigh half a billion dollars apiece were able to buy or defy legislatures and make or break laws as they pleased; and since such corporations, instead of individuals, more and more became the employers of labor, not only did the old-time kindliness between help and hirers die out, but men the most cool and intelligent feared the new power as a menace to democracy. Strikes, therefore, commanded large public sympathy. Stock-watering and other vicious practices, involving the ruin of corporators themselves by the few holders of a majority of the shares in order to repurchase the property for next to nothing, contributed to this hostility. So did the presence, in many great corporations, of foreign capital and capitalists, and also the mutual favoritism of corporations, showing itself, for instance, in special freight rates to privileged concerns. Minor interests, and particularly employés, powerless against these Titan agencies by any legal process, resorted to counter-organization. Labor agitation was facilitated by the extraordinary increase of urban population, it being mostly manufacturing and mechanical industry which brought the hordes of workmen together. Trades-unions secured rank development. The Knights of Labor, intended as a sort of union of them all, attained a membership of a million. The manufacturers' "black list," to prevent any "agitator" laborer from securing work, was answered by the "boycott," to keep the products of obnoxious establishments from finding sale. Labor organizations so

LABOR WAR IN PENNSYLVANIA

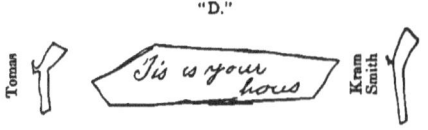

Notice you have Caried this as far as you can By cheating thy men you three Bosses Be Carefull if the Above dont Be your home in A short Time.

From a Stranger
he nowes you

A "*Mollie Maguire*" *Notice*

strong often tyrannized over their own members, and boycotting became a nuisance that had to be abated by law. In the Pennsylvania mining districts labor troubles early became acute. The great coal barons, offending the public by pricing their indispensable product extortionately high, long received no sympathy and no aid in repressing employés' crimes. During 1873, 1874 and 1875, these grew frightfully common. Usually the motive seemed to be not so much to injure employers' property as to scare " scab " help from the mines during contests against " cuts " in wages. A cut at the Ben Franklin Colliery had been accepted by the men, who were peaceably at work, when the " breaker " was burned, throwing them all out. Another " breaker " near by a gang of strikers fired almost by daylight, first driving the workmen away.

A common method of intimidation was for ten or twelve roughs to form a gang, and, armed, to sweep through a mining camp, forcing every man to join; the numbers so collected being soon sufficient to overawe any inclined to resist. June 3, 1875, one thousand men thus gathered stopped work at several mines near Mahanoy City, and a similar band did the same at Shenandoah. At night there was an attempt to derail a passenger train approaching Shenandoah, but the plot was discovered in time. The same night a "breaker" near Mount Carmel went up in smoke, and a few days later two contractors at the Oakdale mine were shot.

For a time every passenger train on the Reading Railroad had to be preceded through the mining districts by a locomotive carrying an armed posse. Watchmen and station agents were beaten; loaded cars and other obstructions were put upon main tracks; switches were misplaced and warehouses plundered. At every cut or forest along the line lay armed assassins to shoot trainmen and passengers. Each engineer ran his train, his left hand on the throttle, his right clutching a revolver.

V.

(Notice found in yard of D. Patchen, Engineer, Cresson.)

from the gap   Daniel Patch
remember you will be running in this coal ragion at night you took an nother mans engin we will give you fair warning in time and some more. V. L.

M. M. H. S. T.

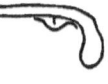

VI.

we hear notify you to leave th Road for you took a nother man chop take a warning to Save your live
             to Yost

A Notice Put in Evidence During the "Mollie Maguire" Prosecution

Bosses and "scabs" specially hated by the desperate miners were served with notices denouncing vengeance on them if they did not leave. Some of these are reproduced on pp. 293, 294, 295.

One admonition ran:

" Now men i have warented ye before and i willnt warind you no mor—but i will gwrintee you the will be the report of the revolver."

A rude drawing of a revolver was subjoined as the author's sign manual.

Others were as follows:

" NOTICE

" Any blackleg that takes a Union Man's job While He is standing for His Rights will have a hard Road to travel and if He don't he will have to Suffer the Consequences."

This " Notice " was followed by a picture of a dead man in his coffin, and signed " BEACHER AND TILTON."

MURDER OF YOST

At Locust Summit, March 31, 1875, was posted the following:

"NOTICE"

" Mr. Black-legs if you don't leave in 2 days time You meet your doom there vill Be an Open war—imeateatly—"

Such threats, unless heeded, were nearly always executed. Among others notified in these ways was one McCarron, a policeman in Tamaqua, who had aroused the enmity of " Powder Keg " Carrigan. Two men were detailed to kill McCarron late on a given night, and hid themselves for this purpose near his beat. But on this night McCarron happened to have changed beats with another policeman named Yost, an old soldier, whom all, even the Mollies, liked. Climbing a lamppost ladder early in the morning to turn out the gas, Yost was fatally shot by the men who had heen lying low for McCarron.

The chief source of these atrocities was a secret society known as the " Mollie Maguires," their name and spirit both imported from Ireland. They terrorized the entire Schuylkill and Shamokin districts. A superintendent or a boss was attacked, beaten or shot down somewhere almost every day. Gangs of these thugs would waylay a victim in the field or by the roadside if they could, but, failing in this, they surrounded his house, forced him

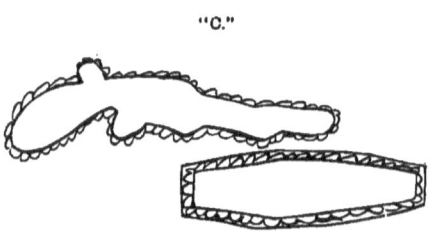

"C."

Notice is here given to you men the first and the last Notice that you will get for no mau to go Down this slope After to Night if yo Do you Can Bring your Coffion Along With you for By the internal Crist We mean What this Notice says you Drift man stop at home and Cut no more Coal let him go and get Coal himself I Dont mean Engineer or firemans let them mine there one Work now men the Next Notice you Will get I Dont mean to Do it With my Pen I Will Do it With that there Rolver I Dou't Want no more Black legs at this Collary.

(No signature)

A "Mollie Maguire" Notice

out, and did him to death. Among the most brutal of their murders was that of Alexander Rea, a mine superintendent, pounded and shot to death in October, 1868. Driving along a lonely road between Mount Carmel and Centralia, supposed to be going to pay off his men, and therefore to have $19,000, more or less, in his buggy, he was set upon by a gang of Mollies, among them Dooley (or Tully), McHugh, and " Kelly the Bum." After filling themselves with liquor, the squad, at dawn, hid in a piece of woods through which their victim was to pass, and, upon his approach, rushed at him, pistols in hand. " Kelly the Bum " fired first. Rea piteously begged for his life. He happened on this occasion to have only $60 with him, having paid at the colliery the day previous, a day earlier than usual; but he offered his assailants all he had, as well as his watch, agreeing also to sign a check for any amount if they would spare him. In vain. Having fired several bullets into the wretched man, they made sure of the work with clubs and the butts of their revolvers. The bloody conspirators were subsequently tried, convicted, and hung for this murder, save " Kelly the Bum," who got off by turning State's evidence.

Law-abiding people feared to stir out after dark, or even by day unless well armed. The Mollies had their signs and passwords for use when necessary, but they grew so bold that such devices were rarely needed. In case of arrest plenty of perjurers were ready to swear an *alibi*, though not a witness could be drummed up for the State. The Mollies nominated officers and controlled elections. Members of the Order became chiefs of police, constables and county commissioners. One of them came very near being elected to the Schuylkill County bench. Superintendents of jobs had to hire and discharge men at the Mollies' behest, or be shot. At a certain State election a high State official gave the Order large money for casting its vote his way. Jack Kehoe, a leading Mollie, when in prison for murder, boasted that if he were convicted

THE TRIAL OF THOMAS MUNLEY, THE "MOLLIE MAGUIRE," AT POTTSVILLE, PA.
Painted by W. R. Leigh, from photographs by George A. Bretz

McPARLAN BECOMES A "MOLLIE"

JAMES McPARLAN,   *THOMAS MUNLEY*   *"JIMMY" KERRIGAN,*
the detective   *the "squealer"*
From photographs by George A. Bretz

and sentenced "the old man up at Harrisburg" would never let him swing. The entire power of the Catholic Church in the region was used against the Order, but in vain.

The principal honor of exposing and suppressing this Pennsylvania Mafia is due to Hon. Franklin B. Gowen, a lawyer, at the time President of the Pennsylvania and Reading Coal and Iron Co. Knowing the uselessness of attempting the work with the local police, he, in 1873, secured from Pinkerton's Detective Agency in Chicago the services of one James McParlan, a young Irishman of phenomenal tact and grit, to go among the Mollies as a secret detective. No bolder, no more dangerous, no more telling work was ever wrought by a detective than that now undertaken by McParlan. Calling himself McKenna, he began operations in the autumn of 1873. By stating that he had killed a man in Buffalo and that his favorite business had been "shoving the queer," he was at once admitted to the Order, and soon became one of its prominent officers. He seems, however, to have been from the first the object of some suspicion, so that the progress of his mission was slow.

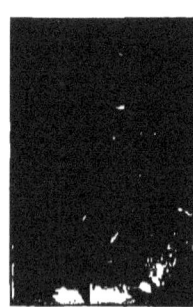

FRANKLIN B. GOWEN
From a photograph by Gutekunst

299

THE LAST QUARTER-CENTURY

It was not till 1875 that McParlan's work began to tell. Two murders to which he was privy he unfortunately could not prevent, so closely was he watched. One of these was that of Thomas Sanger, a young English boss miner. Early on the morning of September 1st Sanger started from his house to his work. Hardly out of sight of his door a man faced him and shot him through the arm. Running round a house near by he was met by a second villain, pistol in hand. Turning, he stumbled and fell, just as a third appeared, who shot him fatally. A fourth deliberately turned the body over so as to make sure of hitting a vital part, and shot him again. Robert Heaton, an employer, heard the firing and rushed, armed, to Sanger's aid. The murderers fled. Poor, brave Sanger, bleeding to death, told Heaton: "Never mind me, give it to them, Bob." Sanger's agonized wife, from whom he had just parted, reached his prostrate form barely in time to hear him gasp: "Kiss me, Sarah, for I am dying."

The assassins escaped Heaton, but went straight to the house where McParlan was, acquainting him with every detail of their bloody deed. Gowen had employed him on the express condition that he should never be called as a witness or be required in any way to show his hand, but when arrests were made the Mollies suspected him, so that it appeared to be his safest course to come out openly for the prosecution. Going upon the witness stand he demolished the sham *alibi* which the culprits sought to establish, and gave clews which led to the extirpation of the entire gang. Schuylkill County, where the worst crimes had occurred, rose in its might and stamped out the conspiracy. A small army of *alibi* witnesses were punished for perjury. Nine of the Mollies were sentenced to death, and most of the other leaders imprisoned for long terms.

"Then," said Mr. Gowen, who acted as counsel for the prosecution, "we knew that we were free men. Then we could go to Patsy Collins, the commissioner of this county,

THE ATTEMPT TO FIRE THE PENNSYLVANIA RAILROAD ROUND-HOUSE IN
PITTSBURG, AT DAYBREAK ON SUNDAY, JULY 22, 1877

Painted by W. R. Leigh, from photographs by Robinson

COLLAPSE OF THE MOLLIE MAGUIRES

and say to him : ' Build well the walls of the new addition to the prison ; dig the foundations deep and make them strong ; put in good masonry and iron bars ; for, as the Lord liveth, the time will come when, side by side with William Love, the murderer of Squire Gwither, you will enter the walls that you are now building for others.' Then we could say to Jack Kehoe, the high constable of a great borough in this county : ' We have no fear of you.' Then we could say to Ned Monaghan, chief of police and murderer and assassin : ' Behind you the scaffold is prepared for your reception.' Then we could say to Pat Conry, commissioner of this county : ' The time has ceased when a governor of this State dares to pardon a Mollie Maguire—you have had your last pardon.' Then we could say to John Slattery, who was almost elected judge of this court : ' We know that of you that it were better you had not been born than that it should be known.' Then all of us looked up. Then, at last, we were free, and I came to this county and walked through it as safely as in the most crowded thoroughfares of Philadelphia.''

The times evoked a specially bitter feeling against great railway corporations, and a widespread desire to set legal limitations to their power. Their reckless rivalries, their ruinous borrowing and extravagance were freely criticised even by such as did not deem themselves injured thereby ; but their employés were rendered frantic.

The most desperate and extensive strike that had yet occurred in this country was that of 1877, by

*Owing to the general congestion of traffic, there were miles of freight cars blocked at this point, which the rioters burned as they stood.

BURNT FREIGHT CARS AT PITTSBURG *

THE LAST QUARTER-CENTURY

Union Station   Round-house

SCENES AFTER THE RAILWAY RIOT OF 1877 IN PITTSBURG

the employés of the principal railway trunk lines—the Baltimore & Ohio, the Pennsylvania, the Erie, the New York Central, and their western prolongations. The immediate grievance was a ten per cent. "wage cut," reinforced, however, by irregular employment, irregular and tardy payment, forced patronage of "pluck-me" hotels, and the like. On some roads the trainmen were assessed the cost of accidents. At a preconcerted time junctions and other main points were seized. Freight traffic on the roads named was entirely suspended, and the passenger and mail service greatly impeded. When new employés sought to work, militia had to be called out to preserve order. Pittsburg was the scene of a bloody riot. At Martinsburg, also at Pittsburg, a great part of the State troops sympathized with the strikers and would not fire upon them. At Pittsburg, where the mob was immense and most furious, the Philadelphia militia were besieged in a round-house, which it was then attempted to burn by lighting oil cars and pushing them against it, until the soldiers were compelled to evacuate. Fortunately they made good their retreat with only four killed. The militia having had several bloody and doubtful encounters on July 21, 22 and 23, at the request of the Governors, President Hayes dispatched United States troops to Pennsylvania, Maryland and West Virginia. Faced by these forces the rioters in every instance gave way without bloodshed.

Scranton's mayor narrowly escaped death, but was rescued by a posse of special police, who killed three of the mob ringleaders. In disturbances at Chicago nineteen were killed, at Baltimore nine. At Reading, endeavoring to recapture a railroad train held by the mob in a cut near the city, the soldiers were assailed with bricks and stones hurled from above, and finally with pistol shots. One militiaman retorted, scattering shots followed, and then a sustained volley. Only 50 of the 253 soldiers escaped unhurt, but none were seriously injured. Of the crowd 11 were killed and over 50 wounded, two of the killed and some of the wounded being mere on-lookers.

The torch was applied freely and with dreadful effect. Machine-shops, ware-houses and two thousand freight-cars were pillaged or burned. Firemen in Pittsburg were at first threatened with death if they tried to stop the flames, and the hoses were cut; but, finally, permission was given to save private property. In that city attacks did not cease till the corporation property had been well-nigh destroyed. 1,600 cars and 126 locomotives were burned or ruined in twenty-four hours. Allegheny County alone became liable for about $3,000,000. Men, women and children fell to thieving, carrying off all sorts of goods—kid ball-shoes, parasols, coffeemills, whips and gas-stoves. In one house the police found seven great trunks full of clothes, in another eleven barrels of flour. It is said that a wagon-load of sewing machines was sold on the street, the machines bringing from ten cents to $1 apiece. The loss of property was estimated at $10,000,000.

One hundred thousand laborers are believed to have taken part in the entire movement, and at one time or another 6,000

THE LAST QUARTER-CENTURY

or 7,000 miles of road were in their power. The agitation began on July 14th, and was serious till the 27th, but had mostly died away by the end of the month, the laborers nearly all returning to their work.

Hosts of Pennsylvania miners went out along with the railroad men. The railway strike itself was largely sympathetic, the ten per cent. reduction in wages assigned as its cause applying to comparatively few. The next years witnessed continual troubles of this sort, though rarely, if in any case, so serious, between wage-workers and their employers in nearly all industries. The worst ones befell the manufacturing portions of the country, where strikes and lock-outs were part of the news almost every day.

CHAPTER XII

ANYTHING TO BEAT GRANT

PRESIDENTIAL POSSIBILITIES IN 1880.—GRANT THE LION.—REPUBLICAN CONVENTION.—A POLITICAL BATTLE OF THE WILDERNESS.—GARFIELD THE DARK HORSE.—GRANT'S OLD GUARD DEFEATED BUT DEFIANT.—DEMOCRATS NOMINATE HANCOCK.—"THE INS AND THE OUTS."—PARTY DECLARATIONS.—THE MOREY FORGERY.—BLAINE CAN'T SAVE MAINE.—CONKLING'S STRIKE OFF.—GARFIELD ELECTED. —"SOAP" VS. INTIMIDATION AND FRAUD.—FROM MULE BOY TO PRESIDENT.—HANCOCK'S BRILLIANT CAREER.—THE FIRST PRESIDENTIAL APPOINTMENTS.—CONKLING'S FRENZY AND HIS FALL.— THE CABINET.—GARFIELD ASSASSINATED.—GUITEAU TRIED AND HANGED.—STAR ROUTE FRAUDS.—PENDLETON CIVIL SERVICE ACT.

MR. HAYES'S very honorable administration neared its end and the presidential campaign of 1880 approached. Spite of the wide unpopularity of resumption, spite of the hard times and the labor troubles, the party in power was now in far better condition to win than it had been in 1876. The Republicans therefore had no dearth of potential standard-bearers. Returning from a remarkable tour around the world, General Grant became, in 1880, a candidate for a third-term nomination. There is reason to think that Grant himself did not greatly desire this but was pushed forward by Senator Roscoe Conkling, of New York, to insure the defeat of James G. Blaine, of Maine, whom Conkling not merely disliked but hated. Conkling was now in effect Republican dictator in his State. Its delegation to the Convention was hence expected to be a unit for Grant, in which case it would form a good nucleus for the third-term forces. Don Cameron, of Pennsylvania, and General John A. Logan, of Illinois, like Conkling, strongly favored Grant, securing for him, not without some contest, the delegations from their respective States and at the same time

THE LAST QUARTER-CENTURY

securing control of the National Committee, which dictated the time and place of holding the Convention. Mr. Blaine had great strength in the West and considerable elsewhere. Senator Edmunds was the cynosure of a knot of Independents, mostly Eastern men. Sherman's masterly handling of the Treasury brought him also into prominence, almost into popularity, as a candidate. He was able, practically, to name the four Ohio delegates-at-large, Warner M. Bateman, William Dennison, Charles Foster and James A. Garfield. The last-named had expressed his wish to be a delegate-at-large, in order that he might more effectively aid the Sherman cause.

General Grant was now more than ever a hero. He had recently visited every prominent court and country on the globe. The Emperors of Germany and Austria, the Czar, the Queen of Great Britain, the Sultan, the Pope, the Kings of Belgium, Italy, Holland, Sweden and Spain, the Khédive of Egypt, the Emperor of Siam, the Mikado of Japan, the Viceroy of India, and with them a host of the world's most distinguished statesmen, soldiers and literary men, had vied with one another in rendering the ex-President's progress from land to land a continuous ovation. No human being in all history had ever received such honors. The ex-President's self-possession amid all this pomp, his good sense and sturdy maintenance of simple, democratic man-

ROSCOE CONKLING

"ANYTHING TO BEAT GRANT"

ners, impressed everyone. Some who had opposed him in 1876 now wished him elected, on the ground that four so honorable years in private station justified renewed promotion, while not transgressing the unwritten law against a third term.

So formidable did Conkling's movement for Grant become that the opponents of the two rallied to the war-cry, "Anything to beat Grant." About this time the superstitious were stirred by Mother Shipton's prophecy,

> "The world to an end will come
> In eighteen hundred and eighty-one."

An anecdote was told of a preacher who dwelt upon the impending cataclysm, urging his hearers by all means to be prepared. While he was describing the peril an earnest voice from the congregation ejaculated, "Thank God!" The minister sought out the possessor of the voice and asked why he was thankful for a prospect at which most men shuddered. "Anything to beat Grant," was the answer. A determined sentiment hostile to the ex-President's candidacy found expression in the resolutions of the Republican Anti-third-term Convention, held in St. Louis on May 6th. These resolutions declared against the Grant movement as likely to revive the memory of old scandals, and certain, if successful, to introduce personal government and to hinder civil service reform.

After the revelations described in Chapter IX the movement to elect Grant President for a third term was sure to awaken bitter opposition in his own party. The story of his second term, which might have been left for posterity to extract from the records as best it could, was vividly recalled to memories which had never fully lost it, being rehearsed in a thousand newspapers, now piecemeal, now in whole chapters, till all intelligent people were perfectly familiar with it.

The Republican Convention met at Chicago on June 2d. Conkling, who had charge of the Grant canvass, sanguine of carrying the Convention but fearing a "bolt" afterward, introduced the following disciplinary resolution, which was passed by a vote of 719 to 3 :

"*Resolved*, As the sense of this Convention, that every member of it is bound in honor to support its nominee, whoever that nominee may be, and that no man should hold his seat here who is not ready to so agree."

An effort was made to expel the three recalcitrants, but it proved abortive. The rule requiring State delegations each to vote as a unit, which had been assailed at the Cincinnati Convention of 1876, was now definitively abandoned. This gift of a voice to minorities in State delegations lopped off ninety votes from Grant's constituency, which was a great victory for his opponents. It was in effect another blow against the Grant cause when Mr. Flanagan, of Texas, uttered the memorable query: "What are we here for if it isn't for the offices?"

The State of New York had seventy votes in the Convention. Knowing that they would all be needed if Grant were to win, Conkling had gotten the New York Convention to instruct the delegation to vote as a unit for the nominee desired by the majority. But nineteen of them, led by Conkling's opponent in New York Republican politics, William H. Robertson, refused to obey this mandate and voted for Blaine. Nine of the Ohio delegation bolted from Sherman to Blaine, a move which solidified the rest of the Ohio delegation against Blaine, and thus "undoubtedly," says Sherman, "led to his defeat." The first ballot showed Grant in the lead, with Blaine a close second, and they maintained this relative position through thirty-five consecutive ballots. The thirty-fourth ballot called attention to James A.

JAMES A. GARFIELD
Before entering college. From a daguerreotype by Ryder

GARFIELD NOMINATED

Garfield, who received seventeen votes, fifteen more than any preceding ballot had given him. As a feeler Wisconsin, near the foot of the list, bolted to him. Galleries and Convention went wild. Garfield had been somewhat prominent in the Convention, having charge of Sherman's cause and being, in some sense, the leader of all the forces opposed to Grant, but scarcely anyone had dreamed of his being nominated. It having become plain that the New York split must defeat Blaine and Grant alike, the bulk of the Blaine and Sherman delegates, under instructions from their chiefs at Washington, went over to Garfield. Conkling was confident till Maine cast her vote for Garfield, when he sent the word around for delay. In vain. Too late. Conkling's old guard of 306 delegates, remaining steadfast to the last, rendered him too confident, and he was outgeneralled. That very morning some one asked Garfield: "Well, General, who is going to win the battle of the Wilderness?" "The same little man that won the first will win it," he replied, deliberately, "and I am afraid it will mean the destruction of the Republican party." The stampede gave Garfield 399 votes, twenty-one more than were needed to make him the choice of the Convention. While the State banners were seized and waved in a circle above his head, while all was enthusiasm and hubbub, Garfield himself sat, as if in a stupor, dazed and benumbed. The second place on the ticket being conceded to a Grant man, Conkling, as a stab at President Hayes, named for Vice-President Chester A. Arthur, the same whom Hayes had deposed from office. "Garfield and Arthur" was therefore the ticket.

The country hailed the presidential nomination with extreme satisfaction. Blaine, in spite of his defeat, hastened to send Garfield his congratulations. So did Sherman, who blamed Governor Foster, and not the nominee, for perfidy. But Conkling sulked, cursing the nineteen rebellious New York delegates, and vowing eternal vengeance upon Robertson in particular. Grant's phalanx, which had stood solid for him from the first, alone failed to partake of the general enthusiasm.

The Democratic Convention assembled at Cincinnati on June 22d. Mr. Tilden could, no doubt, have had the nomination had he signified his willingness to accept it, but his friends were wholly ignorant of his wishes until just as the Convention met, when he wrote declining renomination. On the third ballot the delegates nominated the hero of Gettysburg, the brave and renowned General Winfield S. Hancock, of Pennsylvania.

WINFIELD S. HANCOCK

The two parties were at this time best classed as "the ins" and "the outs." Though not exactly one upon the fading issue of intervention at the South, or upon that of "incidental protection" *versus* a "tariff for revenue only," neither these issues nor any others were kept steadily in sight during the campaign. The Republicans had not yet wearied of reminiscences, while the Democrats nursed their party fealty by calling Hayes "the fraud President." On the people at large the ceaseless repetition of this phrase had not the slightest effect, particularly after the publication of the "cipher despatches," which involved certain Democratic leaders in attempts, pending the Hayes-Tilden controversy, to bribe electors representing doubtful States.

The Republicans' platform charged Democrats with "a supreme and insatiable lust of office," yet their own *devoir*

PLATFORMS AND ISSUES

to civil service reform they paid only as an afterthought, amid the jeers of delegates. To detach the Republican reform vote, the Democratic platform made three distinct allusions to that subject, indorsing a general and thorough reform, "execrating" the course of the Administration in using offices to reward political crime, and promising " a genuine and lasting improvement in case of a change." The Republicans suspected the other party of coquetting with the Roman Catholic Church, and urged an amendment forbidding State appropriations for sectarian schools; but both parties applauded public education and separation between Church and State. They were at one also in decided opposition to Chinese immigration. The pensioner was becoming conspicuous. Republicans boasted of paying annually more than thirty millions of dollars in pensions, and promised the old soldiers—sincerely, as events showed—undiminished gratitude in future. They further declared against polygamy. The Democrats avowed themselves in favor of "free ships and a chance for American commerce on the seas and on the land;" also for gold, silver and convertible paper money.

Though living issues were little discussed in the campaign, it was not wanting in warmth or movement. Republicans were incessantly "waving the bloody shirt," a Democratic phrase which became familiar at this time. The Democrats, as we have said, harped upon the "fraud" that they ascribed to the Electoral Commission which "counted out" Mr. Tilden. Incidentally, as election-day grew near, protection to home industry and restriction to Chinese immigration were more or less discussed, with, perhaps, considerable local effect, but the election was in no sense decided by either. Seizing upon a luckless utterance of General Hancock's, to the effect that the tariff was "a local issue," the Republicans took occasion to ridicule his ignorance of economic and political affairs. Garfield was accused of disreputable connection with the Credit Mobilier, and with the Washington Ring back in the seventies, but nothing worse than indiscretion was proved against him. Shortly before election-day Democratic politicians sowed broadcast *facsimiles* of a letter signed with Garfield's name, and representing him as so lovingly attached to "our great manufacturing and corporate interests" as to favor Chinese immigration until laborers should be sufficiently abundant to satisfy capital. This letter was proved to be a forgery, and one of the authors of it was sentenced to prison for eight years.

In 1878 Maine had surprised everyone by electing a Democratic governor, through a fusion of Democrats with Greenbackers. After the next annual election, acting as a Canvassing Board, professedly under the law, this governor, Garcelon, and his counsel declared a Democratic legislature to be elected—a proceeding denounced as a "counting in" worthy of the most approved Louisiana model. This course contravened the judgment of the State Supreme Court. It was not upheld by public opinion either in the State or elsewhere, not even by Democratic opinion, unless as a species of "poetic justice." Most fatal of all, the new legislature was unsupported by the State militia, upon which, as no federal troops were at command, devolved, during the interregnum, the charge of keeping order. The fusionists, therefore, gave up in discouragement. But in the State election of the presidential year, in September, renewed success came to them. Their candidate, Harris M. Plaisted, was elected Governor, spite of the Republicans' activity under the personal lead of Mr. Blaine.

Until this reverse in Maine most supporters of Grant had sulked, but they did so no longer. The "strike" was now declared "off," and all the available resources of the party called into requisition for the election of Garfield. Persuaded by Grant, Conkling himself took the stump, working for the nominees with all his might. Popular audiences found his eloquence irresistible. No man did more than he to carry the

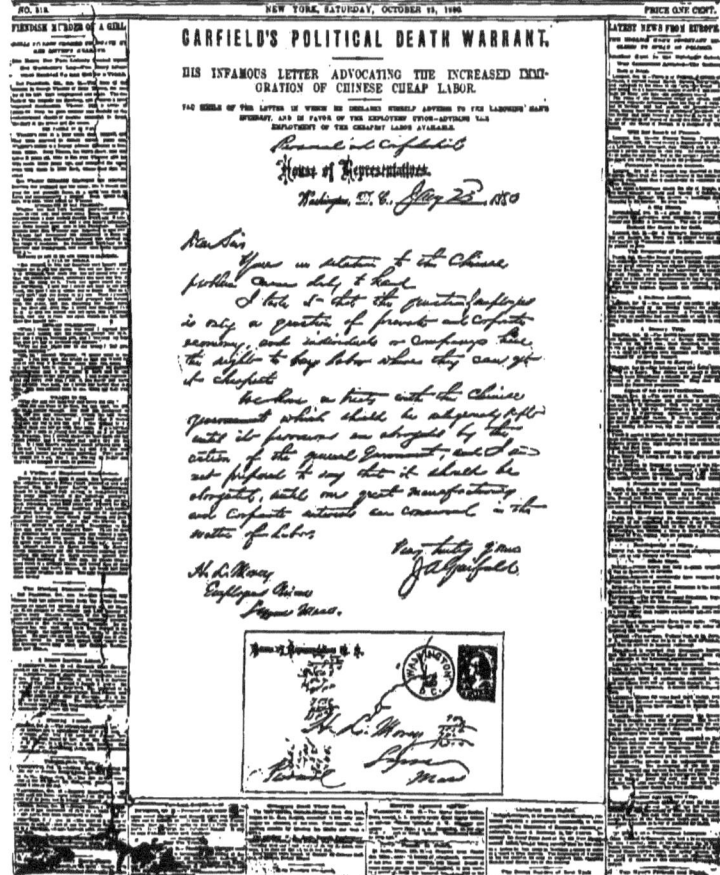

Facsimile of the front page of the issue of "*Truth*" containing the "*Morey Letter*"

GARFIELD AND ARTHUR VICTORIOUS

important State of New York. He took Grant with him throughout the State, exhibiting him for five-minute speeches, while he himself made long orations. This occasioned much comment, but probably "did good." Conkling and his supporters deemed his agency decisive of the result in the nation as well as in New York, and considered President Garfield as under the deepest obligation on this account. Hancock swept every Southern State. Garfield carried every Northern one except New Jersey, Nevada, and California. For the first time in our history the presidential electors were all chosen by popular vote, and for the first time their votes were counted as cast.

Thus the victory was won for Garfield and Arthur. It was not obtained, however, without employing, to some extent, illegitimate means. At a dinner in honor of Hon. S. W. Dorsey, Vice-President Arthur, in a vein of pleasantry, remarked that the Republicans had been victorious in Indiana by a liberal use of "soap." After the election discreditable exposures were made respecting contributions by government civil servants to the Republican campaign-fund.

But if machine politics had much to do with Garfield's election, machine politics no more determined it than intimidation and fraud solidified the South for Hancock. Garfield had a highly honorable record—literary, military, and civil. From a mule-boy on the tow-path of the Ohio Canal between Cleveland and Marietta — which rough life, it seems, bade fair for a time injuriously to affect his character—he had risen to a college presidency and to the Senate of Ohio, all before the war. Entering the service early, he rose rapidly in

HARRIS M. PLAISTED

rank—as he deserved, for no civilian commander had proved a better soldier. His martial quality came out at Middle Creek, Shiloh, and pre-eminently at Chickamauga, where his gallant and meritorious services made him a major-general. At Chickamauga, when the right wing of Rosecrans's army was in full retreat, leaving to its fate the left, under General Thomas, Garfield, through a fiery storm of shot, fatal to most of his escort, had ridden back to acquaint Thomas with the state of affairs, encourage him, and arrange for the safe re-formation of the Union forces on a new line. Entering Congress in December, 1863, he at once became a leader, serving with distinction on the most important committees, a power in debate and on the stump, eloquent, sensible, patriotic—not, indeed, an adroit politician, but no little of a statesman. While in Congress he probably had a more thorough acquaintance with important public questions than any other man in official life. His firm and decisive stand for honest money when a formidable faction in his party was for fiat greenbacks has already been alluded to in this History. That his State made him its Senator, and his country made him its President, were in nowise mere accidents.

Hancock's record, too, was altogether spotless and proud. A West Point graduate and a patriot to the backbone, brevetted for gallantry at Contreras and Cherubusco, at the front whenever he could possibly get there in any serious engagement of our army in Virginia during the entire Civil War, always a fighter, the bravest of the brave, the cause of Union victory at Gettysburg if any one man could be so called, Hancock at the time of his nomination came before the public as perhaps the most consummate specimen of a mere military man in the whole history of the country. Grant said Hancock's name "was never mentioned as having committed in battle a blunder for which he was held responsible." Nor can any well doubt that Hancock would have made a successful President. Few, in fact, questioned this. It was his

BLAINE VERSUS CONKLING

party that was distrusted. Had the Democracy held the place in public esteem which was accorded to the candidate, Hancock would almost certainly have been elected. As it was, Garfield's popular majority was trifling, though in the Electoral College he had 214 votes to Hancock's 155.

If it was Garfield's wish, as he again and again declared, to treat all stripes of the party alike, it is hard to understand what led him to select Blaine as Secretary of State in his Cabinet. The mere rumor of this purpose roused Conkling's utmost ire. Blaine and Conkling had long been openly and bitterly at feud. Their quarrel, beginning in empty trifles, had grown by incessant fanning until it menaced the party with fatal schism. Tried and wise friends of both besought Blaine not to accept the offered portfolio. Senator Dawes was one of these. He says: "I warned Mr. Blaine that if he entered the Cabinet with the intent or hope of circumventing his rival, it would be fatal to him and to the administation of Garfield, and I expressed the opinion that it would be impossible for him to keep the peace if he took the office. He replied with frankness, and, I have no doubt, with entire sincerity, that it would be his purpose if he accepted the office to ignore all past differences, and so deport himself in it as to force reconciliation. He said also that he could not agree with me, even if the effect should prove otherwise, that he should for that reason be debarred from the great opportunity, for which he felt himself qualified, to administer the Foreign Office on the broad and grand scale he did afterward undertake but was not permitted to perfect. I foresaw the rocks all too plainly, and advised him to remain in the Senate. But he determined otherwise and accepted the position."

Garfield and Blaine probably thought that Conkling's influence against them might be safely ignored (in which they proved not wholly right), considering him a very shallow man (wherein they were not wholly wrong). It is among William Winter's reminiscences that Conkling and George William

THE LAST QUARTER-CENTURY

Curtis once compared judgments touching poetry and oratory, each citing passages that seemed to him ideal. Conkling named Mrs. Hemans's "Casabianca," "The boy stood on the burning deck," etc., as his model poem, and some fine sentences from Charles Sprague as what suited him best in eloquence. It was Sprague, we recall, whose Fourth of July oration at Boston, in 1825, contained the smart period beginning: "Not many generations ago, where you now sit, circled by all that adorns and embellishes civilized life, the rank thistle nodded in the wind and the wild fox dug his hole unscared." Curtis, for eloquence, presented the following from Emerson's Dartmouth College oration, delivered on July 24, 1838: "You will hear every day the maxims of a low prudence. You will hear that the first duty is to get land and money, place and name. 'What is this Truth you seek? What is this Beauty?' men will ask, with derision. If nevertheless, God have called any of you to explore Truth and Beauty, be bold, be firm, be true. When you shall say, 'As others do, so will I. I renounce, I am sorry for it, my early visions; I must eat the good of the land, and let learning and romantic expectations go until a more convenient season;' then dies the man in you; then once more perish the buds of Art and Poetry and Science, as they have died already in a thousand thousand men."

This Conkling thought rather tame.

Conkling looked upon Blaine's promotion as nothing but a deliberate attempt to humiliate himself, and his friends concurred in this view. " Garfield, of whose great brain-power political sagacity formed no part, could not be made to see in the opposition anything but an attempt by dictation to trench upon his constitutional prerogatives in the choice of his own councillors, and all Blaine men agreed with him."

Bad was made worse when Garfield offered the post of Secretary of the Treasury to Charles J. Folger, of New York, not only without consulting Conkling but against Conkling's

Platt   Arthur   Conkling   Garfield
THE INTERVIEW AT THE RIGGS HOUSE

CONKLING DENOUNCES GARFIELD

warm recommendation of Mr. Morton. That Mr. Folger declined the portfolio did not pacify Conkling. No man in the Cabinet represented Conkling, whereas he and his friends thought that on account of his great service in the campaign all New York appointments, at least, should be filled by him from among his friends. Garfield, undoubtedly influenced by Blaine, would not consent to this. He was willing to do what he reasonably could to pacify Conkling, but he refused to renounce his constitutional privilege of personally selecting the men who were to aid him in discharging his arduous duties.

Shortly before the inauguration, in the spring of 1881, Senator Platt, who was politically and sympathetically in accord with his colleague, received the information that Mr. James had been selected for the position of Postmaster-General. Up to this time the two New York Senators had received assurances from the President-elect that the Empire State was to be favored with the portfolio of the Treasury Department, which was regarded as a more dignified and more influential position in every respect. As soon as Mr. Platt heard of the President's change of mind, he repaired at once to Chamberlain's, where he found Vice-President Arthur and Senator Conkling at breakfast. He broke the news to them. Arthur and Conkling at once left the table and all three repaired to the Riggs House, where Garfield had rooms. They received an audience without delay, and for over an hour Conkling stormed up and down the room, charging Garfield with treachery to his friends in New York and asserting that he was false to his party. Garfield sitting on the side of the bed listened in silence to the tirade, violent and unseemly as all thought it. Both General Arthur and Senator Platt subsequently declared that for invective, sarcasm and impassioned eloquence this was the speech of Conkling's life.

On March 23, 1881, Conkling's dearest foe, Mr. Robertson, was nominated by the President as Collector of Customs at the Port of New York, the then incumbent, E. A. Merritt, being nominated for the post of Consul-General at London. Both appointments were opposed by Conkling and his colleague, Mr. Platt, but in spite of this they were subsequently confirmed by the Senate. Conkling's ire grew into a frenzy. Sober Republicans were aghast at the chasm widening in the party. A committee of conciliation, consisting of five gentlemen representing different attitudes to the litigants, was appointed to try and harmonize them. Conkling met these gentlemen to recount his wrongs. Said Mr. Dawes, who was chairman of the committee: " On that occasion he surpassed himself in all those elements of oratorical power for which he was so distinguished. . . He continued for two hours and a half to play with consummate skill upon all the strings known to the orator and through all the notes from the lowest to the highest which the great masters command, and concluded in a lofty apostrophe to the greatness and glory of the Republican party and his own devotion to its highest welfare. 'And,' said he, 'I trust that the exigency may never arise when I shall be compelled to choose between self-respect and personal honor on the one side and the temporary discomfiture of that party on the other; but if that time shall ever come I shall not hesitate in the choice, and I now say to you, and through you to those whom it most concerns, that I have in my pocket an autograph letter of this President, who is now for the time being its official head, which I pray God I may never be compelled in self-defence to make public; but if that time shall ever come, I declare to you, his friends, he will bite the dust.'"

This letter proved to be one like the " My dear Hubbell" epistle mentioned below. It had been written in the course of the campaign to press collections from government officials and clerks for campaign expenses. President Garfield had retained a copy. His friends urged him to publish it forthwith, thus anticipating Conkling; and he, at first, consented, but Mr. Blaine dissuaded him. True to his threat, Conkling gave it out, but too late, so that it fell flat. The conciliation

H. L. Dawes, Mass.   J. P. Jones, Nevada   Roscoe Conkling
   E. H. Rollins, N. H.

"*I DECLARE TO YOU, HIS FRIENDS, HE WILL BITE THE DUST*"
Conkling's speech before the "Committee of Conciliation"

committee waited on the President to see if there was not some way by which he could consistently accord Conkling fuller recognition. Nothing came of the effort, as Conkling would be satisfied only by the President's utter neglect and humiliation of the Robertson faction in New York. Conkling was labored with again and begged to be magnanimous, but he would not yield a hair. Instead of placing the good of the party before his personal spite, he proposed to rule or ruin. "Should I do as I am urged," he said, "I should myself go under, and should be burned in effigy from Buffalo to Montauk Point, and could not be elected a delegate to a county convention in Oneida County." It is said that he did actually seek, later, an election to a convention in that county, but without success.

Republicans after the heart of Conkling and Arthur, constituting "the Prince of Wales's Party," now called themselves "Stalwarts," a term invented by Mr. Blaine, at the same time styling administration Republicans "Half-breeds." Those declining to take sides either way they dubbed "Jelly-fish." On May 16th, before Robertson's confirmation, the two New York Senators, Conkling and Platt, resigned their places, expecting the honor and indorsement of an immediate re-election. In this they were disappointed. They were defeated in the New York Legislature by E. C. Lapham and Warner Miller, administration or "Half-breed" Republicans. Mr. Conkling never again reappeared in politics. Mr. Platt, on the contrary, suffered only a temporary loss of influence. Disliked by a large section—perhaps a majority—of the New York Republicans, he still did not cease to be the determining factor of the fortunes of the party in his State. It is not unlikely that Mr. Bryce had Conkling and Platt in mind when, in his chapter upon "Rings and Bosses," he wrote: "There have been brilliant instances of persons stepping at once to the higher rungs of the ladder in virtue of their audacity and energy, especially if coupled with oratorical power. However,

THE LAST QUARTER-CENTURY

*THE ANTI-CHINESE RIOT OF 1880, IN DENVER, COL.**

the position of the rhetorical boss is less firmly rooted than that of the intriguing boss, and there have been instances of his suddenly falling to rise no more."

Mr. James was well succeeded in the New York Post-office by Mr. Pearson, who had been the Assistant Postmaster. Robert T. Lincoln, of Illinois, Secretary of War, was not well known, but the illustrious name of his father made the selection a popular one. He had supported Grant in the convention, and his appointment was an acknowledgment of the Logan faction. Of Mr. Kirkwood, Secretary of the Interior, it is sufficient to say that he was indorsed by Carl Schurz, his predecessor in the department. Judge William H. Hunt was placed in charge of the navy portfolio. He was an Old-Line

---

*The publication of the "Morey Letter" (see p. 315) stirred up a general anti-Chinese feeling, particularly through the West. On October 31, 1880, a mob attacked the Chinese quarter in Denver, and were only driven back when the firemen turned the stream from their hose on them.

GARFIELD'S CABINET

Whig, born in South Carolina, who had moved to Louisiana. Throughout the war he was a staunch Union man, and afterward a consistent Republican. He had been counsel for Governor Kellogg against McEnery in the famous Durell case, and also a candidate for the office of Attorney-General on the Louisiana State ticket with Packard. President Hayes made him a judge of the Court of Claims, a position which he held till he received this promotion from Mr. Garfield.

Wayne MacVeagh, of Pennsylvania, Attorney-General in Garfield's Cabinet, was universally respected for his high character and ability. Though a son-in-law of Simon Cameron, he was an Independent, and therefore, politically, no friend to either of the Camerons. William Windom, of Minnesota, Secretary of the Treasury, the East suspected of monetary "unsoundness," but this occasioned little anxiety, as Garfield was well known to be perfectly trustworthy in this regard. Windom was immensely popular in the West because of his antagonism to monopolies, some of which had already made themselves formidable and odious. By this time telegraph and railway lines had become consolidated and one or two "Trusts" had arisen.

In the fall of 1880 a Mr. Hudson, of Detroit, confided to Senator Sherman a fear that General Garfield would be assassinated, giving particulars. Being at once apprised, Mr. Garfield, under date of November 16, 1880, replied: "I do not think there is any serious danger in the direction to which he refers, though I am receiving what I suppose to be the usual number of threatening letters on that subject. Assassination can no more be guarded against than death by lightning; and it is not best to worry about either." Hardly had President Garfield entered upon his high duties when Mr. Hudson's fears were realized. This was only six weeks after the murder of Czar Alexander II. The President had never been in better spirits than on the morning of July 1, 1881. Before he was up one of his sons entered his room. Almost the boy's first words were "There!"—taking a flying leap over his bed —"you are the President of the United States, but you can't do that." Whereupon the Chief Magistrate arose and did it. Later in the morning, thus healthy and jovial, he entered the railway station at Washington, intending to take an Eastern trip. Charles J. Guiteau, a disappointed office-seeker, crept up behind him and fired two bullets at him, one of which lodged in his back.

The country already had a deep affection for Mr. Garfield, all except those immediately interested in party politics and many of these, sympathizing with him against Conkling in the struggle that had arisen over appointments. Democrats honored him for his course in this business. The terrible misfortune now come upon him ostensibly in consequence of his boldness in that matter wonderfully endeared him to the popular heart. He was likened to Lincoln, as another "martyr President." In all the churches throughout the North often as the congregations met for worship, earnest prayers were offered for the President's recovery. In every city crowds watched the bulletin boards daily from morning till night to learn from the despatches constantly appearing the distinguished sufferer's condition. The bullet had pierced the tissues by a long, angry and crooked course, leaving a wound that could not be properly drained. Spite of treatment by the most famous medical practitioners—whom, however, high authorities deemed somewhat fussy and irresolute in handling the case—blood-poisoning set in, and at length proved fatal. The President's hardy constitution enabled him to fight for life as few could have done. He languished on and on through weeks of dreadful suffering, till September 19th, when he died.

On the 21st of December the Houses of Congress passed resolutions for memorial services, to occur on February 27, 1882, to which were invited the President and ex-Presidents, the heads of departments, Supreme Court Judges, Ministers of

James G. Blaine, State   *William Windom, Treasury*   *Robert T. Lincoln, War*   *Wayne MacVeagh, Att'y-Gen.*

W. H. Hunt, Navy   *Thos. J. Kirkwood, Interior*   *T. L. James, Post.-Gen.*

PRESIDENT GARFIELD'S CABINET

BLAINE'S ORATION ON GARFIELD

JAMES A. GARFIELD
After a photograph by Bell—the last picture made before the assassination

foreign countries, Governors of States, and distinguished officers of the army and the navy. Upon that occasion Mr. Blaine delivered an oration on the life and character of the dead Chief Magistrate. The closing periods ran: " As the end drew near, his early craving for the sea returned. The stately mansion of power had been to him the wearisome hospital of pain, and he begged to be taken from its prison walls, from its oppressive, stifling air, from its homelessness and its hopelessness. Gently, silently, the love of a great people bore the pale sufferer to the longed-for healing of the sea, to live or to die, as God should will, within sight of its heaving billows, within sound of its manifold voices. With wan, fevered face tenderly lifted to the cooling breeze, he looked out wistfully upon the ocean's changing wonders; on its far sails, whitening in the morning light; on its restless waves rolling shoreward to break and die beneath the noonday sun; the red clouds of evening, arching low to the horizon; on the serene and shining pathway of the stars. Let us think that his dying eyes read a mystic meaning which only the rapt and parting soul may know. Let us believe that in the silence of the receding world he heard the great waves breaking on a further shore, and felt already upon his wasted brow the breath of the eternal morning."

THE LAST QUARTER-CENTURY

The sorrow over President Garfield's death, said George William Curtis, in another eulogy, was "more worldwide and pathetic than ever before lamented a human being. In distant lands men bowed their heads. The courts of kings were clad in mourning. The parish bells of rural England tolled, and every American household was hushed with pain as if its first-born lay dead."

It may be doubted whether posterity will give Mr. Garfield quite the high place assigned him by contemporary judgment; yet he was certainly among our greater men. Somewhat vacillating and passive, and too much dominated by Blaine's stronger nature, Garfield was a man of solid character, no little personal magnetism, and great information. In many respects he and Blaine were alike. In aptness for personal intercourse with men, and in the power of will, he was Blaine's inferior, while in logic, learning and breadth of view he was in advance of Blaine.

Guiteau had been by spells a politician, lawyer, lecturer, theologian and evangelist. He pretended to have been inspired by Deity with the thought that the removal of Mr. Garfield was necessary to the unity of the Republican party and to the salvation of the country. He is said to have exclaimed, on being arrested: "All right, I did it and will go to jail for it. I am a Stalwart, and Arthur will be President." His trial began in November and lasted over two months. The defense was insanity. The prosecution showed that the man had long been an unprincipled adventurer, greedy for notoriety; that he first conceived the project of killing the President after his hopes of office were finally destroyed; and that he had planned the murder several weeks in advance.

The public rage against Guiteau knew no bounds. Only by the utmost vigilance on the part of his keepers was his life prolonged till the day of his execution. Sergeant Mason, a soldier set to guard him, fired into Guiteau's cell with the evident intention of applying to the assassin assassins' methods.

GUITEAU IN COURT

The sergeant was tried by court-martial, dismissed from the army, deprived of his back pay, and sentenced to eight years in the Albany Penitentiary. Two months later, as they were taking the wretched Guiteau from jail to court, a horseman, dashing past, fired a pistol at him, the bullet grazing his wrist.

The prisoner's disorderly conduct and scurrilous interruptions of the proceedings during his trial, apparently to aid the plea of insanity, impaired the dignity of the occasion and

PRESIDENT GARFIELD'S REMAINS LYING IN STATE AT THE CAPITOL

elicited, both at home and abroad, comment disparaging to the court. Judge Cox threatened to gag the prisoner or send him out of court; but as neither of these courses could be taken without infringing Guiteau's right to confront his accusers and to speak in his own behalf, the threats were of no avail.

THE LAST QUARTER-CENTURY

Guiteau was found guilty in January, 1882. As the last juror signified his assent to the verdict the condemned man sprang to his feet and shrieked: "My blood will be upon the heads of that jury. Don't you forget it! God will avenge this outrage!" He was executed at Washington on June 30, 1882, and his skeleton is now in the Army Medical Museum in that city. The autopsy showed no disease of the brain.

Although it had no logical connection with the spoils system, the assassination of President Garfield called the attention of the country to the crying need of reform in the civil service. Through March, April, May and June, 1881, Washington streets had been blockaded with office-seekers and political adventurers, bearing "testimonials" of their worth, seeking indorsers and backers and awaiting chances to "interview" the President himself. Contributors to the election fund were especially forward in demanding positions. The President's time and strength were wasted in weighing the deserts of this or that politician or faction of a State to control patronage there. All who had known him in the army, in Congress or at home now made the most of such acquaintance.

We have seen that Hayes's administration marked in this respect, as in others, an immense improvement. Secretary Schurz in the Interior Department enforced competitive examinations. They were applied by Mr. James to the New York Post-office, and, as a result, one-third more work was done with less cost. Similar good results followed the adoption of the "merit system" in the New York Custom-house after 1879. President Hayes also strongly condemned political assessments upon office-holders, but with small practical effect, as his effort lacked full legislative sanction and sympathy.

But the corruption which had enjoyed immunity so long could not be put down all at once. During Hayes's last years, and thereafter, much public attention was drawn to the "Star Route" frauds. The Star Routes were stage-lines for

SCENE AT A STATION ON THE PENNSYLVANIA RAILROAD AS THE GARFIELD AMBU-
LANCE TRAIN PASSED ON ITS WAY TO ELBERON*

*On September 6th, the President was removed to Elberon, N. J., in a specially designed car, the bed being arranged so as
to minimize the jolting. It was an extremely hot day and the train went very fast, the President sending a message to the engineer to increase the speed. At the stations and in the fields knots of people congregated to watch the
passage of the train, instinctively removing their hats as it came into sight.

THE STAR ROUTES

THE GARFIELD FUNERAL CAR ABOUT TO START FROM THE PUBLIC SQUARE,
CLEVELAND, O., FOR THE CEMETERY
Drawn by T. L. Thulstrup from a photograph by Ryder

carrying the mails in sections of the West where railroads and steamboats failed. In 1878 there were 9,225 of these Star Routes, for the maintenance of which Congress in that year appropriated $5,900,000. A Ring made up on the one hand of Democratic and Republican public men, some of these very prominent, and on the other hand of certain mail contractors, managed to increase the remuneration for service on 135 pet routes from $143,169 to $622,808. On twenty-six of the routes the pay-roll was put up from $65,216 to $530,319. The method was, first, to get numerously signed petitions from the districts interested, praying for an increase in the number of trips per week and shortening the schedule

THE LAST QUARTER-CENTURY

time of each trip, get "estimates" from the contractors vastly in excess of actual cost for the service, get these estimates allowed at Washington, and then divide profits between the "statesmen" and citizens interested in the "deal." Over some of these lines, it was asserted, not more than three letters a week were carried.

Attention was drawn to the Star Route matter before the close of Hayes's term, but exposure was staved off until Mr. James, "the model New York Postmaster," assumed the office of Postmaster-General. On May 6, 1881, Mr. James wrote Thurlow Weed: "Rest assured I shall do my whole duty in the matter of the Star Route swindlers. It is a hard task, but it shall be pushed fearlessly, regardless of whom it may involve."

Thomas W. Brady, Second Assistant Postmaster-General, was supposed to be a member of the Ring. At any rate, he threatened, unless proceedings were stopped, to publish a letter of President Garfield's written during the campaign. This he did. It was the famous "My dear Hubbell" epistle. The writer, addressing "My dear Hubbell," hoped that "he" (referring to Brady) "would give them all the assistance possible." According to Brady, this meant that he should, among other things, get money from the Star Route contractors. Garfield insisted that it was simply a call on Brady to contribute from his own pocket. In the next sentence of the letter, however, the presidential candidate asks: " Please tell me how the departments generally are doing." This will hardly bear any other construction than that of party extortion from the government employés, especially since this same Hubbell, as chairman of the Republican Congressional Committee, was

GEORGE H. PENDLETON

PENDLETON CIVIL SERVICE ACT

Dorman B. Eaton *John M. Gregory* *Leroy D. Thoman*
THE CIVIL SERVICE COMMISSIONERS APPOINTED BY PRESIDENT ARTHUR

later called to account by the reformers for levying two per cent. assessments upon the clerks—styled by him and his friends "voluntary contributions." Whether Brady's *tu quoque* availed him, or for some other reason, his trial was postponed and he was never convicted. Senator Dorsey, of Arkansas, was also arraigned, but, upon his second trial, in 1883, was acquitted. Indeed, of those prosecuted for fraud in connection with the Star Routes, only one was ever punished; and in this case the Government was in error, as the man was innocent.

The tragic fate of President Garfield, taken in connection with these and other revelations of continuing political corruption, brought public sentiment on Civil Service Reform to a head. A bill prepared by the Civil Service Reform League, and in 1880 introduced in the Senate by Senator Pendleton, of Ohio, passed Congress in January, 1883, and on the 16th of that month received the signature of President Arthur.

Renewing, in the main, the provisions adopted under the Act of 1871, it authorized the President, with the consent of the Senate, to appoint three Civil Service Commissioners, who were to institute competitive examinations open to all persons desiring to enter the employ of the Government. It provided that the clerks in the departments at Washington, and in every customs district or post-office where fifty or more were employed, should be arranged in classes, and that in the future only persons who had passed the examinations should be appointed to service in these offices or promoted from a lower class to a higher, preference being given according to rank in the examinations. Candidates were to serve six months' probation at practical work before receiving a final appointment.

The bill struck a heavy blow at political assessments, by declaring that no official should be removed for refusing to contribute to political funds. A Congressman or government official convicted of soliciting or receiving political assessments from government employés became liable to $5,000 fine or three years' imprisonment, or both. Persons in the government service were forbidden to use their official authority or influence to coerce the political action of anyone, or to interfere with elections. Dorman B. Eaton, Leroy D. Thoman, and John M. Gregory were appointed commissioners by President Arthur. By the end of the year the new system was fairly in operation. Besides the departments at Washington, it applied to eleven customs districts and twenty-three post-offices where fifty or more officials were employed.

CHAPTER XIII

DOMESTIC EVENTS DURING MR. ARTHUR'S ADMINISTRATION

MR. ARTHUR'S DILEMMA.—HIS ACCESSION.—RESPONSIBILITY EVOKES HIS BEST.—THE PRESIDENTIAL SUCCESSION QUESTION.—SUCCESSION ACT PASSED.—ELECTORAL COUNT ACT PASSED.—ARTHUR'S CABINET.—CONDITION OF THE COUNTRY IN 1881.—DECADENCE OF OUR OCEAN CARRYING.—TARIFF COMMISSION OF 1882 AND THE TARIFF OF 1883.—MAHONE AND THE VIRGINIA "READJUSTERS."—MAHONE'S RECORD.—HIS ENTRY INTO THE SENATE.—PRESIDENT ARTHUR AND THE CHINESE.—ORIGIN OF THE CHINESE QUESTION.—ANSON BURLINGAME.—THE 1878 EMBASSY.—CHINESE THRONG HITHER.—EARLY CALIFORNIA.—THE STRIKE OF 1877 AFFECTS CALIFORNIA.—RISE AND CHARACTER OF DENIS KEARNEY.—HIS PROGRAM.—THE "SAND-LOT" CAMPAIGN.—KEARNEY'S MODERATION.—HE IS COURTED.—AND OPPOSED.—HIS CONSTITUTIONAL CONVENTION.—ITS WORK.—KEARNEYISM TO THE REAR.—THE JAMES DESPERADOES.—THEIR CAPTURE.—THE YORKTOWN CELEBRATION.—MEMENTOES OF OLD YORKTOWN.—THE PAGEANT.—"SURRENDER" DAY.—THE OTHER DAYS.—CLOSE OF THE FÊTE.—FLOOD AND RIOT IN CINCINNATI.

DURING Garfield's illness Mr. Arthur's predicament had been most delicate. The second article of the Constitution provides that "in case of the removal of the President from office, or of his death, resignation or inability to discharge the powers and duties of said office, the same shall devolve on the Vice-President." What is here meant by a President's "inability," and how or by whom such inability is in any case to be ascertained, had never been determined. Was the question of "inability" to be decided by the President himself, by the Vice-President, or by Congress? Could the Vice-President take up Presidential duties temporarily, giving way again to the President in case the latter recovered, or must he, having begun, serve through the remainder of

THE LAST QUARTER-CENTURY

the four years, the once disabled President being permanently out of office? These problems doubtless weighed heavily upon Mr. Arthur's mind while his chief lay languishing. They were everywhere discussed daily. A popular view was advocated by General Butler, to the effect that the Vice-President himself was charged with the duty of deciding when to take up the higher functions. As Garfield's was a clear case of "inability to discharge the powers and duties of the Presidency," Mr. Arthur may actually have felt it, from a technically legal point of view, incumbent upon him to assume these " powers and duties." In a Cabinet meeting Mr. Blaine suggested that Mr. Arthur be summoned to do this, intimating that the chief direction ought certainly to be devolved on Arthur should an extraordinary emergency in administration arise. It was fortunate that no such emergency occurred, and that Mr. Arthur did not feel for any reason called upon to grasp the reins of government. At this critical juncture he might easily have acted, or even spoken, in a manner seriously to compromise himself and his country. Far from doing anything of the sort, he was singularly discreet through the whole trial.

Hardly had Garfield breathed his last, when, the same night, in the small morning hours of September 20, 1881, Mr. Arthur took oath as President. This occurred in his house in New York City, Judge Brady, of the New York State Supreme Court, officiating. The next day but one, the oath was again administered by Chief Justice Waite in the Senate Chamber at Washington. On this occasion Mr. Arthur delivered a brief inaugural address. He said: " The memory of the murdered President, his protracted sufferings, his unyielding fortitude, the example and achievements of his life and the pathos of his death, will forever illuminate the pages of our history. Men may die, but the fabrics of our free institutions remain unshaken. No higher or more assuring proof could exist of the strength and power of popular

PRESIDENT ARTHUR TAKING THE INAUGURAL OATH AT HIS LEXINGTON AVENUE RESIDENCE

IMPORTANT LEGISLATION

government than the fact that, though the chosen of the people be struck down, his constitutional successor is peacefully installed without shock or strain."

Responsibility brought out the new President's best qualities. He had little special preparation for his exalted office. Save among the New York Republicans, he was almost unknown till his nomination as Vice-President, and when he succeeded Garfield there was much misgiving. Yet his administration was distinguished as few have been for ability, fairness, elevation of tone and freedom from mean partisanship. He was extremely diligent, circumspect, considerate and firm. That he had nerve men saw when, in 1882, he resolutely vetoed a portentously large River and Harbor Bill. His public papers were in admirable spirit, thoroughly considered, and written in a style finer than those of any preceding President since John Quincy Adams.

The country's ordeal in connection with Garfield's death led to an important piece of legislation. Few were then or are now aware by what a slender thread the orderly government of our country hung between the shooting of Garfield in July, 1881, and the second special session of the Senate of the Forty-seventh Congress the following October. Had Mr. Arthur died at any moment during this period—and it is said that he was for a time in imminent danger of death—or had he become in any way unable to perform a President's duties, there could have been no constitutional succession to the Presidency. The law of March, 1792, declares that in case the Vice-President as well as the President dies, is removed, or is disqualified, "the President of the Senate *pro tempore*, or, if there is none, then the Speaker of the House of Representatives for the time being, shall act as President until the disability is removed or a President elected." But at the time of Garfield's assassination, neither a President *pro tempore* of the Senate nor a Speaker of the House existed. It had been customary for the Vice-President before the end of a session of the Senate to retire, and so require the appointment of a President *pro tempore* who should continue as such during the recess; but on this occasion the special session of the Senate in May had adjourned without electing any such presiding officer. On October 10th Senator Bayard was made President *pro tempore* of the Senate, followed on the 13th by Senator David Davis. Of course there could be no Speaker at this time, as the Forty-sixth Congress had ceased to exist in March, and the House of the Forty-seventh did not convene till December.

In his first annual message President Arthur commended to the "early and thoughtful consideration of Congress" the important questions touching the Presidential succession which had so vividly emerged in consequence of his predecessor's assassination. It had been a question whether the statute of 1792 was constitutional. The ground of the doubt was that, according to the doctrine agreed to when, in 1798, an attempt was made to impeach Senator Blount, of Tennessee, Speakers of the House and temporary Presidents of the Senate are not, technically, "officers of the United States." Hence, were either a speaker or a temporary head of the Senate to take a President's place, Presidential duties would be devolved on an official who could not be impeached for malfeasance. The law of 1792 was objectionable for other reasons. It originally passed only by a narrow majority. Many then wished that the Presidential succession should take the direction of the Secretary of State, and had not Jefferson held this office at the time the law would probably have so provided.

On the second day of its first regular session the Senate of the Forty-seventh Congress ordered its Judiciary Committee to consider the question of the Presidential succession, inquire whether any, and if so, what, further legislation was necessary in respect to the same, and to report by bill or otherwise. A bill to meet the case was soon introduced by Senator Garland, of Arkansas. The matter was briefly debated both then and

PRESIDENTIAL SUCCESSION ACT

at intervals for a number of years; but no legislation upon it occurred till January, 1886, when the Forty-ninth Congress passed a law based on Garland's draft. It provided that if the Presidency and the Vice-Presidency are both vacant the Presidency passes to the members of the Cabinet in the historical order of the establishment of their departments, beginning with the Secretary of State. If he dies, is impeached or disabled, the Secretary of the Treasury becomes President, to be followed in like crisis by the Secretary of War, he by the Attorney-General, he by the Postmaster-General, he by the Secretary of the Navy, and he by the Secretary of the Interior. To be thus in the line of the Presidential succesion a Cabinet officer must have been duly confirmed as such and must be constitutionally eligible to the Presidency. If Congress is not in session when one of these officers thus comes to the Presidency, and is not to convene in twenty days, the new President must issue a proclamation convening Congress after twenty days, and Congress must then order a new election for President.

The Forty-ninth Congress also passed, on February 3, 1887, an act to fix the day for the meeting of the electors of President and Vice-President, and to provide for and regulate the counting of the votes for President and Vice-President and the decision of questions arising thereon. The ascertainment of the electors

CHESTER A. ARTHUR

within and for any State is so far as possible made the business of that State, any judicial determination made for this purpose within six days of the electors' meeting being binding on Congress. In case of a single return fixing the *personnel* of the electors the vote of any elector can be rejected only by the two Houses concurrently agreeing that it was not legally cast. In case of conflicting returns one of which a State tribunal has adjudged to be legal, only those votes denoted by this return can be counted. If there is question which of two or more authorities or tribunals had the right to determine the legal electoral vote of the State, the votes, being regularly cast, of the electors whose title the two Houses acting separately concurrently decide to be the legal ones, are counted. If there has been no determination of the question of electors' legitimacy, those votes and those only are counted which the two Houses concurrently decide to have been cast by the lawful electors; unless the two Houses acting separately concurrently decide that such votes were not the legal votes of the legally elected electors.

We still have no legal or official criterion of a President's "inability to discharge the powers and duties of his office," nor has any tribunal been designated for the settlement of the question when it arises. We do not know whether, were another President so ill as Garfield was, it would be proper for the Cabinet to perform Presidential duties, as Garfield's did, or whether the Vice-President would be bound to assume those duties. Barring this chance for conflict, it is not easy to think of an emergency in which the chief magistracy can now fall vacant or the appropriate incumbent thereof be in doubt.

The only member of Garfield's Cabinet whom Arthur permanently retained was Robert T. Lincoln, Secretary of War. However, the old Cabinet did not dissolve at once. Not till December 19, 1881, did Mr. Blaine, who had practically been at the head of the Government from the President's assassination till his death, surrender the State portfolio.

CONDITION OF THE COUNTRY

Frederick T. Frelinghuysen, of New Jersey, took his place. Ex-Governor Edwin D. Morgan, of New York, had been nominated and confirmed as Secretary of the Treasury, but had declined on account of ill health. Judge Charles J. Folger took the Treasury portfolio November 15, 1881. In April, 1882, William E. Chandler, of New Hampshire, and Henry M. Teller, of Colorado, were called to the Navy and Interior Departments respectively. January 5, 1882, Timothy O. Howe, of Wisconsin, was confirmed as Postmaster-General, but he died in March, 1883. Walter Q. Gresham succeeded him. Benjamin H. Brewster, of Pennsylvania, was confirmed Attorney-General in December, 1881. Secretary Folger died in 1884. Gresham was then transferred to the Treasury, Assistant Postmaster-General Frank Hatton being advanced to the head of the Post-office Department. Mr. Gresham soon resigned to accept a Circuit Judgeship on the Seventh Circuit. His place as Secretary of the Treasury was filled by Hugh McCulloch, who had administered most acceptably the same office from 1865 to 1869.

In addressing Congress for the first time, President Arthur was able to represent the condition of the country as excellent. Colorado had been admitted to the Union in 1876. During the decade ending in 1880 our population had grown somewhat over twenty-five per cent., that is, from thirty-eight millions to fifty millions. The net public debt, December 31, 1880, was a trifle less than $1,900,000,000, a decrease in the face of the debt of $600,000,000, in the ten years. Agricultural production was found to have advanced one hundred per cent., while, according to the ninth census, the increase from 1870 to 1880 had been but twelve per cent. The tenth census corrected certain figures relating to our national area, making the country eight hundred square miles smaller than it had been supposed to be.

Americans thought it a serious matter that for the year 1879 the foreign trade of Great Britain exceeded $3,000,000,-

000, two and a half times the amount of ours. It was also a source of solicitude that we were the only civilized country in the world whose ocean-carrying had absolutely decreased since 1856. In that year American ships bore seventy-five per cent. of all we exported and of all we imported. In 1878 American ships bore twenty-five per cent.; in 1882 fifteen per cent. Though our foreign commerce had increased seventy per cent. in amount, the cargoes transported in American ships were $200,000,000 less valuable in 1878 than in 1857. In 1856 foreign vessels entered at our ports had a tonnage of 3,117,034. By 1881 it had increased 308 per cent. or to 12,711,392 tons, of which 8,457,797 sailed under the Union Jack. On the other hand, American tonnage from foreign ports, in the same period, increased from 1,891,453 to 2,919,-149, or only 54 per cent. "The continuing decline of the merchant marine of the United States," wrote President Arthur, "is greatly to be deplored. In view of the fact that we furnish so large a proportion of the freights of the commercial world, and that our shipments are steadily and rapidly increasing, it is a cause of surprise that not only is our navigation interest diminishing, but it is less than when our exports and imports were not half so large as now either in bulk or in value."

An Act of Congress passed May 15, 1882, created a Tariff Commission consisting of prominent manufactures and others, viz.: J. L. Hayes, H. W. Oliver, A. M. Garland, J. A. Ambler, Robert P. Porter, J. W. H. Underwood, A. R. Boteler and Duncan F. Kennon. After long investigation and deliberation, having examined many witnesses, these gentlemen brought in in December an able, luminous and comprehensive report of 2,500 printed pages, forming an invaluable exhibit of our then customs laws, their merits and defects. Part of it ran: "In the performance of the duty devolved upon them, all the members of the Commission have aimed, and, as they believe, with success, to divest them-

TARIFF COMMISSION AND BILL

selves of political bias, sectional prejudice or considerations of personal interest. It is their desire that their recommendations shall serve no particular party, class, section or school of political economy."

In this report the Commission recommended an average reduction in tariff rates of not less than 20 per cent. In certain rates a lowering of 50 per cent. was urged. The Senate amended a House internal revenue measure by adding a tariff bill calculated to effect some reduction, though less radical and less impartial than that wished by the Commission. "If the Senate Finance Committee had embodied in this bill the recommendations of the Tariff Commission, including the schedules, without amendment or change, the tariff would have been settled for many years. Unfortunately, this was not done, but the schedules prescribing the rates of duty and their classification were so radically changed by the Committee that the scheme of the Tariff Commission was practically defeated. Many persons wishing to advance their particular industries appeared before the Committee and succeeded in having their views adopted."*

A two-thirds vote was required to bring this Senate bill before the House. Wishing it referred to a conference committee, which would be to their advantage, the high-protection leaders in the House adroitly got the rules revised, enabling a bare majority to non-concur in the Senate amendment, but not to concur therein so as to pass the bill. The measure, therefore, went to the Conference Committee. There it took on features much more highly protectionist. The resulting act, the tariff law of 1883, in some instances advanced customs rates even over their former figures, making them higher than either Commission, Senate or House had proposed, closely approximating those of the old War tariff. The average diminution from the tariff as it previously stood was, perhaps, about four per cent.

*John Sherman, Recollections.

This Act paved the way for infinite trouble over the tariff. It was full of irrational and contradictory provisions, and, as a whole, pleased nobody. Each industry wished what it purchased treated as raw material, to be tariffed low or not at all, and what it sold considered as the finished article, to receive the highest rates. Struggle over these conflicting interests was apparent in the many incongruous features of the Act.

It was significant that Mr. Arthur's first message made no allusion to the Southern question. All felt, so well had Mr. Hayes's policy worked, that that section might now be safely left to itself. Meantime the "Readjuster" controversy in Virginia bade fair to be the entering wedge for a split in the solid South. The Readjusters were a Democratic faction taking name from their desire to "readjust" the State debt on a basis that meant partial repudiation. In 1879, by a fusion with the Republicans, the Readjusters controlled the State and elected their leader, William Mahone, to the United States Senate. Mahone had been a major-general in the Confederate Army, and his bravery greatly endeared him to the Southern heart. He it was who commanded the slender contingent of Confederates at Petersburg on July 30, 1864, when the mine on Burnside's front was exploded. He there fought like a tiger, and made his dispositions with the utmost skill and coolness. To him almost alone was due the credit that day of keeping Petersburg from Union hands and of replacing the Confederate lines by sunset exactly where they were at sunrise. Had the Confederacy endured, he should have been one of its presidents for his meritorious services in this battle. The negro vote helped Mahone. He had always favored fair treatment for the black man. In his county the blacks had voted freely and their votes had been counted as cast. Good provision for colored schools had also been made there.

The Virginian's entry into the Senate in 1881 was marked by a dramatic passage at arms. His personal appearance drew

MAHONE ENTERS THE SENATE

attention. He had been a striking figure in battle uniform, and he was hardly less so in citizen's attire. He wore a close-bodied suit of brown broadcloth, frilled cuffs extending beyond the sleeves. He had a small head and spindle legs. His hair and beard were long, his stature diminutive. One described him as "a spry midget, full of Irish fire, who enjoyed cutting a national figure." As elected, the Senate of the Forty-seventh Congress had a small Republican majority, but Garfield's Cabinet appointments, calling away the three Republican Senators—Blaine, Kirkwood and Windom—left the two parties in the body equally divided. When the fight for organization came on there were thirty-seven sure Republicans and thirty-seven sure Democrats, not counting David Davis or Mahone, both of whom were expected to act more or less independently of party. Davis, favoring the *status quo* and evidently expecting Mahone to vote with the Democrats in organizing, declared himself resolved "to support the organization of the Senate as it stood." It had till now been Democratic. Had Mahone sided with him, the committees as made up by the Democratic caucus would have been elected. But in spite of Democtratic pleadings and denunciation, Mahone concluded to support the Republicans. This tied the Senate, even if Davis voted with the Democrats, and Vice-President Arthur could of course be counted on to turn the vote the Republican way. This he did in postponing indefinitely the motion to elect the Democratic committees and in electing the Republican list. When it came to choosing sergeant-at-arms and clerks, Davis, now favoring the new status, as before he had the old, voted with the Republicans.

WILLIAM MAHONE

Mahone's course aroused great wrath, especially among the Southern Senators. "Who is that man?" cried Senator

THE LAST QUARTER-CENTURY

Hill, of Georgia, amid laughter from the Republican side of the Chamber: "Who is that man so ambitious to do what no man in the history of this country has ever yet done—stand up in this high presence and proclaim from this proud eminence that he disgraces the commission he holds? Such a man is not worthy to be a Democrat. Is he worthy to be a Republican?" In rejoinder Mahone, while declaring himself a Democrat in principle, denied that he was indebted to the Democratic party for his place in the Senate. He concluded: "I want that gentleman to know henceforth and forever that here is a man who dares stand and defend his right against you and your caucus." Senator Hill's query was forthwith answered. Mahone was welcomed by the Republicans with open arms. A bouquet of flowers, said to be from President Garfield, was sent to his desk, and Federal patronage in Virginia was placed at his disposal.

A storm of indignation from the Pacific Coast fell upon President Arthur's head when, in 1882, he vetoed a bill for restricting Chinese immigration. To understand the reason of his act and of his unpopularity, a brief review is necessary.

What originally brought the Chinaman to our shores was the discovery of gold in California. At first he was not unwelcome. Said the *Alta California* of May 12, 1851: "Quite a large number of Celestials have arrived among us of late, enticed hither by the golden romance which has filled the world. Scarcely a ship arrives that does not bring an increase of this worthy integer of our population." The "worthy integer" was soon engaged in an exciting though not enviable part of the "golden romance," for the next year we read that gangs of miners were "running out" Chinese settlers. This race strife on the coast was incessant both during and after the war.

Meantime, Anson Burlingame, our Minister to China, who during an intercourse of some years had come to possess the confidence of the Chinese in an unusual degree, had been

"UNITE THE EAST AND THE WEST UNDER AN ENLIGHTENED AND PROGRESSIVE CIVILIZATION"

Drawn by W. R. Leigh

RELATIONS WITH CHINA

entrusted by them with a mission which at first seemed as though it might lead to new relations. On his return he bore credentials constituting him China's ambassador to the United States and to Europe. He proceeded to negotiate with this country a treaty of amity, which was signed on July 4, 1868. But anti-Chinese agitation did not cease. In 1871 occurred a riot in the streets of Los Angeles, when fifteen Chinamen were hanged and six others shot, Chinamen having murdered one police officer and wounded two others. In 1878 an anti-Chinese bill passed Congress, but was vetoed by President Hayes as repugnant to the Burlingame treaty. Rage against the Celestials, to which all forces in the Pacific States had bent, being thus baffled at Washington, grew more clamorous than ever.

On September 28, 1878, a new Chinese embassy waited upon President Hayes. The ambassador, Chen Lan Pin, wore the regulation bowl-shaped hat, adorned with the scarlet button of the second order and with a depending peacock plume, caught by jeweled fastenings. His garments were of finest silk. He had on a blouse with blue satin collar, a skirt of darker stuff, sandal-shaped shoes and leggings of the richest kid. His letter of credence was drawn by an attendant from a cylinder of bamboo embellished with gold. In this document the Emperor expressed the hope that the embassy would " eventually unite the East and the West under an enlightened and progressive civilization." The indirect issue of this embassage was a fresh treaty, ratified in March, 1881, amending the Burlingame compact.

That compact, recognizing as inalienable the right of every man to change his abode, had permitted the free immigration of Chinamen into the United States. The new treaty of 1881 so modified this feature that immigration might be regulated, limited or suspended by us for no specified period should it threaten to affect the interests of the United States or to endanger their good order. A bill soon followed

THE LAST QUARTER-CENTURY

TYPES OF THE OFFICIAL CLASS. THE CHINESE CONSULATE IN IN SAN FRANCISCO
After a photograph by Taber

prohibiting Chinese immigration for a period of twenty years, on the ground that the presence of the Mongolians caused disorder in certain localities. This was the bill which President Arthur vetoed as contravening the treaty, he objecting, among much else, to the systems of passports and registration which the bill would impose upon resident Chinese. But the advocates of the exclusion policy were in earnest, wrought up by the growing hordes of Celestials pressing hither.

Only sixty-three thousand Chinese had been in the country in 1870; in 1880 there were one hundred and five thousand. Another bill was at once introduced, substituting ten for twenty years as the time of suspension, and it became a law in 1882. China sent a protest, which availed naught.

Interwoven with the Chinese agitation, as well as with

AFFAIRS IN CALIFORNIA

nearly all the national problems of that day and this, was the movement known as Kearneyism, which took form in California in 1877 and found expression in the State Constitution of 1879. His habits of mental unrest engendered by speculation and the gold fever, had marked California society since 1849. A tendency existed to appeal to extra-legal measures for peace and justice. The golden dream had faded. Although wages were higher in California than in most parts of the country, working people there showed much discontent. In no State had land grants been more lavish or the immense size of

A " MIXED FAMILY" IN THE HIGHBINDERS' QUARTER, "CHINATOWN"
From a photograph by Taber

landed estates more injurious. Farming their vast tracts by improved machinery, the proprietors each season hired great throngs of laborers, who, when work was over, betook themselves to the cities and swelled the ranks of the

GOD IN JOSS TEMPLE, "CHINATOWN," SAN FRANCISCO
After a photograph by Taber

unemployed. Worse yet, California was in the hands of a railroad monopoly which by threats or blandishments controlled nearly every State official. Politics were corrupt and political factions, with their selfish and distracting quarrels, were numerous. The politician was hated next to the " Nob " who owned him.

The immediate occasion of Kearneyism was the great railroad strike at the East in 1877. The California lines, having announced a reduction of wages, were threatened with a similar strike, but took alarm at the burning and fighting in Pittsburg and rescinded the notice. Nevertheless a mass-meeting was called to express sympathy with the Eastern strikers. It

THE MERCHANT CLASS—TYPES OF CHINESE ACCOUNTANTS
After a photograph by Taber

THE "NOBS" IN TERROR

AN ALLEY IN "CHINATOWN"
After a photograph by Taber

was held on July 23d. The new-rich grandees trembled. Authorities took precautions, but at the meeting no disorder occurred. During this and the two following evenings a number of Chinese wash-houses were destroyed and some persons killed. The violence was naturally ascribed to the workingmen. A Committee of Public Safety was organized under William T. Coleman, President of the Vigilance Committee

DINING ROOM OF A CHINESE RESTAURANT IN WASHINGTON STREET, SAN FRANCISCO
After photograph by Taber

of 1856. The laboring men denied their alleged complicity with the lawlessness, and a number enlisted in Mr. Coleman's "pick-handle brigade," which patrolled the city for a few days. Among the pick-handle brigadiers was Denis Kearney, a man at once extreme in theories and language and singularly temperate in personal habits. Born in 1847, at Oakmount, Ireland, from eleven years of age to twenty-five he had followed the sea, but since 1872 had prospered as a drayman in San Francisco. He was short, well built, with a broad head, a light mustache, a quick but lowering blue eye, ready utterance and a pleasant voice. He was of nervous temperament, and had the bluster and domineering way of a sailor, withal possessing remarkable shrewdness, enterprise and initiative. For two years he had spent part of each Sunday at a lyceum for self-culture, where he had levelled denunciations at the laziness and

A SAND LOT MEETING IN SAN FRANCISCO
The Workingmen passing a Resolution by Acclamation
Composition of B. W. Clinedinst, with the assistance of photographs by Taber

KEARNEY AN AGITATOR

extravagance of the working-classes, at the opponents of Chinese immigration, and at anti-capitalists in general.

For some reason, whether from a change of heart, or on account of unlucky dabbling in stocks, or because rebuffed by Senator Sargent, Kearney determined to turn about and agitate against all that he had held dear. On September 12, 1877, a company of the unemployed in San Francisco assembled and organized "The Workingmen's Party of California." Its salient principles were the establishment of a State Bureau of Labor and Statistics and of a State Labor Commission, the legal regulation of the hours of labor, the abolition of poverty along with all land and moneyed monopoly, and the ejection of the Chinese. Kearney, conspicuous among the extremists, was chosen president. His advanced ideas were incorporated into the party's creed, as follows:

"We propose to wrest the government from the hands of the rich and place it in those of the people. We propose to rid the country of cheap Chinese labor. We propose to destroy land monopoly in our State. We propose to destroy the great money power of the rich by a system of taxation that will make great wealth impossible. We propose to provide decently for the poor and unfortunate, the weak, the helpless and especially the young, because the country is rich enough to do so, and religion, humanity and patriotism demand that we should do so. We propose to elect none but competent workingmen and their friends to any office. The rich have ruled us till they have ruined us. We will now take our own affairs into our own hands. The republic must and shall be preserved, and only workingmen will do it. Our shoddy aristocrats want an emperor and a standing army to shoot down the people. When we have 10,000 members

DENIS KEARNEY

we shall have the sympathy and support of 20,000 other workingmen. The party will then wait upon all who employ Chinese and ask for their discharge, and it will mark as public enemies those who refuse to comply with their request. This party will exhaust all peaceable means of attaining its ends, but it will not be denied justice when it has power to enforce it. It will encourage no riot or outrage, but it will not volunteer to repress, or put down, or arrest or prosecute the hungry and impatient who manifest their hatred of the Chinamen by a crusade against John or those who employ him. Let those who raise the storm by their selfishness suppress it themselves. If they dare raise the devil, let them meet him face to face."

Soon began the memorable sand-lot meetings, made famous by the San Francisco *Chronicle*, which sent its best reporters to describe them. From his new eminence the agitator returned this favor by advising his hearers to boycott the *Morning Call* and subscribe for its rival, the *Chronicle*. His speeches were directed partly against the Chinese, but chiefly against the "thieving politicians" and "blood-sucking capitalists." At one gathering he suggested that every workingman should get a gun, and that some judicious hanging of aristocrats was needed. The sand-lot audiences were largely composed of foreigners, Irishmen being the most numerous, but even the Germans caught the infection. The orator could cater to their prejudices with effect, as he did in an address before the German Club in March, 1878 : " Pixley said to me that the narrow-faced Yankees in California would clean us out, but I just wish they would try it. I would drive them into the sea or die." On the other hand, in the Kearneyites' Thanksgiving-day parade, appealing to the whole people, none but United States flags were carried and none but Union veterans carried them. The leader affected the integrity and stoicism of a Cato. As Cato concluded every oration of his with the impressive "*Carthago delenda est*," so Kearney intro-

Drawn by G. W. Peters

"THE CHINESE MUST GO!"

Denis Kearney Addressing the Workingmen on the night of October 29, on Nob Hill, San Francisco

KEARNEY'S MODERATION

duced each of his harangues with "The Chinese must go!" The contest against the Chinese, he said, would not be given up till there was blood enough in Chinatown to float their bodies to the bay. Still, on one occasion a poor Chinaman at the mercy of hoodlums owed his rescue to the Kearneyites alone.

Much as Kearney delighted in scaring the timid nabobs of San Francisco, he was careful to keep within the law. More than once, while himself breathing out threatenings and slaughter, he tactfully restrained his devotees from excesses. Shrewdly estimating the value of martyrdom, he once said: "If I don't get killed I will do more than any reformer in the world. But I hope I will be assassinated, for the success of the movement depends upon that." The horns of this dilemma crossed, but each pointed in a hopeful direction. The leader's yearning for persecution was gratified. On October 29th about two thousand workingmen collected at Nob Hill, where the railway magnates lived. Bonfires being lighted, Kearney launched his philippic. The "Nobs" heard the jeers at their expense, and looked out upon the lurid scene in alarm. They had Kearney and other leading spirits arrested on the charge of using incendiary language. The city government passed a sedition ordinance known as the Gibbs gag law, and the legislature enacted a ridiculously stringent riot act.

The two laws were still-born and harmless. The only effect of the arrests and of the new legislation was to give Kearney additional power. On his release from jail he was hailed as a martyr, crowned with flowers and drawn in triumph on his own dray. A Yorkshire shoemaker and evangelist named Wellock—"Parson Wellock" he was called—preached Kearneyism as a religion. He was tall, with a narrow head, high forehead and a full, short beard. At each Sunday sand-lot assembly he used to read a text and expound its latter-day bearings. Speaking of the monopolists, he said: "These men who are perverting the ways of truth must be destroyed. In the Bible the Lord is called a consuming fire. When he commands we must obey. What are we to do with these people that are starving our poor and degrading our wives, daughters, and sisters? And the Lord said unto Moses, 'Take all the heads off the people and hang them up before the Lord.' This is what we are commanded by the Supreme Being to do with all that dare to tread down honesty, virtue and truth."

Both parties began to court Kearney. Aspirants for office secretly visited him. Office-holders changed from hostility to servility. The railroad kings, if they failed to moderate his language, found ways to assuage his hatred. Hirelings of corporate interests joined the Kearneyites and assisted them to carry out their wishes. Even the better classes more and more attended his harangues, partly from curiosity, partly from sympathy, partly from disgust at the old parties. The enthusiastic compared him with Napoleon and Cæsar. The party of the sand lots, Kearney nominally its president, really its dictator, spread over and controlled the State. This result assured, "reform" needed only that a new State constitution should be adopted, properly safeguarding the people against monopolies and the Chinese. Agitation for a Constitutional Convention was at once begun and pushed till successful.

The very immensity of the new party's growth begot reaction. The monopolists intensely hated Kearney at the very moment when they most sought to use him. His chief strength lay in the city populace. The Grangers sympathized and in many measures co-operated with him, yet maintained a becoming independence. In the city, too, there was a rival labor organization, set on foot at that first mass-meeting held to express sympathy for the Pittsburg strikers. Though Kearney's braggadocio "took" wonderfully with the people, this body let slip no chance for denouncing the man's extreme notions and assumption. Numerous and active enemies were made by Kearney's inability to brook aught of opposition or rivalry. By a motion of his hand he swept out of existence

DENIS KEARNEY BEING DRAWN THROUGH THE STREETS OF SAN FRANCISCO AFTER
HIS RELEASE FROM THE HOUSE OF CORRECTION
The procession passing the Lotta Fountain in Market Street
Painted by Howard Pyle from photographs by Taber and a description by Kearney himself

OPPOSITION TO KEARNEY

THE OLD CHRONICLE BUILDING IN SAN FRANCISCO
(It was here that Charles De Young was shot in 1880 by Isaac Kalloch, Jr., son of the
Workingmen's Mayor)
After a photograph by Taber

the Central Committee of his party. He liked best his most fulsome eulogists, and selected lieutenants whom he could fling aside the instant they hampered or crossed him. Many so treated beset him afterward like fleas. The Order of Caucasians, a species of anti-Mongolian Ku-Klux, with headquarters at Sacramento, was opposed to Kearney. Many men of influence and apparent impartiality, notably Archbishop Alemany, criticised his incendiary speeches, alienating some of his supporters.

Democrats now felt that by "united action" the Constitutional Convention which the Kearneyites had succeeded in getting called might be saved from their control. Accordingly

THE LAST QUARTER-CENTURY

a non-partisan ticket was started, which, notwithstanding some grumbling from the old "wheel-horses" of the two parties, received pretty hearty support. Despite all, by coalescing with the Grangers, the Kearneyites controlled the convention. The new California Constitution which resulted was an odd mixture of ignorance and good intentions. To hinder corruption in public office it reduced the power of the legislature almost to a shadow, and made the bribery of a legislator felony. To lighten taxation, particularly where it bore unduly upon the poor, the Constitution set a limit to State and local debts, taxed uncultivated land equally with cultivated land, made mortgage debts taxable where the mortgaged property lay, and authorized an income tax. However, for the benefit of the school fund, a poll tax was laid on every male inhabitant. Corporations were dealt with in a special article, which restricted them in many ways. Among other things it instituted a commission with extraordinary powers, enabling it to examine the books and accounts of transportation companies and to fix their rates for carriage. This commission, when placed in the hands of any party, uniformly violated pre-election pledges, and proceeded against the unanimous wish of Californians. Only the Commission of 1895 seemed to have taken some steps toward lowering freight rates.

ISAAC KALLOCH
Elected Mayor of San Francisco by the Workingmen

After the adoption of the Constitution a more powerful reaction set in and Kearneyism soon became a thing of the past. The *Chronicle* abandoned Kearney and "exposed" him. He was called to the East in the interest of labor agitation, but had little popularity or success. He returned to San Francisco, but never again became a leader. The most pronounced result, or sequel, which the Kearney movement left behind was a fixed public opinion throughout California

PROCESSION H'ONG FONG—THE MOST REPRESENTATIVE PUBLIC CELEBRATION CUSTOMARY AMONG THE CHINESE IN SAN FRANCISCO

Painted by Thulstrup from photographs by Taber

FALL OF THE JAMES GANG

and all the Pacific States against any further immigration of the Chinese. The new California Constitution devoted to these people an entire article. In it they were cut off from employment by the State or by corporations doing business therein. "Asiatic coolieism" was prohibited as a form of human slavery. This sentiment toward the Celestials spread eastward, and, in spite of all opposition by interested capitalists and by disinterested philanthropists, determined the subsequent course of Chinese legislation in Congress itself.

During the years under survey Missouri as well as the Pacific States had to contend with aggravated lawlessness. When hardly a week passed without a train being "held up" somewhere in the State, Governor Crittenden was driven to the terrible expedient of using crime itself as a police power. In the spring of 1882, Jesse James, the noted desperado, was assassinated by former members of his gang, who then surrendered to the authorities and were lodged in jail—none too soon, as an angry populace, gathering in thousands, hotly beset the slayers. Slayers and slain had been Confederate guerrillas in the war. On the return of peace they became train-robbers as easily as privateers turn pirates. James, at any rate, had not been inspired by lust of gain, for in spite of robberies amounting to hundreds of thousands of dollars he died poor. He had been a church member, concerned for "his wayward brother" Frank's salvation. After his death his sect in Missouri repudiated him, while expressing strongest disapproval of the treachery used in his taking off. For nearly twenty years every effort to capture the fellow had proved futile. The nature of the country aided him, but not so much as the enthusiastic devotion of his neighbors.

> This murderous chief, this ruthless man,
> This head of a rebellious clan,

had made himself a hero. The Sedalia *Democrat* said: "It was his country. The graves of his kindred were there. He refused to be banished from his birthright, and when he was hunted he turned savagely about and hunted his hunters. Would to God he were alive to-day to make a righteous butchery of a few more of them."

By thus fighting fire with fire, Governor Crittenden succeeded in dispersing three other desperado bands. Upon being arraigned the men-killers pleaded guilty and were sentenced to be hanged, but they were at once pardoned. The Governor's policy, however, was most unpopular. Infinite hate and scorn were visited upon the betrayers. James's wife and mother cursed them bitterly; Dick Little, chief traitor, being the object of their uttermost loathing. "If Timberlake or Craig (the county sheriff and his deputy) had killed my poor boy," cried the mother, "I would not say one word; but, O God! the treachery of Dick Little and those boys! Craig and Timberlake are noble men, and they have done too much for me. My poor boy who now lies there dead told me if they killed him not to say one word." Craig and Timberlake were pall-bearers at James's funeral. The Hannibal & St. Joseph Railroad extended courtesies to the bereaved widow and mother, who were on all hands treated as the heroines of the hour.

Close after President Garfield's funeral followed an event which for some days attracted the world's attention—the centennial celebration of Cornwallis's surrender at Yorktown, Va. The hamlet of Yorktown was seated on a sandy river-bank among the vestiges of the two sieges it had sustained, that of 1781 and that of 1861, the Confederate works thrown up in the last-named year not having completely erased the defences erected by Cornwallis. The Confederate fortifications were to be seen in 1881, as also some of McClellan's approaches. The site of Washington's headquarters, still known as "Washington's Lodge," was pointed out two and a half miles back from the river. The buildings were burned during the civil war, but the house had been rebuilt. The old Nelson House,

MOORE HOUSE AT YORKTOWN

gray, ivy-grown, massive, was standing; also the West House, built by Governor Nelson for his daughter, Mrs. Major West, midway between the Nelson House and the Monument; while a mile away was the Moore House, Cornwallis's quarters at the time of his surrender. Its exterior was tricked out with red, yellow and green paint, effects which, inside, æsthetic wall-paper and fine carpets strove to match.

The Moore House was, in a very true sense, the central spot of American History. It was historic sixty years before the Revolution, when it was Governor Spottswood's residence. In

THE NELSON HOUSE IN 1881
(Showing holes made in brick wall by cannon shot)

the "Temple," near by, was presented the relic of a still older strife, the tomb of Major William Gooch, who died in 1655. In the chimney of the Moore House was a cannon-ball hole, and in one of its corner rooms was still preserved the table whereon the articles of Cornwallis's surrender had been drawn. Its roof sheltered Lafayette and Rochambeau; also Washington in the proudest moment of his life. It was in 1896 the residence of Mr. A. O. Mauck. Standing in the midst of Temple Farm, it commanded a beautiful view of Chesapeake

THE LAST QUARTER-CENTURY

Bay, of Yorktown Monument and of quaint old Yorktown. Near by was a mill, built on the very foundations of the one where was fired the first shot in the Cornwallis siege. A shaft fifteen feet high, made of brick taken from the first court-house in York County, laid in German cement, has been erected by the Superintendent of the National Cemetery on the spot where Cornwallis's sword was delivered to General Lincoln.

THE WEST HOUSE AT YORKTOWN
(Showing the shot holes)

This shaft was dedicated on October 19, 1895, and placed in the care of the school children of our country to preserve.

Once redeemed from the British and once from Confederate rule, Yorktown was now, for a few days, rescued from its own loneliness. There was some complaint that locality was not ignored and the anniversary celebrated where modern conveniences were at hand. Such were the dust and heat at and about the village on the first day of the *fête* that pilgrims admired Cornwallis's good sense in surrendering as quickly as decency allowed, that he might go elsewhere. The second day was twenty degrees colder, and dusters gave way to ulsters. Truly vast preparations had been originally planned, but so obvious were the discomforts which could not but attend a long sojourn at the place, that the programme was radically docked. The events that were left, however, amply repaid for their trouble all who saw them.

Arrangements had been making at Yorktown for a month,

YORKTOWN DURING THE FÊTE

during which time the sandbanks all about were in a stir, such as neither Cornwallis's nor Magruder's cannon-wheels had occasioned. When the day marking the anniversary of the Briton's surrender arrived, a score of great war-ships, with other craft of various sorts, lined the river up and down, while shanties and tents covered the landscape in all directions. Wagons, buggies and carriages by hundreds came and went, frequent among them the two-wheeled family vehicle of the Virginia negro, attached by a rope harness to a scrawny "scalawag." Strains of martial music, the thunder of heavy guns, throngs of civilians and of soldiers, thieves and gamblers plying their art unmolested till a welcome detachment of Richmond police arrived—all conspired to waken the little place from the dead. To the credit of the Post-office Department, no hitch occurred when mails multiplied from three a week to two a day, and the daily delivery of letters mounted from fifty to five thousand.

The celebration began on October 18th, "Surrender Day." Troops had been pouring in all night and the influx in-

THE MEMORIAL MONUMENT
Corner-stone laid Oct. 19, 1881

THE LAST QUARTER-CENTURY

M. GLENNAN
The Virginia Commissioner of the Yorktown Centennial Celebration

R. C. WINTHROP

creased at dawn. Some had marched far and swiftly. Captain Sinclair's battery of the Third Artillery had covered the distance from Fort Hamilton, New York Harbor, to Yorktown, 470 miles, in twenty-one marching days. At ten o'clock the *Tallapoosa*, bearing the President and most of his Cabinet, came up the river, being saluted as she passed the batteries. At this notice " the yards of the ships of war were manned "— the account read quaintly after the lapse of but fourteen years. For ten minutes smoke-clouds covered the river and the boom of ponderous cannon quenched all other sounds. Behind the *Tallapoosa* were vessels bringing the Secretary of the Navy, the Secretary of War and General Sherman. Distinguished foreign guests came, too, descendants of de Grasse, de Rochambeau, de Lafayette, and von Steuben, the heroes who had shared with Washington the glory of humbling England's pride a hundred years before. Each dignitary being saluted according to his rank, the deafening cannonade was kept up for a number of hours.

Wednesday, October 19th, was devoted to the ceremony of laying the corner-stone of the Yorktown Centennial Monument. Commemorative exercises formed the feature of Thursday. President Arthur delivered an address, the Marquis de Rochambeau responded in French, and Baron von Steuben in German, all three being loudly applauded. Hon. Robert C. Winthrop pronounced the oration of the day.

CLOSE OF THE YORKTOWN CELEBRATION

The presence of Steuben and Rochambeau, of Generals Sherman and Wade Hampton, of Hancock, the favorite and hero of the festival, and FitzHugh Lee, hardly second to him in receipt of applause, naturally suggested the themes of concord and reunion. Among those who shook hands with President Arthur was the widow of President John Tyler. At the conclusion of these exercises all the troops passed in review before the President. It was the most brilliant military pageant seen since the war. Northern visitors noticed with pleasure that many of the Southern commands wore uniforms of blue. On Thursday evening fireworks were displayed. All the war vessels were illuminated. The steam corvette *Vandalia*, commanded by Captain (subsequently Rear-Admiral) Meade, so disposed her lights as to bring out the outlines of her hull and rigging with charming effect. The splendor was produced by the use of Chinese lanterns, which Captain Meade purchased for the occasion. The celebration ended on Friday with a naval review, embracing all the men-of-war in the harbor. A graceful and handsome deed, acknowledged by the British press, was the salute paid by the entire fleet to the Union

LAURENCEBURG, INDIANA, DURING THE FLOODS OF 1884
Copyright, 1884, by Rombach & Groene

THE LAST QUARTER-CENTURY

SECOND STREET, CINCINNATI, LOOKING EAST

Jack hoisted at the foremast of each vessel.

Freshets in February, 1884, had induced an unprecedented rise in the Ohio River, submerging country and city along the banks. At Cincinnati houses were wrecked, lives lost, destitution and suffering the lot of thousands. To add to the horrors, the gas-works were under water, and night whelmed the city in Cimmerian darkness. As the news spread, practical responses came from all quarters, in the shape of food and clothing, which steamers

THE GAS TANKS IN SECOND STREET, CINCINNATI

RIOT AND FLOOD IN CINCINNATI

THE CINCINNATI RIOTS OF 1884
The Barricade in South Sycamore Street
From a Photograph by Rombach & Groene

distributed up and down the swollen stream. Highest water was reached on February 14th, the highest ever recorded, the river at Cincinnati standing on that date at seventy-one feet and three-quarters of an inch.

Riot followed flood. In March two confessed murderers had come off with a conviction for mere manslaughter. As twenty other murderers were in prison, respectable citizens assembled to demand reform in murder trials. Noisy leaders of the mob element tried to capture the meeting, which was adjourned to prevent mischief. A young man rushing out shouted, "To the jail! Come on! Follow me and hang Berner." The door was burst open, but Berner had been smuggled to Columbus at the first alarm. Meantime the militia were secretly introduced through the same tunnel which afforded him exit. After a skirmish the rioters were driven out, leaving some of their number prisoners. Partly from chagrin, partly to secure the release of the captured leaders, and partly to indulge their lawless humor, the hoodlums set the court-house on fire, robbing an armory and two gun-stores to provide themselves arms. Other shops were broken into and sacked. They fired volley after volley of musketry at the militia, and fiercely attacked barricades which these had erected against them. After repeated warnings retaliation was meted out with terrible effect. The disorders continued six days, when the law was so far vindicated that business could be resumed. The most authentic list put the killed in this riot at forty-five, the wounded at one hundred and thirty-eight.

THIS BOOK IS DUE ON THE LAST DATE
STAMPED BELOW

AN INITIAL FINE OF 25 CENTS

WILL BE ASSESSED FOR FAILURE TO RETURN THIS BOOK ON THE DATE DUE. THE PENALTY WILL INCREASE TO 50 CENTS ON THE FOURTH DAY AND TO $1.00 ON THE SEVENTH DAY OVERDUE.

DEC 18 1962

LIBRARY

MAY 29 REC'D

95100		E661
Andrews, E. B.		A5
The hist.	of the last	v.1
quarter-cent	in the	

www.ingramcontent.com/pod-product-compliance
Lightning Source LLC
Chambersburg PA
CBHW050847300426
44111CB00010B/1159